Author: INGHAM, Patricia
Title: The Brontes

823 BRON

Class no.

To avoid overdue charges please return this book to a
Reading library on or before the last date shown above.
If not required by another reader it may be renewed by
personal visit, telephone, post or online.

D1375406

AUTHORS IN CONTEXT

OXFORD WORLD'S CLASSICS

═

PATRICIA INGHAM

The Brontës

═

OXFORD
UNIVERSITY PRESS

OXFORD
UNIVERSITY PRESS

Great Clarendon Street, Oxford OX2 6DP

Oxford University Press is a department of the University of Oxford.
It furthers the University's objective of excellence in research, scholarship,
and education by publishing worldwide in

Oxford New York

Auckland Cape Town Dar es Salaam Hong Kong Karachi
Kuala Lumpur Madrid Melbourne Mexico City Nairobi
New Delhi Shanghai Taipei Toronto

With offices in

Argentina Austria Brazil Chile Czech Republic France Greece
Guatemala Hungary Italy Japan Poland Portugal Singapore
South Korea Switzerland Thailand Turkey Ukraine Vietnam

Oxford is a registered trade mark of Oxford University Press
in the UK and in certain other countries

Published in the United States
by Oxford University Press Inc., New York

British Library Cataloguing in Publication Data

Data available

Library of Congress Cataloging in Publication Data

Data available

Typeset in Ehrhardt
by RefineCatch Limited, Bungay, Suffolk
Printed in Great Britain by
Clays Ltd., St. Ives plc

ISBN 0–19–284035–5   978–0–19–284035–6

For Li Pasternak Slater

ACKNOWLEDGEMENTS

I am much indebted to Jenny Harrington for her help in preparing this book and to Boyd Hilton and Judith Luna for invaluable advice and suggestions. I am also grateful to Anne Evans, Rosemary Kelly, Bonnie McMullen, Emma Plaskitt, Sue Usher of the Oxford English Faculty Library, the staff of St Anne's College Library, Phil Wickham of the British Film Institute, the staff of the Brontë Parsonage Museum, and the News International Research Fund.

P. I.

CONTENTS

LIST OF ILLUSTRATIONS

A CHRONOLOGY OF THE BRONTËS

	Lives	*Historical and Cultural Background*
1811		Prince of Wales becomes Regent because of George III's madness.
1812	Patrick Brontë's marriage to Maria Branwell.	Lord Byron, *Childe Harolde's Pilgrimage*, cantos I and II
1812–14		Luddite Revolts: some in Yorkshire.
1813		Robert Southey becomes Poet Laureate. Jane Austen, *Pride and Prejudice* Walter Scott, *Rokeby* Byron, *The Giaour*
1813/14	Birth of Maria Brontë in late 1813 or early 1814.	
1814		Austen, *Mansfield Park* Scott, *Waverley* William Wordsworth, *The Excursion* Byron, *The Corsair*
1815	Birth of Elizabeth Brontë.	Battle of Waterloo: Napoleon exiled to St Helena. Corn Law passed protecting homegrown wheat and intended to keep price high.
1816	Birth of Charlotte Brontë.	Income Tax abolished because Napoleonic Wars over. Austen, *Emma* Scott, *The Antiquary* Byron, *Childe Harolde*, canto III
1817	Birth of Branwell Brontë. Births of Mary Taylor and Ellen Nussey.	*Blackwood's Edinburgh Magazine* (a favourite of the Brontës) instituted. Scott, *Rob Roy* Byron, *Manfred* and *Childe Harolde*, canto IV
1818	Birth of Emily Jane Brontë.	Austen, *Northanger Abbey*, and *Persuasion* Mary Shelley, *Frankenstein* Byron, *Beppo* and *Childe Harolde*, canto V
1819		Birth of (Queen) Victoria. Peterloo Massacre in Manchester to repress discontented working-class demonstrators.

Lives	*Historical and Cultural Background*
	Scott, *The Bride of Lammermoor* and *Ivanhoe*
	Byron *Don Juan*, cantos I and II
1820 Birth of Anne Brontë. Brontë family moves to Haworth Parsonage.	Death of George III and accession of George IV.
	Scott, *The Monastery* and *The Abbott*
	Thomas Malthus, *Principles of Political Economy*
1821 Elizabeth 'Aunt' Branwell comes to nurse her sister Maria through terminal cancer until she dies, aged 38, in September.	Death of Napoleon.
	Byron, *Don Juan*, cantos III–V
1823	Byron, *The Island* and *Don Juan*, cantos VI–XIV
1824 Maria and Elizabeth go to Clergy Daughters School, Cowan Bridge. Later Charlotte and Emily follow. Tabitha Ackroyd ('Tabby') engaged as servant.	
1825 Maria and Elizabeth brought home to die of tuberculosis in May and June.	Stockton to Darlington Railway opened.
1826 Patrick brings home wooden soldiers which stimulate his children's early writings and Angrian and Gondal sagas.	Unemployed weavers destroy power looms.
1827 Children begin composing Our Fellows' Play and the Islanders' Play.	Scott, *Life of Napoleon*
1829 First evidence of the Brontës' interest in *Blackwood's Edinburgh Magazine*.	Catholic Emancipation Act. Sir Robert Peel established Metropolitan Police.
1829–30 Brontë children given art lessons by John Bradley of Keighley.	
1830	Death of George IV and accession of William IV. Agitation for political and social reform including the Swing Riots opposing the mechanization of farming which created job losses. Stephenson's Rocket wins speed contest.
	Thomas Carlyle, *On History*

	Lives	*Historical and Cultural Background*
1831	Charlotte sent to Roe Head School, Mirfield, near Huddersfield, run by Margaret Wooler, and meets Ellen Nussey and Mary Taylor. Aunt Branwell begins to take *Fraser's Magazine* which the children read.	
1832		Parliamentary Reform Act enfranchises a section of the middle classes. Deaths of Scott and Goethe.
1833	Patrick joins Keighley Mechanics Institute and gains access to library and lectures. Ellen Nussey visits Haworth.	Factory Act limiting child labour. Oxford Movement develops as an extreme section of Anglican High Church. First steam ship crosses the Atlantic.
1834		Poor Law Amendment Act limiting relief available outside workhouses. Houses of Parliament accidentally burnt down. Slavery abolished in the British Empire.
1835	Branwell applies to the Royal Academy of Arts. Charlotte returns to Roe Head as a teacher and Emily goes as a pupil. After a few weeks Emily is replaced by Anne because she pines for home.	Turner paints *Burning of the House of Lords and Commons*
1836	Branwell becomes a Freemason. Emily's first dated poem. Charlotte sends a specimen of her verse to Robert Southey and a letter asking his advice about her ambition to become a great poet.	Chartist movement for parliamentary reform begins. Charles Dickens, *Sketches by Boz*
1837	Branwell sends a poem to William Wordsworth and writes of *his* ambition to become a poet but receives no reply. Southey responds to Charlotte by recognizing her talent for verse but advising her not to write with the unwomanly ambition of becoming a celebrity. Anne also pines, as Emily did, at Roe	Death of William IV, accession of Queen Victoria. Dickens, *Pickwick Papers*

Lives	*Historical and Cultural Background*
	Head and returns to Haworth in December while Charlotte continues there, although she too is depressed.	

1838   Charlotte leaves Roe Head School which has now moved to Dewsbury. Emily, after three years at home, takes a teaching post at Law Hill near Halifax.

People's Charter drawn up. Anti-Corn Law League set up to fight for free trade.

1839   Emily returns from Law Hill after six months. Anne becomes governess to the Inghams at Mirfield in April but leaves in December. Charlotte goes as a governess to the Sidgwicks near Skipton but leaves after two months. She writes her last Angrian novelette *Caroline Vernon* and her *Farewell to Angria*. Charlotte refuses two marriage proposals: one from Ellen Nussey's brother, the other from the Reverend David Pryce.

Chartist riots. Custody of Infants Act allows women to petition for custody of children under 7.
Dickens, *Nicholas Nickleby*
Carlyle, *Chartism*

1840   Anne becomes governess to the Robinsons of Thorp Green, near York. Branwell becomes tutor to the Postlethwaites at Broughton in Furness in January, but is dismissed in June. He is now translating Horace's *Odes* and sends specimens to Hartley Coleridge whom he visits. Coleridge encourages him. Branwell becomes assistant clerk in charge at Sowerby Bridge Railway Station.

First (unsuccessful) presentation of the People's Charter. Queen Victoria marries the German prince Albert. New Houses of Parliament begun by Barry and Pugin. Introduction of Penny Post.
Charles Darwin, *Voyage of HMS Beagle*

1841   Charlotte goes as governess to the Whites, Rawdon, near Bradford, and stays only until December. She, Emily, and Anne devise a plan to start a school and persuade Aunt Branwell to provide funds to enable Charlotte and Emily to

Dickens, *Old Curiosity Shop* and *Barnaby Rudge*
Carlyle, *On Heroes and Hero Worship*

Lives

Historical and Cultural Background

go to Brussels to perfect their
French. Branwell goes to
Luddenden Foot as clerk in
charge of the station.

1842   Patrick escorts Charlotte and
Emily to Brussels where they
become pupils at Mme Heger's
Pensionnat. There the sisters
meet Mary and Martha Taylor.
Branwell dismissed from the
railway over financial
discrepancies. In October
Patrick's curate William
Weightman dies; Martha Taylor
dies in Brussels; Aunt Branwell
dies at Haworth. Charlotte and
Emily return home to find that
Aunt Branwell has left each
niece £350

Underground labour banned for
women and children. Unsuccessful
presentation of the Charter to
Parliament. Mudie's Lending
Library opened.
Edwin Chadwick, *Report on the
Sanitary Conditions of the Working
Class*
Dickens, *American Notes*

1843   Branwell becomes tutor to the
Robinsons' son at Thorp Green
where Anne is already the
governess. Charlotte returns
alone to Brussels as both teacher
and pupil at the Hegers. She is
increasingly attracted to M.
Heger and hostile to his wife,
leaving her lonely and
depressed. She leaves Brussels
at the end of the year. She writes
to Heger but he does not reply.
She intends to start a school but
fails to find pupils.

Wordsworth becomes Poet Laureate.
Dickens, *A Christmas Carol*
Carlyle, *Past and Present*

1844

Factory Act limits working hours for
women and children.

1844–5

Potato blight causes famine in Ireland
and one million people die.

1845   Charlotte continues to write to
Heger until November. Anne
leaves Thorp Green. Branwell is
dismissed from Thorp Green
for unspecified misbehaviour,
presumably his affair with Mrs
Robinson. He starts to drink
heavily. Mary Taylor emigrates
to New Zealand and starts a shop.

John Henry Newman joins the
Roman Catholic Church.
Benjamin Disraeli, *Sybil*
F. Engels, *Condition of the Working
Class in England 1844*

	Lives	*Historical and Cultural Background*
	Charlotte, after finding a notebook of Emily's poems, plans a publication of poems by all three sisters.	
1846	The sisters pay for the publication of the poems which are well reviewed but do not sell. Charlotte sends *The Professor*, *Wuthering Heights*, and *Agnes Grey* to five publishers who reject them. Patrick Brontë operated on for cataract in Manchester, accompanied by Charlotte who starts to write *Jane Eyre* there.	Corn Laws repealed. 'Railway Mania' year: 272 Railways Acts passed.
1847	*Wuthering Heights* and *Agnes Grey* accepted for publication by Newby. Publisher George Smith rejects *The Professor* but encourages Charlotte to write a three-decker. She sends him the newly completed *Jane Eyre* which is published under her pseudonym in October and is an immediate success. *Wuthering Heights* and *Agnes Grey* published in December. Branwell, desperate that the now widowed Mrs Robinson will not marry him, relies heavily on alcohol and opium.	Ten Hour Factory Act limits working hours.
1848	Anne's *The Tenant of Wildfell Hall* published in June. Anne and Charlotte travel to London to call on George Smith to prove their separate identities. Branwell dies in September, and Emily in December after refusing treatment for tuberculosis.	Year of revolutions in Europe. Charter again unsuccessfully presented to Parliament and Chartism fails. Cholera outbreak in London. Public Health Act inspired by Chadwick's 1842 report. Dickens, *Dombey and Son* William Makepeace Thackeray, *Vanity Fair* Elizabeth Gaskell, *Mary Barton* Karl Marx and Engels, *The Communist Manifesto*
1849	As Anne's tuberculosis worsens, Charlotte and Ellen Nussey take her to Scarborough where she dies and is buried in May.	

	Lives	*Historical and Cultural Background*
1850	*Shirley* is published in October. Charlotte, now desperately lonely, stays with the Smiths, visits the Royal Academy, and sees her hero the Duke of Wellington. She also stays with the Kay-Shuttleworths near Windermere, and with Harriet Martineau in Ambleside.	Thomas Wiseman created cardinal to restore the Roman Catholic hierarchy in England. North London Collegiate School for Girls founded. Dickens, *David Copperfield* Thackeray, *Pendennis*
1851	Charlotte refuses a proposal from James Taylor, an employee of George Smith, but corresponds freely with another employee, William Smith Williams. She visits the Great Exhibition five times.	The Great Exhibition at the Crystal Palace in Hyde Park is backed by Prince Albert and is a great success.
1852	Patrick's curate, Arthur Bell Nicholls, proposes to Charlotte but her angry father forbids the match.	Wellington, Charlotte's hero, dies. Thackeray, *Henry Esmond* Ruskin, *The Stones of Venice*
1853	*Villette* published.	Vaccination against smallpox becomes compulsory. Gaskell, *Cranford* Dickens, *Bleak House*
1854	After a clandestine correspondence, Charlotte accepts Nicholls after arranging that they will stay with her father. They marry in June.	Crimean War begins: Britain and France defend European interests in the Middle East against Russia. Florence Nightingale goes out to Scutari. Dickens, *Hard Times* Gaskell, *North and South* Anthony Trollope, *The Warden* (first of the Barchester novels)
1855	Charlotte dies, possibly as a result of complications to her pregnancy; and Nicholls stays on with Patrick. Patrick asks Elizabeth Gaskell to write Charlotte's biography.	
1856		Crimean War ends; Victoria Cross instituted for bravery.
1857	Gaskell's *Life of Charlotte Brontë* published. *The Professor* published with a Preface by Nicholls.	Matrimonial Causes Act gives divorce on roughly equal terms to men and women. Dickens, *Little Dorrit*

	Lives	*Historical and Cultural Background*
1859		Darwin, *Origin of Species* Dickens, *A Tale of Two Cities* Samuel Smiles, *Self-Help* George Eliot, *Adam Bede*
1861	Patrick dies, aged 85, and Nicholls only then returns to Ireland.	Death of Prince Albert. Abolition of Paper Tax.
1864	Nicholls marries his cousin, Mary Anna Bell.	

ABBREVIATIONS

Alexander	Christine Alexander, *The Early Writings of Charlotte Brontë* (Oxford: Basil Blackwell, 1983)
Allott	Miriam Allott (ed.), *The Brontës: The Critical Heritage* (London and Boston: Routledge and Kegan Paul, 1974)
Barker	Juliet Barker, *The Brontës* (London: Weidenfeld and Nicholson, 1994)
BST	*Brontë Society Transactions*
Gérin	Charlotte Brontë, *Five Novelettes*, ed. Winifred Gérin (London: Folio Press, 1971)
Gezari	Emily Jane Brontë, *The Complete Poems*, ed. Janet Gezari (Harmondsworth: Penguin, 1992)
Letters	*The Letters of Charlotte Brontë*, ed. Margaret Smith, 2 vols. (Oxford: Oxford Clarendon Press, 1995–2000)
LFC	T. J. Wise and J. A. Symington (eds.), *The Brontës: Their Lives, Friendships and Correspondence*, 4 vols. (Oxford: Basil Blackwell, 1980)
McGann	Lord Byron, *The Major Works*, ed. Jerome J. McGann (Oxford: Oxford University Press, 2000)
Shorter	Clement Shorter, *Charlotte Brontë and Her Circle* (New York: Dodd, Mead and Co., 1896)

CHAPTER I

THE LIVES OF CHARLOTTE, EMILY, AND ANNE BRONTË

The Family Circle

'HAPPINESS', wrote Charlotte Brontë in *Villette*, 'is not a potato to be planted in mould and tilled with manure'. This was her response to the advice that one should 'cultivate' happiness and is to be accounted for by the fact that she and her siblings were able to achieve little of it during their short lives. By contrast, the reputation and impact of their novels have been growing of their own accord, ever since they were written, to prodigious extremes. The events of their lives were, as many dramatic reconstructions have shown, melodramatic: early deaths, sudden success, alcoholism, adultery, unrequited and unrequitable love all feature. But these happenings took place on a limited stage and the reference to a family circle is doubly apt here. The Brontës were a numerous and tightly linked group; and their ties were drawn closer by the setting in which they lived and by the early deaths of family members. If chronology had allowed Branwell to paint the whole family in his well-known triple portrait, it would have included not only their father, Patrick, and mother, Maria, but two older sisters: Maria (born 1814) and Elizabeth (born 1815). Charlotte had been born in 1816, Branwell in 1817, Emily in 1818, and Anne in 1820. For Patrick and Maria had six children, not four, when they moved to the Yorkshire village of Haworth in 1820 to take up Patrick's living as 'perpetual curate'.

This was the setting for their somewhat theatrical lives, despite its apparently unexciting nature. The cobbled main street of the village curved steeply uphill to the Parsonage at the top, with the moor behind it. The façade of the house looked over to the church and the graveyard which, contrary to the popular view, is not the burial place of the Brontë family—they are buried in the church itself. Haworth, with its population of more than 4,500 inhabitants, was not a healthy place: over 40 per cent of children there died before the age of 6. Its water was of poor quality and was sometimes contaminated; there was no adequate sanitation. In the neighbourhood or chapelry there were some thirteen textile mills as well as home-workers in the woollen industry. So it was by no means the remote natural wilderness sometimes depicted in films: though three or four miles from the neighbouring town of Keighley, it was situated on a main route between Yorkshire and Lancashire. But to Charlotte, Emily, and Anne, the Parsonage and moors represented a home to which they were always drawn back. When they left it they longed to return and Charlotte on one occasion described it as paradise. If Patrick has often been portrayed as harsh, he was not harsh enough to spoil this home for them.

Elizabeth Gaskell in her *Life of Charlotte Brontë* (1857) sees Haworth somewhat differently and describes it as variable in its impression 'according to the mood of mind in which the spectator may be'. She focuses on the moors which may appear 'grand, from the ideas of solitude and loneliness which they suggest, or oppressive from the feeling they give of being pent up by some monotonous and illimitable barrier' (volume i, chapter 1). Ellen Nussey, another friend of the Brontës, was struck above all by the neatness and cleanliness of the sparsely furnished parsonage.

Haworth was a busy and populous village but the Brontë sisters were to some extent isolated socially—apart from their dealings with Patrick's curates. They did not mix on equal terms with the textile workers, shopkeepers, and tradesmen or their households, though Branwell found local drinking companions. Their relatively well-to-do friends were small in number and were mainly acquired by Charlotte after 1831 when she went to Roe Head boarding school near Mirfield. These friends lived at a distance so that contact was maintained through letter-writing or infrequent visits. Large numbers of Charlotte's letters remain but very few from Emily and Anne. This isolation turned the children in on their own resources, and close bonds developed through their communal reading and acting games. The bonds grew tighter with the death of their mother within a year of their arrival at Haworth from what appears to have been cancer. Maria, the eldest child, who was now 7 years old, is said to have tried to act in her mother's place while two local girls, Nancy and Sarah Garrs, acted as housekeeper and nursemaid.

Patrick tried somewhat ineptly to find a second wife to act as mother to his children by proposing unsuccessfully, perhaps to three women and certainly to two. He fell back, however, on the services of his late wife's sister, Elizabeth Branwell, who had come to act as nurse to the dying woman and who remained at Haworth until her death in 1842. In this way the gap in the family circle left by Maria's death was filled by another blood-relative. She may be assumed to have had some considerable influence on the children's lives. Branwell certainly regarded her as a second mother and after her death wrote of her as 'the guide and director of all the happy days connected with my childhood' (Barker, p. 404). The fact that she was a Wesleyan Methodist, enforcing strict discipline, has led to an assumption that she was another harsh figure in the Parsonage but Branwell's tribute to her and her financial generosity to her nieces suggest a more kindly and less censorious woman than she has sometimes been portrayed.

The imaginative and intellectual talents that all the Brontë children displayed and on which they drew in their reading, writing, and role-playing activities seem likely to have been inherited from their talented father. Patrick Prunty/Brunty/Bruntee/Brontë (the family name evolved) was born in 1777 in a two-roomed cottage in County Down as the eldest of ten children in an Anglican family surrounded by Roman Catholics. He wrote an account of his upbringing for Gaskell when she was writing her biography of Charlotte. He referred to the belief that his father was of an ancient family as a matter which he had never bothered to enquire into. It was, he said, thanks to his mother's industry that she had brought up ten children to respectability. Though he left school at 16, he soon opened a small school of his own and eventually became a tutor in the family of an evangelical clergyman, Thomas Tighe. It is assumed that his astonishing scholarship to study at Cambridge University was due to the patronage of Tighe and other evangelicals whom his talent had impressed since, like Oxford, Cambridge was still virtually entirely the preserve of the upper classes rich enough to study there.

After his ordination in 1807 to the Anglican priesthood, Patrick secured several curacies, first in Essex and then in 1809 in Yorkshire, presumably again with the help of evangelical patrons. Yorkshire at this time was in a turbulent state as a result of unrest in the woollen industry following the introduction of machines which threatened to destroy the workers' jobs. In 1811–12 there were attacks on the machines brought to the mills by a group of workers known as Luddites. There were also threats to murder employers and at least one murder actually took place. Over the next few years Luddite threats recurred. There is evidence that Patrick recounted some of these events to friends and a strong presumption that he regaled his children with such tales: for the violence in Charlotte's novel *Shirley* draws on the doings of the Luddites, whose activities she researched in back numbers of the *Leeds Mercury*.

Patrick's rise even to a perpetual curacy was startling for the time but it still left him in straitened circumstances on an annual salary of £170 with six children to provide for. His own education made him anxious to secure that of his children. To Branwell, his only son, he acted as tutor in the classics. Some knowledge of Latin literature, at least in translation, must have rubbed off on Charlotte who confidently makes classical references in her writing. For his daughters Patrick did his best to provide outside help in giving them the conventional feminine education in French, Italian, and possibly German; drawing; music; and needlework.

In 1824 when his eldest daughters were 10 and 9 years old, he took the further step of sending them to a boarding school at Cowan Bridge, Tunstall, where fees were subsidized for the daughters of evangelical clergymen to a mere £14 per year. The school was later to become notorious as the origin of the terrible Lowood School in *Jane Eyre*. The evidence of sources other than Charlotte's novel confirms that conditions were indeed harsh and that the details of life at Lowood match those at Cowan Bridge. The school was founded on a basis of extreme evangelicalism which regarded all humanity as innately sinful and in need of regeneration by discipline. Hence the early rising to wash in ice-covered water, followed by a breakfast of porridge, often too burnt to eat. Other meals were equally unappetizing: a dinner of potatoes and meat together; half a slice of bread and coffee, followed by the last food of the day—oatcake and water. Study was undertaken from 9 a.m. till midday; after dinner there was more study until 5 p.m. and also for part of the evening, and study meant largely learning by rote. The regime at Cowan Bridge varied on Sundays when the girls walked two miles to church where they attended morning and afternoon services, eating a cold lunch there in between. This kind of programme was common in charity schools and there has been critical discussion of whether or not Charlotte's account in *Jane Eyre* is too condemnatory; however, the argument that such cruel conditions were usual does not remove or reduce the suffering for the individuals involved.

Charlotte and Emily joined Maria and Elizabeth towards the end of 1824 and did not impress the compiler of the school register. Charlotte was thought clever for her age but not to know anything systematically; Emily was said to read well and sew a little. Maria, the surrogate mother to her siblings, was of an uncomplaining nature and perhaps for this reason was particularly ill-treated. This is certainly what Charlotte believed when she insisted later that Maria was the model for the long-suffering and angelic Helen Burns in *Jane Eyre*. Soon, however, both Maria and later Elizabeth developed tuberculosis, which at the time was usually fatal. Presumably conditions at Cowan Bridge exacerbated the disease and in early 1825, some six months after their arrival, Patrick took the two girls home where they died within a month of each other. These deaths broke another link in the family circle and Patrick now brought Charlotte and Emily home too. For the next five years the four remaining siblings stayed at Haworth in an ever more closely knit group in which Charlotte often paired with Branwell and Emily with Anne.

The manifestation of the children's closeness took the form of the imaginative worlds which they created together. These worlds arose out of acting games sparked by the twelve toy soldiers that Patrick brought home for Branwell in 1826. The Brontës christened them 'The Young Men', each chose one and gave it the name of a figure with whom they half-identified: Charlotte chose as her hero the Duke of Wellington; Branwell decided on Napoleon; Emily at first chose 'Gravey' for her serious-looking soldier; and Anne named hers 'Waiting Boy'. On reflection the two younger girls, now aged 8 and 7, renamed their characters after Parry and Ross, two notable explorers whom they had read about in *Blackwood's Magazine*. The choice of names is significant: it reflects the interest of all the children (still under 10 years old) in current affairs, politics, and the Napoleonic Wars. From naming the characters they moved on—or perhaps developed existing games—to make up stories about them which they acted out. These turned into dramas which were shaped or, as Charlotte records, gradually 'established'. First came the Young Men's Play in June 1826, then Our Fellows' Play and the Islanders' Play in December 1827. By 1829 the children began to write down the stories and plays in minuscule handwriting on the tiny sheets of paper that they were obliged to use. These pages were then stitched into small books, some of which survive to the present day. Later these laborious scribes prepared miniature journals for their characters, based on the periodicals of the day: Charlotte and Branwell created the 'Young Men's Magazine' as well as 'Branwell's Blackwood's Magazine'. These writings were the beginning of two alternative worlds that the children were gradually to create, and the apprentice work for their mature novels.

The tales were often set in exotic places such as Africa where the Duke of Wellington confronts the hostile native Ashantees. This and other colourful events form a complex and inconsistent narrative. It is presumably these tales that Charlotte is referring to when she writes at the beginning of a long poem 'We wove a web of child-hood'. Within this web, at once a refuge and an obsessive activity, Charlotte and Branwell developed their imaginary country of Angria, and Emily and Anne their Gondal. A considerable amount of material survives from the Angrian saga and its antecedents but not from Gondal apart from Emily's Gondal poems from which she carefully removed Gondalian references.

In Angria politics and wars preoccupied Branwell while Charlotte concentrated on love affairs and exotic descriptions. She luxuriated in lush accounts of 'blooming and fragrant paradises'. Already in the Glass Town saga she gives details of such a paradise, a desert oasis:

Here the tufted olive, the fragrant myrtle, the stately palm-tree, the grace-ful almond, the rich vine and the queenly rose mingled in sweet and odorous shadiness, and bordered the high banks of a clear and murmuring river over whose waters a fresh breeze swept which cooled delightfully the burning air of the desert which surrounded [it]. (Alexander, p. 57)

Massive buildings gave similar scope for elaborate and admiring accounts: 'Out of the barren deserts arose a palace of diamond, the pillars of which were ruby and emerald illuminated with lamps too bright to look upon' (Alexander, p. 31).

The central focus of these plays and stories, however, is clearly the characters. The children themselves often play an ambivalent role amongst them. As authors they sometimes adopt an identity as nar-rators which gives them a part to play in the story. So Charlotte narrates the story as Charles Wellesley (later Charles Townshend), brother of Arthur Wellesley, elder son of the Duke of Wellington and later Marquis of Douro, then Duke of Zamorna, then King of Angria. 'Charles' (alias Charlotte) takes a satirical view of his brother's life, and when Branwell takes on the identity of the young Soult, a gifted poet, Charlotte also treats him satirically in the stories. Originally all four Brontë children identified with their chosen characters, Wellington, Napoleon, Parry, and Ross, but already in the Young Men's Play they appear collectively as a powerful group called the Chief Genii. Branwell claims leadership of the four when he asserts in the text:

I am the chief Genius Brannii, with me there are 3 others: she, Wellesly who protects you is named Tallii; she who protects Parry is named Emmii; she who protects Ross is called Annii . . . We are the Guardians of this land, we are the guardians of you all. (Alexander, p. 30)

A similar role is taken by the four in the Islanders' Play where they form a group given to intervening in events as 'The Little King and Queens'. In this way the geographical boundaries between the Haworth world and the one that the children created are removed: authors and their creations tread the same world.

Nor are the imaginary worlds separate in time from life at Haworth. This is confirmed by the interweaving of events in Angria or Gondal with daily life in the Parsonage in the Diary Papers written by Emily and Anne in 1834, 1837, 1841, and 1845 to mark their birthdays. They record the events around them as they occur and Emily writes in 1834:

This morning Branwell went down to Mr Driver's and brought news that Sir Robert Peel was going to be invited to stand for Leeds. Anne and I have been peeling apples for Charlotte to make an apple pudding. Charlotte said she made puddings perfectly and she is of a quick but limited intellect. Taby said just now, Come Anne pillopatate (i.e. pill a potato) Aunt has come into the kitchen just now and said Where are your feet Anne Anne answered On the floor Aunt . . . The Gondals are discovering the interior of Gaaldine. Sally Mosley is washing in the back kitchen.[1]

Here events in Gondal are made contemporaneous with those in the Parsonage kitchen as well as those heard of from the political scene. This is echoed in all the other Diary Papers and it is also true of Angria in the Paper of 1837 where Zamorna and Northangerland are always at odds:

Tabby in the Kitchin—the Emperors and Empresses of Gondal and Gaaldine preparing to depart . . . for the coronation which will be held on the 12th of July Queen Victoria ascended the throne this month. Northangerland in the Monceys Isle—Zamorna at Eversham. all tight and right in which condition it is to be hoped we shall all be on this day 4 years. (Barker, p. 271)

The source of the worlds of Angria and Gondal was ultimately the creative faculties of the four Brontës but the materials that they drew on and transformed in Tolkien fashion were the worlds they dis-covered in their reading. Patrick had grown up in the Regency period which was notoriously more liberal and less censorious in outlook than the mid-Victorian era. Perhaps this accounts for the freedom he gave his children to read whatever they could lay hands on and perhaps also for the mid-Victorian reaction to *Jane Eyre*, *Wuthering Heights*, and *The Tenant of Wildfell Hall*. All were found coarse and shocking by many, for by the late 1840s novelists were writing in a climate of moral hypocrisy. This attitude of Patrick's offers a more likely explanation of the unconventional content of the Brontës' novels than the suggestion sometimes offered by their defenders that it was the outcome of an upbringing in barbaric backwoods. Patrick did not prevent them from reading the danger-ous poems of the dashingly wicked Byron or those of the equally disreputable and atheistic Shelley, as well as the harmless Wordsworth and Southey.

But the everyday world was not absent from their reading: they had standard textbooks of history and geography. They were also familiar with reproductions of famous paintings and had a particular taste for the large, apocalyptic canvases of Robert Martin as well as being able to sketch or paint themselves. Branwell even aspired in early adulthood to a career as a portrait painter. But the yeast in this mixture of literary and religious reading is the unlikely element pro-vided by messages from the real world in the shape of newspapers and periodicals. These included the *Leeds Mercury* and the *Leeds Intelligencer*, two local newspapers which they read aloud to each other and discussed avidly. Then crucially their source of current affairs expanded when Patrick began to borrow *Blackwood's Maga-zine*. This too the children fell upon: Branwell later even claimed (albeit to the editor of Blackwood's) that as a child it formed his 'chief delight' (Alexander, p. 20). Added to this in 1831 was *Fraser's*

Magazine to which Aunt Branwell began to subscribe. *Blackwood's*, however, was their main resource. It was a Tory periodical, enlivened by what seemed to some rather sensational writing as contemporaries understood the term. It included accounts of national events, political machinations, travel and exploration, scientific news, stories, poems, translations, and literary reviews. It was this journalism that familiarized the children with the idea of the publication of magazines and books. Their mother also had written some religious works and their father had a substantial amount of writing published between 1810 and 1818. These were religious writings in verse and prose such as *Winter Evening Thoughts: A Miscellaneous Poem*; *Cottage Poems*; *The Rural Minstrel: A Miscellany of Religious Poems*; *The Cottage in the Wood*; and *The Maid of Killarney*. From an early age, therefore, Charlotte and Branwell aspired to literary careers. Both wrote to Wordsworth for advice and Charlotte also wrote to the poet Robert Southey.

Though the juvenilia, as the children's early writings are called, were a discontinuous and complex web, they are in many ways continuous with the three sisters' novels, as we shall see. The structuring of the Angrian saga, however, already resembles the novels in some formal aspects. All three Brontës use first-person narrators in their later fictions: *The Professor*, *Jane Eyre*, *Wuthering Heights*, *Agnes Grey*, and *The Tenant of Wildfell Hall*. It is also significant that, just as Charlotte adopts a male persona in the saga under the names of Charles Wellesley/Charles Townsend, the narrator of her first novel, *The Professor*, is a man, as are those of Emily in *Wuthering Heights* and of Anne in *The Tenant of Wildfell Hall*. This shape-shifting is potentiated in Emily's novel by the doubling of these male narrators who are each distinct individuals, although Charlotte, Emily, and Anne knew few men who could serve as a model. In their own family there were merely two extremes: Patrick—dominant, eccentric, but compassionate—and Branwell—talented, vain, ambitious, but given to dissipation and depression. Angria provided scope for Charlotte, for instance, to create men based on the Duke of Wellington, a renowned politician and military hero, as well as others from his entourage of whom she had read in *Blackwood's*. For all the sisters the acting out of many roles in their plays and stories provided material from which to create the many very different characters in their novels.

Haworth Parsonage at the time of the Brontës

A family portrait by Branwell: (l. to r.) Anne, Charlotte, Branwell, Emily

Pupils and Teachers

For six years, then, from 1825 to 1831, the four Brontës only knew the outside world in forms filtered through the words of others. Consequently it reached them not in a mundane but in an exciting and even glamorous shape as the doings of those who lived the high life of politics and travel to exotic places. As has been shown, this served to provide material for their own half-real, unreal world. But by 1831 Patrick was still a perpetual curate on a low income. He had no means at the advanced age of 54 to make provision for his children financially in the event of his death. There now came a time when, to prepare his daughters to become self-supporting as governesses or teachers, he needed to improve their education.

In 1831 Patrick sent Charlotte to Roe Head school near Huddersfield as a boarder. This was a reputable and pleasant institution, quite unlike Cowan Bridge. It was run from 1830 by Margaret Wooler and her four sisters in a humane way. When Charlotte arrived there, she was one of no more than ten pupils in a peaceful and well-run school. The other pupils, however, clearly saw her as a misfit, a kind of alien; two of them described the impression she made on them to Elizabeth Gaskell. Significantly Ellen Nussey, a politely conventional and religious woman, wrote later mainly of Charlotte's physical appearance:

certainly she was at this time anything but *pretty*, even her good points were lost. Her naturally beautiful hair of soft silky brown being then dry and frizzy-looking, screwed up in tight little curls, showing features that were all the plainer from her exceeding thinness and want of complexion, she looked 'dried in'. A dark, rusty green stuff dress of old-fashioned make detracted still more from her appearance. (Barker, p. 172)

Mary Taylor, a strong-minded and intelligent woman, confirms this visual appearance but with more insight into Charlotte's feelings:

I first saw her coming out of a covered cart, in very old-fashioned clothes, and looking very cold and miserable . . . She looked a little old woman, so short-sighted that she always appeared to be seeking something, and moving her head from side to side to catch a sight of it. She was very shy and nervous, and spoke with a strong Irish accent.[2]

Charlotte's shock at being uprooted from her family made her very homesick but of the three sisters she was the one most able to adapt. Since at Roe Head teaching was reasonably good, she applied herself vigorously to the standard textbooks on English grammar, geography, history, and French. She also had music and drawing lessons, showing some flair for drawing but none at all for music. She was by no means limited in intellectual abilities and her absence of arrogance won her respect; she became popular as a storyteller. Furthermore she made the extraordinary discovery that she could form friendships outside her own family. The chief of these were made with the two girls from whom much later Gaskell was to solicit their memories of Charlotte as a schoolgirl. Both Ellen Nussey and Mary Taylor were to become lifelong friends and through them also other members of their families and family friends. Ellen and Mary were totally unlike each other, as becomes evident in their correspondence with Charlotte and Charlotte's with them. Just before Anne's death in 1849 Charlotte wrote from Scarborough:

My friend Ellen is with us. I find her presence a solace. She is a calm steady girl—not brilliant, but good and true. She suits and has always suited me well. I like her, with her phlegm, repose, sense and sincerity, better than I should like the most talented without these qualifications. (*Letters*, ii. 213)

Ellen appealed to the side of Charlotte that always struggled to be a dutiful and womanly person with orthodox religious views. For this, as her letters show, Ellen was her early model.

Mary Taylor by contrast appealed to her more rebellious side, which was always at odds in life and writing with the Ellen within Charlotte. Mary comes across as strong-minded and unconventional in her thinking in her letters from New Zealand to which she had emigrated in order to support herself. Since she destroyed Charlotte's letters to her, it is from her replies that we gather her advanced views on the role of women and their need to work that so appealed to Charlotte. Mary was above all an intelligent and pragmatic person to whom Charlotte wrote freely on intellectual matters that she never touched on with Ellen. With the latter she did in a general way write seriously at one period of her own perceived lapses from religious dutifulness but she did not tell her, as she told Mary, of the publication of *Jane Eyre* nor of her meeting in far-away London with its publishers. She even concealed her authorship from Ellen in response to direct questioning. Presumably she knew that

Ellen would disapprove of a novel that many saw as shocking for its depiction of passion in a woman, and a plot involving attempted bigamy.

Charlotte persisted as a pupil at Roe Head until she completed her studies in July 1832. She was now in theory prepared to start working life as a teacher but did not do so for three years until in 1835 she was invited by Miss Wooler to return to Roe Head as a teacher. Despite the preparation, she did not welcome the prospect: 'I am sad, very sad at the thoughts of leaving home but Duty—Necessity—these are stern Misstresses [*sic*] who will not be disobeyed' (*Letters*, i. 140). Meantime Emily had been living at home since their return from the disastrous school at Cowan Bridge in 1825. She was now sent some ten years later as a pupil to the school where her sister was to become a teacher. Shortly before Emily went to Roe Head, Ellen Nussey had met her and, as with her first sighting of Charlotte, perceived a somewhat alien figure. She admired Emily's graceful litheness but disliked her frizzy hair. She also observed that Emily was too reserved, talked too little, and avoided eye contact.

Like Charlotte, Emily found the separation from home and family painful but in her case it proved too painful to endure. She underwent some kind of physical-psychological collapse later described by Charlotte:

Every morning when she woke, the vision of home and the moors rushed on her, and darkened and saddened the day that lay before her . . . In this struggle her health was quickly broken: her white face, attenuated form, and failing strength threatened rapid decline. I felt in my heart she would die if she did not go home, and with this conviction obtained her recall. (*Letters*, ii. 753)

The recall came only three months after her arrival at the school and Emily went home to be replaced by Anne as a pupil. It is this episode that has led to the suggestion that Emily intermittently showed symptoms of anorexia, though there is no firm evidence for such a diagnosis. But in any event her collapse served as a means of returning to Haworth, where she recovered. To judge from her poems and frequent statements by Charlotte, she had a passion for physical freedom and autonomy. Certainly, if taken as literally expressing Emily's own wish, the poem 'The Old Stoic' suggests as much:

> And if I pray, the only prayer
>   That moves my lips for me
> Is, 'Leave the heart that now I bear
>   And give me liberty!'
>   (Gezari, p. 31)

Although the title of this poem refers to the ascetic philosopher Epictetus, it seems unlikely that Emily would have disagreed. After this, Emily only once attempted a working life like Charlotte's away from home, when in 1838 she went as a teacher to Law Hill School near Halifax. The attempt lasted only about six months when, after a decline similar to that which had taken place at Roe Head, she retreated again to Haworth. With the exception of an extraordinary and unhappy year at Brussels, from which retreat was less easy, she remained at home immersed in Gondal and her poetry for the rest of her life.

Though Charlotte too found life in the outside world very painful, she persevered at Roe Head. Her unhappiness increased after the school moved to a new location and at Christmas 1838 she left behind what she described as 'the concentrated anguish of certain insufferable moments and the heavy gloom of many long hours—besides the preternatural horror which seemed to clothe existence and Nature—and which made Life a continual waking Night-Mare' (*Letters*, i. 505). More persistent than Emily, she later made two more abortive attempts to work as a governess but each was short-lived. The first, in 1839, was with a family called Sidgwick who lived near Skipton, and it lasted only a few months. So too did her second post with the White family (who lived near Bradford) which she took in 1841. It is clear that she found the life of a governess even more unpalatable than that of a teacher in a school. She thought both sets of children unruly and indulged: the Sidgwicks were 'pampered spoilt & turbulent'; and the Whites 'wild and unbroken' (*Letters*, i. 193 and 246). On top of this she found the condescension of her female employers ignominiously intolerable, since she wished to be treated as a gentlewoman and their social equal, not as a superior kind of servant. Underlying these discomforts was her pain at separation from the home and family where she knew only respect, affection, and like minds. She wrote at the time:

it is indeed a hard thing for flesh and blood to leave home—especially a *good* home—not a wealthy or splendid one—my home is humble and unattractive to strangers but to me it contains what I shall find nowhere else in the world—[the] profound, and intense affection which brothers and sisters feel for each other when their minds are cast in the same mould, their ideas drawn from the same source—when they have clung to each other from childhood and when family disputes have never sprung up to divide them. (*Letters*, i. 255)

Anne's forays into a life away from Haworth followed the same pattern. Ellen Nussey describes her appearance approvingly: 'Her hair was a very pretty light brown and fell on her neck in graceful curls. She had lovely violet blue eyes, fine pencilled eyebrows, a clear, almost transparent complexion'. But her approval of Anne's character took a somewhat misleading form when she eulogized her as 'Anne, dear gentle Anne' (*Letters*, i. 598). The phrase became fixed and fostered the idea of Anne as weakly and compliant, though her behaviour and her writing suggest a hidden strength. Although Anne was homesick at Roe Head, she evidently had a streak of steel within and persevered there for two years just as she was later to persevere in her post as governess. But eventually in 1837 she became what Charlotte called wretchedly ill with pain of an unspecified kind and difficulty in breathing. Her state seems to have resembled Emily's and, like hers, was cured by a return to Haworth which took place again at Charlotte's insistence since Miss Wooler was dismissive about its seriousness.

Later, more valiant than Emily or more consciously dutiful, Anne made two attempts to become self-supporting by taking up successive posts as a governess. In April 1839 she went to the Ingham family who lived outside Mirfield. Like her sister she found that the children were unmanageable and that, as Charlotte put it, they were 'desperate little dunces . . . the worst of it is the little monkies are excessively indulged' (*Letters*, i. 189). But at Christmas it was the Inghams who decided that she was unable to manage their children and dismissed her. With admirable determination in 1840 she found another post with the family of Reverend Edmund Robinson and his wife, Lydia. The Robinsons lived in grand style and some luxury and Anne remained with them until 1845. In 1843 Branwell joined her as tutor to the Robinsons' son and both remained there until 1845 when Branwell was dismissed and Anne resigned. It seems likely that the length of her stay there from 1840 to 1845 was a conscientiously endured one, resulting from a strong sense of duty. What the three sisters' excursions into the outside world of Yorkshire had shown was that their attempts to acquire an education and to become self-supporting were largely a failure. But the time that Charlotte and Anne spent as governesses or teachers provided experiences that they could draw on in *Jane Eyre*, *The Professor*, *Villette*, and *Agnes Grey*. For Emily the experiences seem to have been shaken off once she was free of them.

During this period of outside encounters, Charlotte had two more experiences which might have transformed her life had she responded differently to them. Her responses, however, are very revealing and would have startled those of her contemporaries who regarded her as the archetypal spinster never likely to receive an offer of marriage. In fact she received two proposals during 1839 and was to receive two more in later life. The first of the four offers of marriage came from Ellen's brother, Reverend Henry Nussey, a curate whom she had known while at Roe Head. In a letter written in March 1839 Charlotte tells him firmly that her answer 'must be a *decided negative*'. She goes on to give her reasons with a wonderful frankness: 'I have no personal repugnance to the idea of a union with you—but I feel convinced that mine is not the sort of disposition calculated to form the happiness of a man like you'. She believes he would only be suited by a wife whose character 'should not be too marked, ardent and original—her temper should be mild, her piety undoubted, her spirits even and cheerful and her "*personal attractions*" sufficient to please your eye and gratify your just pride'. She sees herself with considerable insight as

not the serious, grave, cool-headed individual you suppose—you would think me romantic and [eccentric—you would] say I was satirical and [severe—however I scorn] deceit and I will never for the sake of attaining the distinction of matrimony and escaping the stigma of an old maid take a worthy man whom I am conscious I cannot render happy. (*Letters*, i. 185)

The second proposal of marriage that year also came from a clergyman, Reverend David Pryce, a young Irishman who visited Haworth on a single occasion with his vicar, William Hodgson. Charlotte found Pryce 'witty—lively—ardent—clever too—but deficient in the dignity & discretion of an Englishman'. She responded to his conversation with ease since she was on home ground, and laughed at his jokes, but 'cooled' when he began to practise his 'Hibernian flattery' on her. Her reaction to a written proposal from him a few days after his visit was to regard it as a joke: in describing the affair to Ellen, she urges her to 'prepare for a hearty laugh'. On receiving the letter, she says 'well thought I—I've heard of love at first sight but this beats all! I leave you to guess what my answer would be—convinced that you will not do me the injustice of guessing wrong' (*Letters*, i. 197–8).

The Wider World: Brussels

The period from 1842 to 1844 opened to Charlotte and Emily a world beyond Yorkshire, or even England. Their stay in Belgium was, however, not a happy experience for either of them. One trigger for the daring trip abroad was a half-formed plan made in 1841 for Charlotte, Emily, and Anne to set up a school together. Charlotte urged the idea that a stay in France or Belgium would be a useful preparation since it would provide a way of improving their knowledge of French and other subjects. But in addition to this practical purpose, the idea was further encouraged by a letter from Mary Taylor which excited Charlotte's imagination. When Mary was touring on the Continent with her brother in August 1841, she wrote to Charlotte who told Ellen:

Mary's letter spoke of some of the pictures & cathedrals she had seen— pictures the most exquisite—& cathedrals the most venerable—I hardly know what swelled to my throat as I read her letter—such a vehement impatience of restraint & steady work. Such a strong wish for wings— wings such as wealth can furnish—such an urgent thirst to see—to know—to learn—something internal seemed to expand boldly for a minute—I was tantalized with the consciousness of faculties increased— then all collapsed and I despaired. (*Letters*, i. 266)

The letter provided an impetus for her to deal with the practical difficulties of arranging a lengthy visit to a foreign country. There was Patrick to be persuaded to approve the scheme; Emily to be coaxed away from Haworth; and the need to find enough money. Charlotte dealt with the latter problem by writing a prudently businesslike letter to Aunt Branwell asking for an advance: friends have advised her of the need to refine her abilities since there are many schools in England competing for pupils; she would choose Brussels rather than France because it is cheaper and 'the facilities for education are equal or superior to any other place in Europe'; she could improve her French and Italian and 'even get a dash of German'; and Mrs Jenkins, wife of the British Consul, would find her 'a cheap and decent residence and respectable protection' (*Letters*, i. 268). The letter convinced her aunt and the money was forthcoming.

In February 1842 Patrick escorted his two daughters to London and then Brussels. What followed was to provide the outline of the story in Charlotte's last novel *Villette* and was to widen her horizons emotionally in a quite unexpected way. The refuge found for the Brontë sisters was the Pensionnat Heger, run by Mme Claire Zoe Heger with the help of her husband, Constantin, who also taught in a boys' school next door. Both the Hegers would appear in *Villette* in the guise of the Becks. The Heger School was built around three sides of a garden. Like the school in *Villette*, it had on the fourth side, closing the square, the boys' school with below its windows an *allée defendue*—a forbidden path. The Brontës' time in Brussels, first as pupils and then as part-time teachers of English (Charlotte) and music (Emily), was spent largely within the Pensionnat.

There were two aspects of the school to which Charlotte, despite her wish for wings that would take her to new worlds, instantly disliked. One was that the pupils were largely Belgian. After only a few months there, she wrote

If the national character of the Belgians is to be measured by the character of most of the girls in this school, it is a character singularly cold, selfish, animal and inferior—they are besides very mutinous and difficult for the teachers to manage—and their principles are rotten to the core—we avoid them—which is not difficult to do—as we have the brand of Protestantism and Anglicism upon us.

The sense of injury in the last comment indicates the other thorn in Charlotte's flesh (and presumably Emily's too): the fact that in a largely Catholic country they were surrounded in the Pensionnat by 'the mummeries' of Papistry, with its 'idiotic mercenary' priests and its feeble childish 'humbug' (*Letters*, i. 289). The effect on Charlotte of all this seems to have been claustrophobic, although she and Emily had friends and acquaintances here. Mary and Martha Taylor were at school just outside Brussels and had cousins, the Dixons, who were also in the city. In addition there were the Jenkins family and an English day-pupil at the Pensionnat, Laetitia Wheelwright, who became a friend of Charlotte.

This situation was easier for Charlotte than for Emily because of the teaching methods of M. Heger who was their instructor. He rigorously trained his pupils by making them read and analyse passages from classic French writers; then instructing them to develop essays, modelled on the style of the author in question, on a topic set by him. He then wrote detailed comments and suggestions which the pupils were to incorporate in a revised version of the essays which they had produced. Such a straitjacket was a far cry from the spontaneity and inventiveness of Gondal and Angria. Emily detested it but Charlotte learnt to kiss the rod when told to cut out mercilessly everything that did not make for clarity, accuracy, and effect. Certainly submissiveness was a form of behaviour which she manifested only with certain men—Patrick, Heger, and finally Arthur Bell. To the rest, she was strong-minded and self-willed.

Charlotte's submissiveness was presumably made easier by the fascination Heger came to hold for her. In May 1842 she described him with ironic humour to Ellen:

he is a professor of Rhetoric a man of power as to mind but very choleric & irritable in temperament—a little, black, ugly being with a face that varies in expression, sometimes he borrows the lineaments of an insane Tom-cat —sometimes those of a delirious Hyena—occasionally—but very seldom he discards these perilous attractions and assumes an air not above a hundred degrees removed from what you would call mild & gentlemanlike (*Letters*, i. 284)

In the same letter, however, she describes in general but revealing terms what has happened to her since her arrival in Brussels:

It felt very strange at first to 'submit to' authority instead of exercising it—to obey orders instead of giving them—but I like that state of things— I returned to it with the same avidity that a cow that has long been kept on dry hay returns to fresh grass—don't laugh at my simile—it is natural to me to submit and very unnatural to command. (*Letters*, i. 284)

The restrictive approach that Heger took to composition may indeed have benefited Charlotte by making her conscious of the rather purple descriptive style she had adopted in the Angrian writings and which does not appear in her published work.

Emily meantime was struggling with the work, not only because of her temperament but, as Charlotte points out to Ellen, because of her inadequate knowledge of French. M. Heger, however, did not underestimate the recalcitrant Emily. According to Gaskell's report of his opinion, he thought Emily had

a head for logic, and a capability of argument, unusual in a man and rare indeed in a woman, . . . Impairing the force of this gift, was her stubborn tenacity of will, which rendered her obtuse to all reasoning where her own wishes, or her own sense of right was concerned. She should have been a man—a great navigator . . . Her powerful reason would have deduced new spheres of discovery from the knowledge of the old; and her strong, imperious will would never have been daunted by opposition or difficulty; never have given way but with life. (Gaskell, *Life*, volume i, chapter 11)

Before their planned six-month stay came to an end, the Hegers offered the sisters free board and lodging for another six months in return for Charlotte giving English lessons and Emily teaching music. This continued until the autumn with Emily unhappy but Charlotte, apart from occasional homesickness, reasonably content with life in Brussels. But in October the first of a series of deaths occurred which disturbed and saddened the Brontës and finally changed their plans. Mary and her younger sister, Martha, the proto-type for Jessy Yorke in *Shirley*, were continuing at the school outside Brussels when Martha was struck down by cholera and in October died. The death of this vivacious young girl came as a great shock to Charlotte and Emily since she was a similar age to them as well as being a friend. Her death and burial in a foreign country presages the death of Jessy Yorke in *Shirley* who, nursed by her sister, dies in her arms, 'alone in a foreign country, and the soil of that country gave Jessy a grave' (book 1, chapter 9).

Other deaths followed and news reached Brussels that one of them, that of William Weightman, a young clergyman, had occurred at about the same time as Martha's. He had become Patrick's curate in 1839 and was a lively and flirtatious young man. Various stories grew up suggesting that Anne or Charlotte became infatuated with him, and the biographer Juliet Barker believes that Charlotte succumbed to Weightman's attractions.

By 2 November Charlotte and Emily had received a letter telling them that Aunt Branwell was dangerously ill. As they prepared to return to England they received another letter to say that she had died. By the time they reached Haworth she was already buried. In addition to their distress over their surrogate mother's death, the three sisters had to rethink their future. With Anne employed by the Robinsons at Thorp Green and Branwell about to join her as a tutor after having been dismissed from his post as a railway clerk, there was need now for someone to take charge of the domestic running of the house and act as a companion to Patrick. This role was willingly accepted by Emily who was now newly solvent as a result of Aunt Branwell's legacy of some £350 to each of her nieces. This was the life Emily wanted: to be in Haworth and free to write her poetry. Charlotte, however, was eager to return to Brussels and took up M. Heger's offer of a teaching post, made in a letter to Patrick Brontë and offered to either her or Emily. She returned this time alone (and unescorted on the journey) to Brussels in January 1843.

According to Charlotte's account to Elizabeth Gaskell, the journey was both pleasurable and frightening and she drew upon it to describe Lucy Snowe's journey to Villette. On arrival she was offered the use of the Hegers' sitting room but avoided it from a feeling that she should not intrude on the family life of her employers. She began to give English lessons to Heger and his wife's brother. The Dixons willingly visited her and all should have been set fair but by April she is rebuking Ellen Nussey for passing on rumours that ' "the future époux [husband] of Mademoiselle Brontë is on the Continent" '. Indignantly she responds that the only man she speaks to is Heger and that rarely. She rejects with contempt women who have 'neither fortune nor beauty' and who set their sights on marriage instead of recognizing that since they are unattractive they had better 'be quiet & think of other things than wedlock' (*Letters*, i. 315). By May 1843 she is becoming unhappy at the cat-like quarrels of two of her fellow teachers and believes that one of them is a 'regular spy' of Mme Heger's. She complains that the latter has influenced her husband against her and that he now regards Charlotte 'as a person to be let alone' (*Letters*, i. 319–20). The implication now seems to be that Mme Heger has recognized Charlotte's attachment to her husband and that the couple are deliberately distancing themselves. To add to Charlotte's isolation, the Dixon and Jenkins families left Brussels.

Though Charlotte's letters to Ellen insist on treating her relationship with Heger as merely one of admiring pupil and teacher, it is evident that her feelings for him became unbearably strong and precipitated some kind of emotional crisis for her in the summer vacation when the pupils went home. Oddly it took a religious form, but then her feelings about Catholicism had always been strangely passionate. Possibly, though she despised it intellectually, its rituals and mystery had an emotional appeal which she needed to suppress. Some such explanation is needed for the episode which occurred during the vacation and which she confided to Emily in September 1843. She tells how, returning from a visit to Martha Taylor's grave, she found herself at the cathedral of St Gudule and went in as a service was about to begin. It is apparent that she felt a need to unburden herself of something she had done that she regarded as sinful. Seeing a confessional, 'I felt as if I did not care what I did, provided it was not absolutely wrong, and that it served to vary my life and yield a moment's interest. I took a fancy to change myself into a Catholic and go and make a real confession to see what it was like' (*Letters*, i. 329–30).

This nonchalant explanation is surprising in view of the passionate hostility to Catholics and Catholicism that recurred throughout her life. She begins by telling the priest that she is a foreigner and a Protestant and, despite his initial resistance, she persuades him to hear her confession. True to her previous belief in the machinating papists, he urges her to come back for instruction and she promises but with no intention of returning. What she confessed is not revealed but she asserts that it was 'a real confession' and the need to unburden herself appears to have been so urgent it might be assumed to relate to her 'sinful' feelings for a married man (*Letters*, i. 329–30). Adultery in Angria was an everyday matter but not so in real life—even in thought. After this the emphasis in her letters shifts slightly from hostility to Mme Heger to thoughts of home. She thinks nostalgically of being in the back kitchen at Haworth 'cutting up the hash', surrounded by the family pets Tiger and Keeper, with 'Tabby blowing the fire, in order to boil the potatoes to a sort of vegetable glue' (*Letters*, i. 331). Shortly after this, during a lesson she writes vehemently into her atlas 'First Class. I am very cold—there is no Fire—I wish I were at home with Papa—Branwell—Emily—Anne & Tabby—I am tired of being among foreigners—it is a dreary life—especially as there is only one person in this house worthy of being liked—also another, who seems like a rosy sugar plum, but I know her to be coloured chalk' (*LFC* i. 307). By the beginning of 1844 she was back in Haworth, free to remain in the back kitchen cutting up the hash.

Gaskell's account of Charlotte's return reveals nothing of her feelings for Heger; instead it concentrates on such matters as Patrick's failing eyesight and his daughter's sense that he needed her. But Gaskell, by the time she wrote her biography, knew of the letters written by her friend to Heger which are the real evidence of her love for him and which were written after her return to England. In theory Charlotte was now well prepared to set up the proposed school with her sisters which it was finally settled was to be at the Parsonage itself. By October 1844 no pupils had been found and the plan fell through. As so often Charlotte was, throughout this time, leading a double life: on the one hand writing to contacts about the proposed school or prospective pupils; and on the other keeping up an anguished and one-sided correspondence with Heger until November 1845. None of her family and friends knew of these letters to her former master.

Their whole tone is beseeching and she becomes increasingly pressing. In July 1844 she confesses that her earlier letter was hardly rational 'because sadness was wringing my heart'. She claims to be afraid of forgetting her French which would be necessary for her to remember when she sees him again—'it must happen since I so long for it, and then I would not like to stay silent in your presence' (*Letters*, i. 357). She writes to him again in August and in October, telling him that however he responds she will be satisfied so long as she receives a letter. In January 1845 when still no reply has come, she grovels: 'Day and night I find neither rest nor peace—if I sleep I have tormenting dreams in which I see you always severe, always saturnine and angry with me' (*Letters*, i. 379). These surviving letters were not discovered until the early twentieth century when they were found, having been torn up and then glued together again. One theory is that Heger tore them up and his Mme Beck of a wife rescued them and stuck them together. Meantime the man Charlotte was later to marry, Arthur Bell Nicholls, had in May 1845 become her father's curate.

The Literary Arena: Triumph and Despair

By the time Charlotte ceased writing to Heger, the family faced a crisis, precipitated as usual by Branwell. In 1840, after an initial failure either to become a student at the Royal Academy or to set up as a portrait painter, he had taken a post as a tutor with the Postlethwaites at Broughton in Furness. From this post he was dismissed, possibly because of drunkenness or sexual misconduct. Things took a turn for the better in the same year when he was appointed as a railway clerk at Sowerby Bridge in Yorkshire and then in 1841 promoted at a salary of £130 a year to chief clerk at Luddenden Foot. But in March 1842, though not accused personally of fraud, he was dismissed for a discrepancy in the accounts. There followed his time as a tutor with the Robinsons at Thorp Green where Anne was already a governess. His stay there lasted from early 1843 to July 1845 when he was apparently accused of an affair with his employer's wife, Lydia Robinson, and dismissed. As Charlotte put it to Ellen, Mr Robinson wrote 'intimating that he had discovered his proceedings which he characterized as bad beyond expression and charging him . . . to break off instantly and forever all communication with every member of his family' (*Letters*, i. 412). Anne too left—of her own accord.

Such a scandal shocked and shamed the family greatly. Some have assumed that Branwell only imagined that Mrs Robinson reciprocated his feelings; others that the scandal involved the seduction of the Robinsons' son, to whom he was tutor. But Branwell, as a well-established womanizer, was rumoured to have fathered at least one illegitimate child at the Postlethwaites'; and Lydia Robinson's behaviour after his dismissal suggests an attempt to keep him quiet. Branwell certainly expected to marry her after her husband's death in 1846. But Lydia and her family moved to Birmingham, though she continued to supply Branwell with money to pay his debts. In 1848, after Branwell's death, she married Sir Edward Scott who had rather more to offer than the disgraced and penniless young man had done. Branwell until his own death continued with his heavy drinking and opium use. According to Charlotte, the later years of his life provided material that Anne was able to use in her portrayal of the faithless and alcoholic husband Arthur Huntingdon, in her novel *The Tenant of Wildfell Hall*. When Branwell and Anne returned home in 1845 none of the Brontë children was now gainfully employed. Charlotte took the lead in casting around for other means of earning money. An opportunity presented itself late in 1845 when, to Emily's fury, her sister discovered and read a manuscript containing her poems. Struck by their quality, Charlotte hatched a plan of publishing a selection of poetry by all three of them. Although Emily was very difficult to persuade, she finally agreed, provided that they all concealed their identity under pseudonyms. She contributed twenty poems, Anne another twenty, and Charlotte nineteen, under the names of Currer, Ellis, and Acton Bell. Publication took place in May 1846 with the sisters contributing to the publisher's costs. Disappointingly the volume sold only two copies but this fact was counterbalanced by very favourable reviews. One reviewer described the work as 'good, wholesome, refreshing, vigorous poetry' amid 'the trash and trumpery' of much contemporary verse (Allott, p. 59). Another critic saw the poems of all three sisters as an example of 'a family in whom appears to run the instinct of song'. This reviewer saw Ellis's work as 'filled with an inspiration and an evident power of wing that may reach heights not here attempted' (Allott, p. 61). None of this was revealed to Patrick.

By April, stirred on by the sight of the poems in print and by the critical approval, Currer, Ellis, and Acton offered their publishers, Aylott and Jones of London, 'a work of fiction, consisting of three distinct and unconnected tales which may be published as work of 3 vols. of the ordinary novel-size, or separately as single vols. as shall be deemed most advisable' (*Letters*, i. 461). The reference to three volumes alludes to the three-decker, a single novel in three volumes: Charlotte is suggesting a pseudo-three-decker but Aylott and Jones declined the offer of Charlotte's *The Professor*, Emily's *Wuthering Heights*, and Anne's *Agnes Grey*. Undaunted, Charlotte sent the manuscripts to several other publishers in succession and eventually Thomas Newby agreed to publish Emily's and Anne's novel but not Charlotte's. *The Professor* was rejected by every publisher it was sent to, but George Smith of Smith Elder wrote, in turning it down, that a talent was discernible in it and a three-volume novel by its author would be looked at with interest. Tenacious as ever, Charlotte was able within a month to send him in August 1847 her second novel, *Jane Eyre*, which she had begun in August 1846 when she spent a month alone with Patrick in Manchester, tending him after a cataract operation. Smith's reader, William Smith Williams, who was to become a close friend of Charlotte, strongly recommended it and passed it on to his employer George Smith himself who 'could not put the book down . . . before I went to bed that night I had finished reading the MS' (Barker, p. 527). By 12 September, less than three weeks after submitting her manuscript, Charlotte was writing to accept Smith's terms and refusing to 'revise' *Jane Eyre*. The novel was published in October while *Wuthering Heights* and *Agnes Grey* did not appear until December. Early in 1848 the fact of Charlotte's authorship—and presumably that of Emily and of Anne—was made known to Patrick. It only slowly spread to the London literary circle and to Yorkshire.

By this time *Jane Eyre* had become a best-seller: 2,500 copies were sold in three months and it was reprinted in January and again in April 1848. *Wuthering Heights* also caused a great stir in the literary world but *Agnes Grey* did not. What Charlotte's and Emily's works were found to have in common was that both were shocking in their handling of sexual matters but both were also powerful and compulsive narratives. But Thackeray had no reservations and wrote to Williams, 'I wish you had not sent me *Jane Eyre*. It interested me so much that I have lost (or won if you like) a whole day in reading it at the busiest period, with the printers I know waiting for copy' (Allott, p. 70). George Eliot struck a sourer note: 'All self-sacrifice is good—but one would like it to be in a somewhat nobler cause than that of a diabolical law which chains a man body and soul to a putrifying carcase. However, the book is interesting—only I wish the characters would talk a little less like the heroes and heroines of news reports' (Allott, p. 92). *Wuthering Heights* troubled readers more than *Jane Eyre* had done but it sold well. Interestingly however, *Agnes Grey* which did precisely what convention required, did not sell anything like so well as the other two novels and received only lukewarm reviews.

Much attention in reviews and elsewhere focused on the identity of the Bells. Were they one, two, or three? Were they male or female? The unscrupulous Newby muddied the waters by suggesting that Anne's second novel, *The Tenant of Wildfell Hall*, which he published in June 1848, was written by the author of all the Bells' novels. Meanwhile reviewers speculated as to gender since they found matters such as the brutality, attempted bigamy, and an unmarried woman's passion for a married man in *Jane Eyre* easier to accept from a male author. Some did suspect female authorship and one saw *Jane Eyre* as a kind of hermaphrodite text in which Currer 'divides the authorship, if we are not misinformed, with a brother and sister' (Allott, p. 98). In a letter to Mary Taylor, now in New Zealand, Charlotte tells how the confusion over the authorship of *The Tenant of Wildfell Hall*, instigated by Newby, led Smith, Elder to send her a letter 'all in alarm, suspicion and wrath' (*Letters*, ii. 111). They believed that Currer Bell's second novel had been given to a rival publisher, a rumour that Charlotte was determined to scotch. She persuaded Anne (but not the reclusive Emily) to accompany her on an unannounced, uninvited visit to Smith, Elder at Cornhill in London. They travelled by train and arrived early on Saturday morning, 8 July, settling themselves at the only lodgings they knew, the Chapter Coffee House, where Charlotte and Emily had stayed with Patrick on the way to Brussels.

The purpose of the trip was to 'prove' their separate identities. At Smith's office, to which they went immediately on arrival, they met George Smith and William Smith Williams (WSW). 'Neither Mr Smith nor Mr Williams knew we were coming they had never seen us—they did not know whether we were men or women—but had always written to us as men' (*Letters*, ii. 112). The tone of Charlotte's letter to Mary suggests a mischievous delight at the 'queer perplexity' of the two men at their sudden arrival and at the contrast between their literary reputation and their demure, old-fashioned appearance. From this point onwards the perplexity must have been transferred to the two sisters who found themselves living out their lives as celebrities in the metropolis. Soon after their identification the Cornhill offices were filled with 'talk talk talk', writes Charlotte,

Mr Williams being silent—Mr Smith loquacious—'Allow me to introduce you to my mother & sisters—How long do you stay in Town?—You must make the most of the time—tonight you must go to the Italian opera—you must see the Exhibition—Mr Thackeray would be pleased to see you—if Mr Lewes knew 'Currer Bell' was in town—he would have to be shut up—I will ask them both to dinner at my house. (*Letters*, ii. 112–13)

Despite an invitation from Smith to stay with his family they insisted on staying on at the Coffee House and also on preserving their incognitos when thrown into the social round that Smith engaged in. For, by their standards, thrown they were. That night without a rest after their journey, Charlotte had to 'put my headache into my pocket' (*Letters*, ii. 113) to accompany the Smith family to the opera to hear *The Barber of Seville*. On Sunday after being accompanied to the Wren church, St Stephen's Walbrook, they dined with the Smiths in grand style in Bayswater. On Monday they visited the Exhibition of the Royal Academy; again dined with the Smiths; and ended the evening with a visit to Williams and his family where a daughter of Leigh Hunt charmed them with Italian songs.

Charlotte's account to Mary takes evident satisfaction in the visual contrast between her own and her sister's old-fashioned and provincial appearance and the VIP treatment which evidently was seen as appropriate to their literary standing. Triumphantly she describes the visit to the opera thus:

we attired ourselves in the plain-high-made country garments we possessed—and went with them to their carriage—where we found Williams likewise in full dress. They must have thought us queer, quizzical looking beings—especially me with my spectacles. I smiled inwardly at the contrast which must have been apparent between me and Mr Smith as I walked with him up the crimson carpeted staircase of the Opera House and stood amongst a brilliant throng at the box-door which was not yet open. Fine ladies & gentlemen glanced at us with a slight, graceful superciliousness quite warranted by the circumstances—Still I felt pleasurably excited—in spite of headache sickness and conscious clownishness. (*Letters*, ii. 113–14)

For Charlotte, always conscious of her plainness, this was the triumph of talent over mere appearance.

On Tuesday they returned to Haworth, laden with books provided by Williams who took up the task of providing them with parcels of books on a permanent basis. For Charlotte several more exciting visits to London were to follow but only after a period of intense grief and depression, during which Williams proved to be a rock in their correspondence. While Charlotte struggled with a new novel, *Shirley*, and Emily evidently began a second novel, Branwell's health grew worse. In addition to advancing tuberculosis, he was in the last stages of alcoholism and drug addiction. Throughout this time, when he was suffering from delirium tremens, Patrick took him to sleep in the same room as himself so that he could care for him. On 24 September Branwell died of what the death certificate described as chronic bronchitis and marasmus but what was probably tuberculosis. Charlotte's reaction to his death is frankly expressed in a letter to Williams some weeks later after she had recovered from a collapse which followed her brother's death: 'I do not weep from a sense of bereavement—there is no prop withdrawn, no consolation torn away, no dear companion lost—but for the wreck of talent, the ruin of promise, the untimely, dreary extinction of what might have been a burning and a shining light' (*Letters*, ii. 122).

Quite soon after Branwell's death, it became apparent that Emily too was gravely ill. She remained stoical but rash, refusing medical help that was anxiously offered from both local and London sources. Emily persisted in ignoring her own condition and on 19 December 1848 again got up, dressed, and came downstairs but by the afternoon she had died 'in the arms of those who loved her'. As Charlotte wrote to Williams, the last three months had seemed to the family 'like a long, terrible dream' (*Letters*, ii. 155). Charlotte, unlike her father, was much more distressed by Emily's death than by Branwell's and wrote that

life has become very void, and hope has proved a strange traitor: when I shall again be able to put confidence in her suggestions, I know not; she kept whispering that Emily would not—*could* not die—and where is she now? Out of my reach—out of my world, torn from me. (*Letters*, ii. 165)

Now, with what seemed like inevitability, the health of Anne, the next in line, declined. For some months Charlotte and Patrick again watched the fluctuations of tuberculosis with anxiety rising and falling. Anne developed an urgent wish to visit a favourite seaside resort, though she was manifestly not fit for the journey. But seeing it as a dying woman's wish, Charlotte and Patrick agreed, and Charlotte and Ellen Nussey took her to Scarborough on 25 May 1849 where she died and was buried three days later.

After a year which had seen literary success and a welter of bereavements shattering the family circle, Charlotte was left alone with Patrick in a house haunted by memories of her sisters and brother. It is to Williams that she describes her unbearable grief:

when evening darkens something in my heart revolts against the burden of solitude—the sense of loss and want grows almost too much for me—I am

not good or amiable in such moments—I am rebellious ... could I do
without bed—I would never seek it—waking—I think—sleeping—I
dream of them—and I cannot recall them as they were in health—still
they appear to me in sickness and suffering. (*Letters*, ii. 224)

The Solitary Life of a Literary Celebrity

In the aftermath of the deaths of all her siblings Charlotte's closest
contact seems to have been her correspondent William Smith
Williams. Though she always addressed him formally as 'My dear
Sir', she is more open with him than with Ellen Nussey. With Ellen
she feels obliged to allude to the consolations of religion; to Williams
she speaks more frankly, confessing that the palliative for her grief is
not religion but writing: 'Labour is the only radical cure for rooted
sorrow'. A calm and cheerful companion such as Ellen is a mildly
soothing opiate but 'work is the best substitute' (*Letters*, ii. 224).

Consequently by the end of August 1849, some three months after
Anne's death, she had completed her new novel. She chose the title
Shirley for the book because, as she told Williams, Shirley 'has
turned out the most prominent and peculiar character in the work'
(*Letters*, ii. 237). This refers to the shift in the focus of the book from
Caroline Helstone to Shirley Keeldar who is popularly seen as a
eulogistic picture of Emily Brontë. This is too simplistic a view and,
like other biographical readings of the Brontës' novels, distorts both
the work and its supposed model. As Charlotte told Williams, writing the narrative 'has been a boon to me—it took me out of dark and
desolate reality to an unreal but happier region' (*Letters*, ii. 241). For
the publication of *Shirley*, Charlotte added a vitriolic preface attacking Elizabeth Rigby who had criticized *Jane Eyre* as the work of a
woman who must be an outcast and possibly a fallen one. With
difficulty Smith and Williams persuaded her to withdraw this embit-
tered and controversial piece. She persisted, however, in rejecting
suggestions for 'improving' *Shirley*, and the manuscript was collected
from Haworth by Smith's managing clerk, James Taylor, and
published in October 1849.

The success of *Jane Eyre* ensured much interest in the author's
next novel and most reviewers chose the easy option of comparing the
two works: the general consensus was positive. Charlotte's impetuous reply to a waspish critique by G. H. Lewes was a single-sentence

letter with no formal opening which read simply: 'I can be on my guard against my enemies, but God deliver me from my friends! Currer Bell' (*Letters*, ii. 330). Lewes's treachery (as Charlotte saw it) may have contributed to the difficulties she experienced when attempting early in 1851 to begin her next novel *Villette*, which she did not complete until the end of 1852. As she struggled with this last novel, she frequently sought distraction from it and from her loneliness and grief by visiting the outside world and particularly London literary society. Between 1851 and mid-1853 she led the life of a celebrity, a literary lion on the London scene, alternating with periods of seclusion in the provincial parsonage. She was all the more sought-after because of her desire to avoid conventional socializing. She had noted during her introductory visit to George Smith that 'I always feel under awkward constraint at table. Dining-out would be a hideous bore to me' (*Letters*, ii. 114). Now she felt confident enough to reject invitations to dinners or receptions with the simple statement that she had made a rule for herself of not going out anywhere during her stay in town. She wanted to meet literary figures, not socialites, and she initiated a correspondence with Harriet Martineau by sending her a copy of *Shirley* and visited her at Ambleside, where she also met Matthew Arnold. On another visit to the Lake District she met Elizabeth Gaskell, her future biographer.

She visited London four times, sometimes prolonging her stay for up to a month and staying as a house-guest of George Smith's mother, with whom he lived. It is often suggested that she fell in love with Smith at this time and took it hard when in 1853 he became engaged to someone else. Certainly she took the daring step of meeting him in the city of Edinburgh, after one of her London trips, where he had gone with his sister to collect a younger brother. She spent two days with them seeing the sights. The question of her feelings for him, however, remains unanswered, though there is a coolness evident after his engagement. Whatever her emotions, she evidently enjoyed her visits to London which provided her with wide-ranging interests and distraction. She visited the Royal Academy, the Turner pictures at the National Gallery, the Chapel Royal for a glimpse of her hero, the Duke of Wellington, the Ladies Gallery of the House of Commons, various private galleries and the Zoological Gardens, as well as a prison and an asylum. She also attended three lectures by Thackeray on English writers and was much impressed by them. She had already become acquainted with him in 1849 and later had given him a grilling about his literary 'shortcomings' which she felt marred his otherwise superlative writings.

Of all the events crammed into her times in London, these lectures and two other experiences were the highlights. These were five visits to the Great Exhibition of 1851 and two performances by the French tragic actress Rachel. Her letters show that her first visit to the Exhibition left her less than overwhelmed:

Yesterday we went to the Crystal Palace—the exterior has a strange and elegant but somewhat unsubstantial effect—The interior is like a mighty Vanity Fair—the brightest colours blaze on all sides—and ware of all kinds—from diamonds to spinning jennies … It was very fine—gorgeous—animated—bewildering—but I liked Thackeray's lectures better. (*Letters*, ii. 625)

Her second visit made it seem almost magical in its splendour and led to three more:

It is a wonderful place—vast—strange new and impossible to describe. Its grandeur does not consist in *one* thing but in the unique assemblage of *all* things—Whatever human industry has created—you find there—from the great compartments filled with Railway Engines and boilers . . . to the glass-covered and velvet spread stands loaded with the most gorgeous work of the goldsmith and silversmith—and the carefully guarded caskets full of real diamonds and pearls worth hundreds of thousands of pounds. It may be called a Bazaar or a Fair—but it is such a Bazaar or Fair as eastern Genii might have created. (*Letters*, ii. 631)

She insists on the quietness of the Crystal Palace: though there were 30,000 people present, 'the living tide rolls on quietly—with a deep hum like the sea heard from a distance' (*Letters*, ii. 631).

The same extreme emotional reaction is even more strongly expressed when she describes the performance of the actress Rachel, from which she drew material for the actress who entrances Lucy Snowe in *Villette*:

On Saturday I went to hear & see Rachel—a wonderful sight—terrible as if the earth had cracked deep at your feet and revealed a glimpse of hell—I shall never forget it—she made me shudder to the marrow of my bones: in her some fiend has certainly taken up an incarnate home. (*Letters*, ii. 648)

Fascination, if not exactly delight, is also evident in a less likely visit to hear a speech by the first English Catholic cardinal and archbishop (of Westminster) since the Reformation. The fact that she went at all indicates something of her ambivalence towards Catholicism, as does her strong reaction to what she saw:

He is a big portly man ... he has not merely a double but a treble and quadruple chin; he has a very large mouth with oily lips, and looks as if he would relish a good dinner with a bottle of wine after it. He came swimming into the room, smiling, simpering, and bowing like a fat old lady, and sat down very demure in his chair and looked the picture of a sleek hypocrite ... A bevy of inferior priests surrounded him, many of them very dark-looking and sinister men. (*Letters*, ii. 640–1)

He spoke, she says, in a 'smooth whining voice' while his Catholic audience regarded him like a god.

While at Haworth in the intervals between trips to London, Manchester, the Lake District, and Ellen Nussey's home, Charlotte was visited by many unannounced and uninvited admirers who wished to view the icon. Throughout all these varieties of distraction she worked on *Villette*, which was published in January 1853. This was her last novel, though not the last to be published: that distinction fell to her much rejected but cherished first novel, *The Professor*, which finally made it into print in 1857.

Marriage and a New Family Circle

During the period of her visits to London from 1851 to 1853 Charlotte received two more proposals of marriage. The first came from Smith's employee, James Taylor, in April 1851 when he was on the brink of a five-year posting to India. Charlotte's letters to Ellen Nussey on the event show her willing herself to accept him but finally unable to do so. She tells how, though 'predisposed as I was to regard him very favourably' (*Letters*, ii. 598), she could not do so. Later she explained her feelings more fully:

with every intention even to look on him in the most favourable point of view at his last visit it was impossible to me in my inmost heart ... [to] think of him as one that might one day be acceptable as a husband ... Dear Nell—I looked for something of the gentleman—something I mean of the *natural* gentleman ... I could not find one gleam ... In mind too; though clever—he is second rate;—thoroughly second rate ... Were I to marry him—my heart would bleed—in pain and humiliation—I could not—*could* not look up to him. (*Letters*, ii. 609)

It is not clear why, in spite of these feelings, she intended to 'favour' him. She evidently found him physically repugnant since 'each moment he came near me . . . my veins ran ice' (*Letters*, ii. 600). She had corresponded with him for some time as a result of the connection with George Smith but never with the openness and evident pleasure that she took in writing to Williams. Why then should marriage to him appear as a duty? True, Patrick favoured him but that in itself was strange since her father did not in general wish her to marry. Perhaps she saw marriage with Taylor as a way of settling her life if Patrick should die, even though she was by now financially secure. Perhaps she simply tried to believe that it was a woman's duty to marry.

Her second proposal in this period (and fourth in her lifetime) came from her father's curate, Arthur Bell Nicholls, who had been in the background of her life since 1845. Charlotte had originally disliked him and told Ellen that it would please everyone if he did not come back from a holiday in his native Ireland. She had also caricatured him as one of the tiresome curates in the opening chapter of *Shirley*. It must have surprised her when, reading the novel aloud to Patrick, he evidently recognized the portrait and roared with laughter. By the end of 1852 she had recognized something of his feelings for her but she was amazed by his manner in proposing to her, 'Shaking from head to foot, looking deadly pale, speaking low, vehemently yet with difficulty'. Before answering him she consulted her father who became passionate in a different way: he 'worked himself into a state not to be trifled with—the veins on his temples started up like whipcord—and his eyes became suddenly bloodshot'. Hastily she promised to reject Nicholls the next day in order to quell Patrick's 'vehement antipathy to the bare thought of anyone thinking of me as a wife' (*LFC* iv. 28–30).

It has been suggested that this antipathy resulted from Patrick's feeling that his celebrated daughter was too good for a mere curate, but later events suggest that at this stage he clung to her as the sole prop in his old age. Whatever the reason, Nicholls was rejected and Charlotte felt it to be an injustice, especially as his shattered state made her realize 'for the first time what it costs a man to declare affection where he doubts response' (*LFC* iv. 28–30). Patrick, however, was in a vengeful mood and wrote a vitriolic note to Nicholls (to which Charlotte added one dissociating herself from her father's sentiments). The curate gave up his post and then, after having second thoughts, wished to withdraw his resignation. Patrick stipulated that he should only do so on condition that he gave up all idea of marrying Charlotte. Finally Nicholls was driven in May 1853 to take another curacy elsewhere. On his final visit to the Parsonage, Charlotte did not see him until he had left her father when she found him 'leaning against the garden-door in a paroxysm of anguish— sobbing as women never sob'. Significantly, though she felt she could not encourage him, she spoke to him in such a way as to let him know that 'I am not cruelly blind and indifferent to his constancy and grief' (*LFC* iv. 68–9).

It seems to have been the passionate nature of Arthur Nicholls's distress that helped to change Charlotte's feeling towards him. Presumably his evident grief at rejection was only too reminiscent of what she had felt about M. Heger in the period after she left Brussels. It is as though the extent of suffering felt was for her the measure of passion the person rejected feels for the one rejecting. Certainly she was prepared, after several letters from Nicholls which she ignored, to start up a clandestine correspondence with him and finally to persuade Patrick to let him visit Haworth Parsonage. Patrick had already suffered one stroke and was shortly to suffer another which affected his eyesight. This evidently brought home to him the folly of alienating a deeply conscientious and supportive curate, a point which Charlotte also recognized. Eventually Patrick agreed to an engagement between the couple with the understanding that Nicholls and Charlotte would move back into the Parsonage after the wedding.

Charlotte is open as to her attitude to her future husband and what life with him would entail: 'he is a Puseyite and very stiff; I fear it will stand in the way of my intercourse with some of my friends' (*LFC* iv. 123). She admits that 'I cannot conceal from myself that he is *not* intellectual; there are many places into which he could not follow me intellectually' (*LFC* iv. 122). She hopes that the marriage will satisfy 'the demands of feeling and duty' and sees in it 'some germs of real happiness' (*LFC* iv. 114). The rationale for the marriage which took place in June 1854, some eighteen months after Nicholls's first proposal, was that it gave Patrick a permanent and reliable curate. As a result of the marriage settlement it also gave financial security in the event of his daughter's death, since he would inherit her earnings which otherwise would have gone to her husband.

While the couple were on the wedding tour, first to North Wales and then to Arthur's home in Ireland, Charlotte was gratified by perceiving his high social status and his popularity amongst his family. On her return she writes of how 'every day makes my own attachment to him stronger' (*LFC* iv. 160). But she also reports how little time she has from her duties as a clergyman's wife, and from Arthur's demands for her company. She tells Ellen how he wishes her to be less open in her letters and he himself requires her friends to burn all Charlotte's letters. Her ties to London have 'waxed very frail' and she does not wish it otherwise (*LFC* iv. 119). Her life now returns to a narrow family circle: her father, her husband, and herself. She stresses Arthur's merits rather than her love for him, and her views on marriage confirm her ambivalence on the subject:

I know more of the realities of life than I once did ... I think those married women who indiscriminately urge their acquaintance to marry— much to blame. For my part—I can only say with deeper sincerity and fuller significance ... Wait God's will ... it is a solemn and strange and perilous thing for a woman to become a wife. Man's lot is far—far different. (*LFC* iv. 145)

Even in this strange and perilous new world Charlotte managed to write two chapters of a new novel, *Willie Ellen*, but got no further. By December 1854 she was pregnant and became ill with what appeared to be a complication of the pregnancy. The seriousness of her condition was not recognized at first and she died in Haworth Parsonage on 31 March 1855. Before her death she wrote a will in which she cancelled the marriage settlement in order to leave everything to Arthur. By this time she was confident of the friendship between her husband and her father, a trust which Arthur discharged until Patrick's death in 1861.

CHAPTER 2

THE FABRIC OF SOCIETY

WE are accustomed to think of the second half of the twentieth century as a period of unparalleled change but in fact the first half of the nineteenth century matches it, at least in qualitative alteration. The period saw the continuation of industrialization, along with its accompanying changes in the way of life for the working classes and many of the middle class. At the same time Britain became more crowded as the population doubled between 1801 and 1851 to over twenty million people. Ease of communication, another twentieth-century preoccupation, increased hugely as a result of simple sounding improvements: new canals, better roads, and better steamships for coastal travel; and in the 1840s came the electric telegraph, the penny post, the pillar box, and the development of photography.

Above all, the pace of life was speeded up as a national railway system developed after George Stephenson in 1815 showed how a steam engine could replace the horses which had sometimes drawn trucks along rails. By 1830 his famous steam engine the *Rocket* had reached a speed of 39 miles per hour on the equally (in)famous day when William Huskisson, the previous president of the Board of Trade, was killed by a passing locomotive. By 1837 the network had spread so that there was a line from London to Manchester; by 1840 from London to Southampton; and by 1841 from London to Bristol. The great London railway termini began to be built like huge temples to the force that could transform landscape with breath-taking viaducts or with man-made valleys, as well as increasing the speed of travel and transport. Sheer disbelief that such progress could occur is evident in a comment in 1820 as to the 'palpable' absurdity of imagining that trains would ever travel as fast as stage-coaches. But by 1848 Charlotte and Anne Brontë could leave Keighley in the late afternoon, journey to Leeds, and thence by train to London for early next morning without finding anything remarkable in the speed, nor in the fact that they had made investments in the railways themselves. Some major industries, such as iron and coal-mining, were boosted by the development of the railways and by the need to supply their products to those building railways outside Britain. Ironically in this way they enhanced the industrial scope of those who were later to become competitors.

Even in this period of continued industrial expansion the country experienced a series of post-war depressions which led to working-class unrest, to which the Tory government responded with severe repression. Forms of protest included attacks on machinery such as those which had already occurred in the Luddite disruption of 1811–16 while there were also bread riots in East Anglia; and in 1819 a mass protest by some fifty or sixty thousand people in St Peter's Field, Manchester. What happened there became known (ironically, on the model of 'Waterloo') as the Peterloo Massacre, when the magistrates panicked and sent in armed troops who left some 400 wounded and 11 dead. The episode stirred up more unrest which led in turn to even more repression in the form of laws specifying powers for magistrates to restrict the size of public meetings and to issue warrants allowing searches for arms. Law and order became a general concern and by 1837 the police force which Robert Peel had initiated in the metropolis in 1829 was replicated in many boroughs in the country. Thus the Brontës' short lifespan was a far from tranquil one nationally: it was marked by a society of haves and have-nots, and the turbulence that such disparity brings.

The Game of Politics 1815–1855

Charlotte, Branwell, Emily, and Anne Brontë were all born in the five years following the triumph of the 'Great Duke' of Wellington over Napoleon at Waterloo, which brought to an end more than twenty years of Napoleonic Wars. Surprisingly the children from an early age took a precocious interest in what went on in the remoteness of Westminster and London, receiving their information from local newspapers; from *Blackwood's Magazine*; and from conversations with their father. It was largely the personalities of the participants in the struggle between the opposing parties, the Tories and the Whigs, which appealed, since they evidently found the 'who's in and who's out' game compulsive and used them as storylines in the Angrian material.

In following this power struggle the children started with a strong inclination to support the Tories, partly because that was Patrick's affiliation; and also because they probably felt a strong inclination to support the party that had governed the country almost continuously since 1783, the party led in turn by William Pitt, the Duke of Portland, Spencer Perceval, Lord Liverpool, George Canning, and the great Duke of Wellington. Only the last of these leaders would have acknowledged the label 'Tory' but, as political conflict polarized in the later 1820s, pundits came increasingly to see the battle in terms of Whigs and Tories, and the ruling party, now led by Wellington and Peel, were characterized simply as Tories. Certainly, it was in this dualistic way that the Brontë girls saw matters. The Tories felt themselves to be the natural rulers of the country since they had ruled for so long and still regarded the landed interest as the 'stamina' of the country. Their first aim was the protection of landowners' interests by suppressing any signs of dissent that might erupt into a bloody revolution such as people of Patrick's generation had seen in France. Increasingly also, in the interest of landowners, they wished to control agricultural commerce through suitable legislation and though Patrick remained a staunch Tory supporter, he believed that retaining the social and political status quo was not incompatible with concern for the physical welfare of the working classes. Hence his role in local matters such as the agitation for clean water at Haworth and his support for the enforcement of the 1833 Factory Act restricting (in a compromised form) the employment of children. The opposing team, the Whigs, were therefore the Brontës' natural enemies whom they wished to see out of power, since in broad terms they represented not only some of the old aristocracy but the commercial and industrial sector of society. They had a more 'liberal' attitude to so-called reform such as extension of the franchise or changes to the Poor Law. These two 'reforms' indicate the ambiguity of the term 'liberal' at this time: the new Poor Law restricting relief only to those in workhouses meant being harsh to the underdogs; extending the franchise meant being generous to the better-off among them.

Neither political grouping, not even the more liberal wing of the Whigs, wished to remove social inequity by reorganizing society, for both Tories and Whigs were led by aristocrats and the recently ennobled whom the Brontë children evidently saw as romantic figures, with Charlotte fascinated by the Duke of Wellington and the

Wellesley family generally. Somewhat surprisingly only Emily, usually in popular imagination an unworldly, fey creature, makes use of the struggle between landed and commercial interests in her writing: *Wuthering Heights*, despite its location, focuses on the rise of the entrepreneur Heathcliff and the fall of the Lintons as landowners.

For the rest, the Brontë children were preoccupied with the alternations in government between Tories and Whigs, and the intrigue and machinations involved as in the post-war years a series of glamorous-sounding aristocrats succeeded each other. Between 1815 and 1852 there were ten changes of government, with six Tory and four Whig administrations. The premiership switched between eight men with some staying in office for only a year or so.

After the ending of the Napoleonic Wars, the Tories moved their attention to the divided society at home. They did their best to secure the interests of landowners by cutting—but not abolishing—income tax which had been introduced during the wars. They also passed the Corn Laws to ensure that the price of corn, a major source of wealth to owners of arable land, did not drop too low because of foreign competition. To prevent this it was enacted that, when the price of corn dropped to a certain level, ports were to be closed to foreign grain. It is not clear that these regulations produced the required effect as there were difficulties in matching the timing of closures to the fluctuations in the price of corn. Since bread, as the word 'breadwinner' (coined in the second decade of the nineteenth century) indicates, was the first food of the working classes, the measures were seen, regardless of their effectiveness, as increasing the price of workers' staple food. The Corn Laws were as unpopular as the Combination Acts of 1799 and 1800, which were aimed at preventing the creation of trade unions: both seemed designed to protect the wealthy at the expense of the poor. The Whig ministries on the other hand provided reforming Acts for factories, public health, and sanitation, as well as the parliamentary Reform Act of 1832 which enfranchised some of the lower middle classes.

As the Angrian stories reveal by their plots, it was largely the manoeuvres in the struggle for control between the two political parties that seem to have fascinated the Brontës. They did not pay much attention to the push for electoral change in the 1830s and 1840s, though Charlotte tells Branwell in the early 1830s of her 'extreme pleasure' at one Reform Bill 'being thrown out by the

House of Lords and of the expulsion or resignation of Earl Grey'. Nor did the Brontës take an interest when the Chartists drew up 'The People's Charter' in 1838, demanding male suffrage, secret voting in elections, equal electoral districts, and payment of MPs. The final Chartist petition was rejected in 1848 when Europe was undergoing revolutions of various kinds but by then the sisters were immersed in publication plans.

One parliamentary event which gripped their imagination, however, was the Catholic Emancipation Act of 1829. The Act was passed to remove the exclusion of 60,000 Catholics in England from many official posts and from both Houses of Parliament. It is unexpected—in view of Charlotte's vehement hostility, and presumably that of her siblings, to Roman Catholicism—that they supported emancipation. Probably the explanation lies with Patrick who, though he had the usual distrust of Papists and their 'mummery', thought that they should have equal rights with the rest of the population. The passage of the Bill involved the Tory Prime Minister, Charlotte's hero the Duke of Wellington, whose hand was virtually forced by the Irish lawyer and Roman Catholic Daniel O'Connell, who managed to win an election for an Irish constituency's MP. He was entitled to stand for election but not to take his seat in Parliament. To annul the election would raise the spectre of an Irish rebellion, only to be avoided by emancipating Catholics from their existing exclusions by passing the Bill.

But to secure his aim of passing the Bill, Wellington had to overcome great difficulties: he needed to placate an angry king who did not like the idea; to conciliate the archbishops of Canterbury and York who were equally opposed; and to persuade his Home Secretary, Peel, who was also opposed in principle to emancipation. Byzantine complications followed, eagerly observed by the Brontës: the King changed his mind; the government resigned—briefly—and then took office again; Wellington was insulted by irate colleagues and fought a duel at Battersea with Lord Winchelsea; Peel sacrificed his principles on tactical grounds and, though regarded as a traitor by some, presented the Bill, which was passed in 1829. All this anticipates the Angrian intrigues and the children loved it.

Charlotte records the excitement that the event generated in the Parsonage amongst the siblings who were still under 12 years old:

O those ... 3 months from the time of the Kings speech to the end! nobody could think speak or write on anything but the catholic question and the Duke of Wellington or Mr Peel I remember the day when the Intelligence extraordinary came with Mr Peels speech in it containing the terms on which the catholics were to be let in with what eagerness papa tore off the cover & how we all gathered round him & with what breathless anxiety we listend [*sic*] as one by one they were disclosed & explained & argued upon so ably and so well. (Barker, p. 157)

Charlotte in her account then begins, as Emily and Anne do in their Diary Papers, to imagine a scene that blots out the room in the Parsonage as Patrick read the account aloud:

the anxiety was almost dreadful with which we listened to the whole affair the opening of the doors the hush the Royal Dukes in theire [*sic*] robes & the Great Duke in green sash & waistcoat the rising of all the peeresses when he rose the reading of his speech papa saying his words were like precious gold & lastly the majority one to 4 in favour of the bill. (Barker, p. 157)

It is evident from this passage that the Angrian chronicles represent a strange political inheritance: mixing ideas of the Napoleonic Wars with current events in the shape of powerful aristocrats, duels, angry kings, and intrigue.

As 'the hungry forties' and their disturbances drew to an end and social conditions were ameliorated, the richer sections of society found a new confidence which is manifest in the Great Exhibition of 1851, instigated by the canny Prince Albert as a display of the art and manufacture of all the nations for the purposes of 'exhibition, of competition and of encouragement'. It was housed in a newly built 'Crystal Palace' of glass and iron in Hyde Park and was a monument not only to consumerism but also, despite its international nature, to self-preening nationalism. The *Illustrated London News* describes it as 'the gayest, most fairy-like, most beautiful and original building in the world' and claims 'London is not simply the capital of a great nation, but the metropolis of the world'.[1]

This optimism was not dented until the 1870s when further economic depression set in and the Crimean War (1854–6) seems only to have encouraged the jingoism, but for Charlotte Brontë what happened in the Crimea in the 1850s helped to bring about a change of heart. Now 39 years old and the last of the siblings to survive, she

The interior of the Crystal Palace as Charlotte knew it

writes of war 'as one of the greatest curses that can fall upon mankind . . . for it really seems to me that no glory to be gained can compensate for the sufferings which must be endured'. She now finds that 'nobleness and patriotism bear a different signification to us to that which we accept while young' (*LFC* iv. 164).

Social Class

The Industrial Revolution involved major shifts in the organization of society and gradually also in the perception of how it was constructed. The region in which the Brontës lived, like the rest of the country, had been a hierarchical society in which superior status depended on inherited rank, ownership of land, or practice in certain professions. The basic unit of society was the individual who was by the presence or absence of these criteria endowed with a core personal identity, a fixed status, and a certain role to play; and in theory the system was held together by mutual respect between individuals: benevolence from 'superiors' and deference from 'inferiors'. Rank was seen as reflecting a divinely ordered pattern with each man or woman striving to play the role to which God had appointed them. Such a scheme did to an extent suit a largely agrarian society, with personal contact between landowning farmers or tenants and their labourers, and somewhere fitting into the pattern between these two groups were the necessary skilled tradesmen such as blacksmiths or saddlers.

As manufacturing industry, commerce, and communication developed from 1775 onwards, the occupations and location of individuals changed: in 1801, when the first national census took place, some two-thirds of the population lived and worked in the countryside, and the rest in towns and cities. By the end of the century these figures were reversed; the urbanized centres, where labourers increasingly lived, were clustered close to the factories, mills, and mines where they worked but employers and employees no longer had direct personal contact as a matter of necessity. Society became organized as a structure with groups of those engaged in the same work as its basic unit: workers, entrepreneurs and professionals, and landowners. By the early nineteenth century a new terminology was used to indicate upper, middle, and lower 'classes'. Each was defined by its function in the country's economy; Adam Smith's *An Inquiry into the Origin and Nature of the Wealth of Nations* (1776) and David Ricardo's *The Principles of Political Economy and Taxation* (1817) were seminal works in spreading the new concept of class. These and other writers were bent on providing a mechanistic account of the economic nature and relationships of the elements composing an industrial society: land, capital, and labour. But discussion of the economic value of these three components lent itself readily in human terms to the idea of their *social* value as correspondingly superior or inferior. In any event the accounts of political economists presented a roughly accurate picture of the power relationships between workers and their employers linked only by the commercial bond. Thus the notion of a three-tier grouping of society seemed to have the support of economic theory. It would have taken a re-examination of the concept of 'value' to change this perception of society. Early writers such as Carlyle, who did challenge such analyses did so vaguely, referring to the past as somehow better: Carlyle disparagingly called the link between employer and employee the 'cash nexus', stressing the increasing distance between rich and poor.

Since Haworth and its surroundings made up a small industrial area, it mirrored these changes. Its industry was based on wool from the outlying sheep farms; and the soft water in the neighbourhood made it ideal for processing the wool. In some ways, therefore, the conditions of the working class resembled those in the account of Manchester given by Friedrich Engels in his *Condition of the Working Class in England* (1845):

these workers have no property whatsoever of their own, and live wholly upon wages, which usually go from hand to mouth. Society, composed wholly of atoms, does not trouble itself about them . . . The dwellings of the workers are everywhere badly planned, badly built and kept in the worst condition, badly ventilated, damp and unwholesome.[2]

Such were the workers' houses clustered at the bottom of the main street that led up to Haworth Parsonage. These were groups of back-to-back cottages with alleys between them. They included some twenty or more two-roomed cellar dwellings: in the Brontës' time one room was still used for wool-combing and the other was home to six or seven people. The only sanitation in Haworth consisted of sixty-nine privies, most of them communal, though the Parsonage had its own. Sewage was periodically carried away by farmers or lay rotting in backyards and alleys. The average age of death, which matched some slum areas in the great cities, was 25. These were the conditions of mill-workers such as those Charlotte describes attacking Robert Moore's mill in *Shirley*.

The details that Engels and others provide are reinforced by accounts of privation in 142 working-class autobiographies written between 1790 and 1850. William Thom, a weaver such as those who worked in Haworth, gives a graphic picture of his family at 11 o'clock one morning during one of the hard times which so frequently occurred in the first half of the nineteenth century:

The four children are still asleep. There is a bedcover hung before the window, to keep all within as much like night as possible; and the mother sits beside the beds of her children, to lull them back to sleep whenever any shows an inclination to awake. For this there is a cause, for our weekly five shillings have not come as expected, and the only food in the house consists of a handful of oatmeal saved from the supper of last night. Our fuel is also exhausted. My wife and I were conversing in sunken whispers about making an attempt to cook the handful of meal.[3]

Times between depressions were not so hard as this and the wages of town workers varied from 5 to 40 shillings a week. The most popular domestic manual in 1824 provided two suitable budgets for a couple and two children which put these wages into perspective: it offers one showing how the family could manage on 21 shillings a week and the other on 33 shillings.[4] Another comparison can be made with Patrick Brontë's salary when he moved with his wife and six children to Haworth: his weekly outgoings would have been approximately 60 shillings a week—hardly luxurious for a family of eight.

INDICATORS OF CLASS

The class to which an individual belonged determined many aspects of life including housing, health, and diet. A simple illustration of this fact is that the lower down the social scale a person came, the less likely they were to eat meat. There may be implications as to social class in the rumour after Charlotte's death that the Brontë children had been brought up on a meatless diet—not eating meat would imply poverty and a working-class household.

A major marker of the 'lower' classes was that they did not have a vote: even after the Reform Act of 1832 the total number of voters was still less than a million. The vote post-1832 went in the boroughs to householders rated at £10 or over and in the counties to £10 copyholders, £50 leaseholders, 40-shilling freeholders. So the newly enfranchised included some but not all of the middle class and none of the working classes. Nor did the Act change the character of the House of Commons: those standing for counties needed an estate worth £600 annually, those standing in boroughs needed one worth £300 annually as well as the cost of standing which ranged between £2,000 and £3,000; and of course MPs were still unpaid. Without a vote the only resource for those wanting change was various kinds of protest, some of which have already been described.

Physical arrangements also spelt out social status: types of clothing, the three different classes of accommodation on trains, saloon bars for the lower middle class and public (or working-class) bars in public houses. Even in churches, rented pews in prominent positions cut off the wealthier from the free seats of those who could not afford to rent. The 1851 census for England and Wales suggested that one reason why 'the labouring classes' disliked going to church was 'the maintenance of those distinctions by which they are kept separate as a class from the class above them'. The census makers suggested that the working classes associated churchgoing with 'having pressed upon their notice some memento of inferiority'[5] and the census itself seems to accept that this 'superiority' and 'inferiority' was real, not just perceived.

There was little chance for the working classes to improve their circumstances by education though, as the autobiographies indicate, there were some notable autodidacts among working men. These self-improvers gradually found reading matter through Mechanics Institutes (such as the one at Keighley used by the Brontës), Sunday school libraries, and religious-tract societies. In his *Autobiography of an Artisan* (1847) Christopher Thomson, born in Yorkshire in 1799, writes of his youth that 'My great want was books', since ' "cheap literature" was not then, as now, to be found in every out-o'-the-way nooking'.[6] At about the same time, in her novel *Mary Barton* (1848), Elizabeth Gaskell gives a fictional account of the self-improving weaver Job Legh, one of a class of working men 'who may yet claim kindred with all the noble names that science recognizes'. She supports this with a comment apparently drawn from her own experience in Manchester where she lived:

In the neighbourhood of Oldham there are weavers, common hand-loom weavers, who throw the shuttle with unceasing sound, though Newton's 'Principia' lie open on the loom, to be snatched at in work hours, but revelled over in meal times, or at night. Mathematical problems are received with interest, and studied with absorbing attention by many a broad-spoken common-looking factory-hand. (chapter 5)

Such men were, however, relatively few and for them and the rest of the working classes there was no state system of education before the enabling Act of 1870, though from the early eighteenth century onwards a number of charity schools had been set up, such as that at Cowan Bridge to which Maria, Elizabeth, Charlotte, and Emily Brontë were sent. The charitable aspect of Cowan Bridge was that it took in the daughters of impoverished clergymen at low fees. In 1800 there were some 179 charity schools, mainly for boys, and there were also increasing numbers of Sunday schools like the ones in *Shirley* where attenders were taught to read the Bible. These schools were of course denominational, with Anglicans and other groups competing as they do in a very literal way in the clash between Anglican and Nonconformist Whitsun marches in *Shirley*.

Such secondary education as existed was in long-established and endowed grammar schools and increasingly, as the century progressed, in fee-paying public schools. Upper-class boys could receive secondary education in such schools or at home with a tutor, like Patrick Brontë, instructing boys in the classics. Thanks to him, Branwell developed considerable aptitude and later in life tried to publish his own translation of Horace's *Odes*. The newly rich in this entrepreneurial period were anxious to fix their sons securely in the gentlemanly caste with the consequence that between 1837 and 1869 thirty-one new public schools were set up.

In practice, of course, society did not consist of three monolithic classes: within each there were uncertain areas and differing perceptions. For class is a two-faced concept: how others perceive us and how we perceive ourselves are often different matters. This is especially true in borderline or grey areas between classes, in which Charlotte and Anne showed an interest, for they themselves belonged to one. Patrick (as his income indicated) was of a lower grade of clergy since he was a 'perpetual curate' at Haworth, with lifetime security of tenure but only a low salary. His education, however, had brought him into the middle class. This meant that, when his daughters felt the need to aim at being self-supporting, they became governesses on very low salaries. Despite the ambiguous status of the governess, the Brontë sisters clearly perceived themselves as middle class even when employed as governesses; but their employers treated them as social inferiors. Charlotte wrote bitterly of her status at the Sidgwicks:

I said in my last letter that Mrs Sidgwick did not know me. I now begin to find she does not intend to know me . . . [I used to think that I should like to be in the stir of grand folks' society] . . . I see now more clearly than I have ever done before that a private governess has no existence, is not considered as a living and rational being except as connected with the wearisome duties she has to fulfil. (*Letters*, i. 191)

Small wonder that governesses figure large in *Jane Eyre*, *Villette*, and *Agnes Grey* as well as to a lesser extent in *Shirley*.

THEORIES ABOUT CLASS

The inequity of the early Victorian social system, with privation for the many and wealth for the few, was plain enough but needed a face-saving rationale which could somehow show that the system was necessary and also that it was compatible with a Christian country's view of itself. The former need was dealt with in terms of economic efficiency which required low wages for the labouring masses; the latter in terms of social mobility. The assumption was that betterment was available for all who were hard-working and prudent enough to grasp it. The idea of the availability of social mobility had existed earlier and persists today but it was particularly widespread amongst the middle and upper classes in the later part of the nineteenth century. Shortly after the death of the last of Patrick Brontë's children the idea found its most well-known expression in Samuel Smiles's *Self-Help* (1859). This work became a best-seller internationally and elaborates the view that society is a gymnasium full of ladders up which the virtuously self-reliant and diligent can climb to respectability and prosperity. The idea is illustrated and validated using brief accounts of the lowly born like Shakespeare or Cardinal Wolsey who rose to great heights.

This simplistic notion was contradicted by another prevalent idea about the working classes which found increasingly frequent expression, especially at times of social unrest. It is captured in the writing of Arthur Helps. This was the idea that the working classes were dangerous, a belief reinforced by accounts in governmental and other reports as to the degree of drunkenness and criminality to be found amongst them. Helps, in his *The Claims of Labour: An Essay on the Duties of the Employer to the Employed*, writes:

I do not seek to terrify anyone into a care for the labouring classes, by representing the danger to society of neglecting them. It is certainly a fearful thing to think of large masses of men being in that state of want and misery which leaves them nothing to hazard; and who are likely to be without the slightest reverence or love for the institutions around them.[7]

Helps spells out the remedy, often proposed by others in different terms, for this threat to the status quo, which he seems to consider needs to be secured permanently: 'I believe that the paternal relation will be found the best model on which to form the duties of the employer to the employed'.[8] Paternalism was a useful and variable concept, especially in a patriarchal society, drawing support from the idea of God as father and creator. It was easy for a Christian father like Patrick Brontë not to question the status quo but to show a fatherly concern for his congregation at Haworth in relation to their physical as well as their spiritual well-being.

Many if not most of the upper classes regarded paternalism as the answer to inequality in society. Carlyle, for example, ranted against what was inflicted on the mass of the population and believed in the end that what was needed was an aristocratic authoritarian regime to do what was best for the lower classes. It took John Stuart Mill in his *Principles of Political Economy* (1848) to see through the hypocrisy of fatherly concern, when he points out ironically that under the shield of this description 'the lot of the poor in all things which affect them collectively' will be 'regulated *for* them, not *by* them'.[9]

The Nature and Roles of Women

During the Brontë sisters' lifetimes, women were second-class people, hardly to be called citizens since none of them was able to vote, a privation shared with lunatics and peers. Even the Chartists, when demanding 'universal suffrage', did not take 'universal' to include women; and when it was suggested, rejected the idea. Women's function in society was constructed as biologically determined and the construction of proper femininity was predicated upon an ideal, domesticated middle-class wife far less rational than a man but intuitive, emotional, with a natural maternal instinct and an equally natural nurturing ability. Men, by contrast, were rational, intelligent, competitive, and adapted to deal with the real world outside the family.

The way that society was structured left few options for women and built perceived inferiority into the system, with many articles and conduct books to reinforce this characterization of women's nature, which frequently seemed the norm even for the women themselves. Indeed those who did not achieve married status became, in the words of a famous article (about what to do with such women), 'redundant'. Sarah Ellis, ignoring such redundancies in her conduct manuals, is absolute in regard to women generally and asks: 'What is your position in society?'. Her reply is: 'As women, the first thing of importance is to be content to be inferior to men—inferior in mental power, in the same proportion that you are inferior in strength'.[10] It is surprising how even Charlotte could internalize these ideas and express them in a letter where she describes how, having been attracted by the title of Lady Morgan's book *Woman & Her Master* (1840), she was dismayed by what she read in it: 'not content with elevating "woman", she seeks to disgrace "man" ' (*Letters*, ii. 756).

Ironically when women did achieve what was seen as their main purpose—marriage—they became not first-class persons but non-persons. The classic statement of a married woman's legal status, or rather absence of one, was made by Sir William Blackstone in the 1760s:

By marriage the husband and wife are one person in law: that is the very being or legal existence of the woman is suspended during the marriage, or at least is incorporated and consolidated into that of the husband: under whose wing, protection, and cover, she performs everything: and is therefore called in our law-french a feme covert.[11]

The consequences of this non-existence of married women in law were crippling. They could not litigate except through a male person who existed in law, such as a father or brother. Legal separation had to be sought by a wife in this indirect way and in the early 1830s she had no right to the legal custody of her children, though this changed in 1839 to allow claims for children under 7. Nor had she any control over money previously hers or earned during the marriage unless a special legal settlement had been made before the marriage. If no such pre-nuptial agreement had been made, money from both sources became her husband's. Divorce required an expensive Act of Parliament until after the Brontë siblings' deaths and was designed to protect wealthy husbands from the danger that an illegitimate child might falsely inherit their estates and possibly titles. The settlement made by Charlotte before her marriage to Arthur Nicholls, in order to ensure that her father inherited her earnings, is an example of how such arrangements might work.

The account of women's nature and role was essentially based on seeing them as lacking in male characteristics; and transforming a negative view into the pseudo-positive one that Ellis presents. But they were even more readily put to misogynistic purposes: intuitive-ness, sensitivity, and quickness of emotion could be represented as the scatterbrained silliness of Mrs Nickleby in Dickens's *Nicholas Nickleby* or Dora Spenlow in *David Copperfield* (1850) whose attrac-tion for Copperfield seems to be her ineptitude. Such frequent accounts, however, did not go entirely unchallenged: works like Marian Reid's *A Plea for Women* (1843) argued that the self-sacrifice crucial to the idealizing view could become a 'most criminal self-extinction'.[12] It was a single individual, Caroline Norton, who brought about the change to the legal position on the custody of children in 1839. In 1839 a Female Political Union was set up in Newcastle to push for women's suffrage, though it had taken almost a hundred years for this to come about. A few enlightened men like John Stuart Mill recognized that enfranchising women was a crucial first step in bringing about change. When an article appeared on the subject in 1848, assumed to be by him, though it was in fact by his wife, Harriet Taylor, Charlotte Brontë read it and found it clear and logical but hugely deficient and she writes to Gaskell:

the writer forgets that there is such a thing as self-sacrificing love and disinterested devotion. When I first read the paper—I thought it was the work of a powerful-minded—clear-headed woman who had a hard jealous heart muscles of iron and nerves of bend leather, of a woman who longed for power and had never felt affection . . . You are right when you say that there is a large margin in human nature over which the logicians have no dominion. (*Letters*, ii. 695–6)

Her comment stands as ironic proof of the truth of her final statement.

WOMEN'S EDUCATION AND WORK

Since women were to prepare for matrimony, the education of middle-class girls took the form of what were called 'accomplishments': a smattering of French or Italian, painting, drawing, singing, and piano-playing. These skills were designed to 'vivify and enlighten the home' once the women were safely ensconced in it. The idea of educating girls for their own sake was seldom mentioned; if they were not, once married, ornamenting the drawing room with their accomplishments, they were expected to be instructing their children. Not until the 1850s, with the founding of Cheltenham Ladies College (1841) and the North London Collegiate School (1850), were there serious attempts to provide secondary education for middle-class girls. The only exceptions to this were individuals with outstandingly enlightened fathers who allowed them to be taught at home as a son might be. Tertiary education was initiated by the founding of two London colleges, Queen's (1848) and Bedford (1849) but for most middle-class girls during the Brontës' childhood the only options were charity schools like Cowan Bridge or small fee-paying schools like Roe Head.

The possibilities for middle-class women to work was summed up by Mary Taylor in a letter to Ellen Nussey in 1849:

There are no means for a woman to live in England but by teaching, sewing or washing. The last is the best. The best paid, the least unhealthy & the most free. But it is not paid well enough to live by. Moreover it is impossible for anyone not born to this position to take it up. I don't know why but it is. (*Letters*, ii. 179)

This state of affairs meant in practice that the only resource left was governessing or, less commonly, teaching in a school.

The 1851 census gives the number of governesses as 25,000, so wages could be kept low. Already in 1841 the Governesses' Benevolent Institution had to draw attention to the problem and help with it. Since the provision of a comfortable home was assumed to make up a large part of the payment for a governess's services, employers sometimes offered no more than this. Otherwise in the 1840s an average salary might be from £25 to £50 per annum and the poverty-stricken governess was a stereotype much discussed in the period leading up to the founding of proper secondary schools in the 1850s, when the Governesses' Benevolent Institution helped with the founding of Queen's College in 1848. It was in the 1850s that Florence Nightingale began to transform training for the nursing profession and to give it a status which made it suitable for middle-class women. In the previous decade, when Dickens was writing *Martin Chuzzlewit*, the stereotype of the nurse was a vulgar, lower-class Mrs Gamp with her lack of skill and addiction to the bottle. Towards the end of Charlotte's life she writes somewhat enviously of the new educational opportunities for women:

The girls of this generation have great advantages; it seems to me that they receive much encouragement in the acquisition of knowledge, and the cultivation of their minds; in these days women may be thoughtful and well-read, without being totally stigmatized as 'Blues' and 'Pedants'. (*Letters*, ii. 364)

There were, of course, many women who worked for even lower pay than governesses, for by 1851 some 36 per cent of women were employed but only 6 per cent of these were middle class and many working-class women toiled for long hours in mines, factories, and as domestic servants. When the governesses' plight was publicized in the 1840s there were thirty times as many domestic servants as governesses but even among those agitating for proper education for middle-class girls, there was little concern for those in the working classes. It was assumed that such women did not require education or were even unsuited to it. Jessie Boucherett, who later set up the Society for Promoting the Employment of Women, wrote:

Among women of the labouring classes a good education is of comparatively little importance, for health and strength are of more service to a labourer's daughter than knowledge or intelligence; but in the middle ranks, a woman cannot become a domestic servant: she would feel that to do so was a degradation; and even if she did not, she would not possess the requisite physical powers from want of early training.[13]

By contrast, Mary Taylor had refreshingly unconventional views on women and work. She writes exuberantly to Charlotte from New Zealand:

I have set up shop! I am delighted with it as a whole—that is it is as pleasant or as little disagreeable as you can expect an employment to be that you earn your living by. The best of it is that your labour has some return & you are not forced to work on hopelessly without result. (*Letters*, ii. 391–2)

This last remark is possibly a reference to work as a domestic servant since both she and Charlotte saw the unproductive repetitiveness of domesticity as a form of imprisonment. Taylor goes on to discuss what *Shirley* has to say about women and work:

I have seen some extracts from *Shirley* in which you talk of women working. And this first duty, this great necessity you seem to think that *some* women may indulge in—if they give up marriage & don't make themselves too disagreeable to the other sex. You are a coward & a traitor. A woman who works is by that alone better than one who does not & a woman who does not happen to be rich & who *still* earns no money & does not wish to do so, is guilty of a great fault—almost a crime. (*Letters*, ii. 391–2)

Not many would have agreed with her.

PROSTITUTION AND FALLEN WOMEN

The work of women in domestic service, mines, and factories, or as seamstresses or washerwomen, was even more poorly paid than that of working-class men. One means of supplementing it was by part-time prostitution which flourished in urban centres and particularly in garrison towns. In the 1840s, partly because of the spread of venereal disease, studies were made of the activities of prostitutes in towns and cities including London, Edinburgh, Glasgow, Liverpool, and Leeds, and by 1850 prostitution was known as 'the Great Social Evil'.

The prostitutes themselves constituted the evil which was to be contained and they were mainly the unskilled daughters of the unskilled classes. This reinforced the idea that working-class women tended to depravity: one common stereotype was that of the girl who had allowed herself to be seduced, was then degraded, and pursued a career selling herself. This facilitated the equation of the compromised middle-class woman with 'fallen' women generally. The reasons for assuming prostitutes were sexually depraved rested on the sexual double standard according to which male sexuality was uncheckable and needed these human outlets. Control was initially attempted by means of institutions for reforming the women and teaching them domestic skills. Charles Dickens, backed by the wealthy Angela Burdett Coutts, organized such an institution and arranged for some of their protégées to emigrate. Men, on the other hand, did not lose social status by 'sowing their wild oats': Rochester in *Jane Eyre* and Huntingdon in *The Tenant of Wildfell Hall*, like Felix Holt in George Eliot's later novel of that name or Angel Clare later still in Hardy's *Tess of the d'Urbervilles*, are fictional examples of such men.

The other basis for regarding 'fallen' women as depraved is the belief that true (not depraved) middle-class women were without sexual feelings. Famously this common view was expressed by a medical doctor, William Acton, who in his *Functions and Disorders of the Reproductive Organs* (1857) wrote,

As a general rule, a modest woman seldom desires any sexual gratification for herself. She submits to her husband's embraces, but principally to gratify him; and were it not for the desire of maternity, would far rather be relieved from his attentions.[14]

This follows naturally after an account of those rare women who do exhibit sexual feelings:

I admit, as the divorce courts show, that there are some few women who have sexual desires so strong that they surpass those of men, and shock public feeling by their consequences. I admit, of course, the existence of sexual excitement terminating even in nymphomania, a form of insanity that those accustomed to visit lunatic asylums must be fully conversant with; but, with these sad exceptions, there can be no doubt that sexual feeling in the female is in the majority of cases in abeyance.[15]

There were those who challenged Acton's view but only a minority shared the opinion of Dr George Drysdale who wrote in *The Elements of Social Science* (1854):

There is a great deal of erroneous feeling attaching to the subject of the sexual desires in woman. To have strong sexual passions is held to be rather a disgrace for a woman, and they are looked down upon as animal, sensual, coarse, and deserving of reprobation . . . This is a great error. In woman, exactly as in man strong sexual appetites are a very great virtue; as they are signs of a vigorous frame, healthy sexual organs and a naturally developed sexual disposition.[16]

But the common beliefs as expounded by Acton were enough to leave Charlotte Brontë and other middle-class women with the belief that passionate feelings in a woman were rightly a source of guilt, possibly of the kind to which she may have confessed to the Catholic priest in Brussels.

Varieties of Religion

Since their father was an Anglican clergyman, the Brontës' lives were dominated by religion; and it was a defining feature of identity for the majority of the population since the nature of different affiliations varied widely. The Anglican Church to which Patrick belonged was, as now, the established church, woven closely into the fabric of existing English society. The idea of an established church has little resonance today but the word 'establishment' has a strong meaning when applied to certain sections of society: the powerbrokers. In the nineteenth century the Church of England was a crucial part of the establishment in this sense and preserved certain public rights and offices for its own members. Roman Catholics were excluded from some of these until 1829. Though Dissenters such as Unitarians, Baptists, Quakers, and Methodists could already, unlike Catholics, become MPs, they too were debarred from some public offices.

Through its right to insist on Anglican membership, the Church could act as gatekeeper for several lucrative professions and, since the government of the day appointed the archbishops of Canterbury and York, church leaders were locked into a power hierarchy grounded in rigid class distinction. Consequently the Church was also closely tied to the natural rulers of the day, the Tory party, which represented the landowners. The bond was drawn tighter by the fact that approximately 12,000 Anglican livings (and the salaries they paid) were in the hands of individual landowners, public schools, or Oxford and Cambridge colleges. Only 1,500 were in the gift of the bishops themselves. Not all of these livings were as poorly paid as Patrick Brontë's: bishops were paid upwards of £1,500 a year and the Bishop of London, for instance, received £15,000 annually.

The income of the church came from rent for land that it owned, from a tithe paid by all farmers in a parish, whether they were Anglicans or not, and from the Church rate, a local tax for the upkeep of church buildings. Furthermore, clergymen were allowed to hold several posts at once. This meant that they could hold two or more livings and hire a cheaply paid curate to provide religious services in those parishes where they did not live. There were evidently many zealous clergy like Patrick but also others who occupied clerical posts as a way of securing a comfortable and pleasant way of life.

From Elizabethan times the Anglican Church had taken up a middle way between that Scarlet Woman, the Roman Catholic Church with its authoritarianism and its pomp, and the more puritanical forms of religion. It had become familiar and fairly low-key with services based on the Book of Common Prayer which laid down details of services for different seasons and events in the life of congregations—births, marriages, deaths. There were also prayers for most kinds of likely petitions to God: rain, good weather, harvests, recovery from sickness. The church services also marked the natural cycle of seasons which was so important as long as the country was largely agrarian, so that its prayers and services provided hands on the clock of existence, offering a stable, and possibly coercive, pattern for its members.

The words of the Bible itself became familiar to many people and it was often the only book they possessed but, though its words may have stuck in people's minds, religious fervour among the mass of Anglicans was much reduced in the eighteenth century. It was revived to an extent by the founding of a sect within the Church initiated by John and Charles Wesley at Oxford in 1729. What was at first nicknamed 'the Holy Club' was eventually to become known as Methodism and by 1783 its adherents had seceded from the Church of England and began to ordain their own ministers. Methodism had a singular and direct appeal because, unlike Anglicanism itself, it focused on the story of human beings lost to God by original sin until Christ, by sacrificing his life on the cross, paid for their sins. In this way Christ both atoned for the sins of humanity and restored the prospect of redemption from the damnation they had earned. This stress on Christ paying the price for others made sense in a commercial society where buying and selling dominated the lives of many along with the idea of reward being earned. The role of the Methodist preacher was thus crystal clear: to bring home to each listener the sense of this divine payment and what it offered in a vivid and moving way and to bring about a personal and felt sense to the individual of the need to seek or accept salvation.

Methodist preachers worked at the grass roots in organizations known as circuits, speaking directly to people as individuals in sermons designed to stir consciences through the emotions they aroused. George Eliot depicts Dinah Morris giving such a sermon in *Adam Bede* (1859) (chapter 2). By 1851 the number of Methodists is estimated at two million, many of them working class. This receptiveness may be explained by the fact that Methodists treated as individuals members of society usually referred to as part of a mass. Methodist sermons also made the assumption that each listener had a soul worth saving, whatever their social position or status.

Not only did this brand of religion make what was on offer sound like a good deal to those whose deals were usually bad, but the emotional sermons were an exciting diversion in lives consisting largely of work and sleep. After 1784 Methodism existed separately from Anglicanism but its direct and emotional approach had spread to a section of the Church of England in a kind of 'back to basics' campaign which became known as evangelical. Patrick Brontë belonged to this wing and had had evangelical patrons both before and after his years at Cambridge. His wife and her sister, Aunt (Elizabeth) Branwell, were both brought up as Methodists but joined the Anglican community, a choice no doubt made easier by Patrick's evangelicalism. So a felt individual faith was the model on which the Brontë children were brought up. Nonetheless, in their youth they satirized Methodists in their writings.

Those in the Anglican Church who did not take to evangelical fervour and emotionalism diverged in a more conservative way from the low-key centre: a group developed in Oxford in 1833 which became known as the Oxford Movement and later Tractarianism. Its chief members were John Keble, Edward Pusey, and John Henry Newman. By contrast with the evangelical wing, it prided itself on its intellectual approach and concerned itself with theological arguments for seeing the Church of England as the true church where authority derived from valid ordinations, traceable back to Christ and his apostles. These arguments were published in ninety learned articles or tracts—hence the name Tractarians—with both the name and the method of communication suggesting the strongly non-populist nature of the sect. Their views were seen by many as the slippery slope to Roman Catholicism and certainly they led some of the proponents to the opinion that if you were looking for the true church in this historical way it was to be found in Rome. As can be seen from the Brontës' attitudes, it is hard to overestimate the dislike and fear of Rome felt by many in the early nineteenth century. It had of course been seen as the enemy of the Church of England from the Reformation onwards and was, as has been said, subject to various kinds of discrimination; and it was widely regarded almost as a secret society, a kind of religious freemasonry, with its Mass in a dead language, statues, incense, bells, pomp and ceremony. Its externals and practices such as confession were also suspected of being half-lures, half-coercion for an ignorant peasant constituency such as the Irish.

For many of the population, as for the Brontës, religion and its implications for the afterlife were living issues which coloured individual attitudes, decisions, and behaviour. In *Jane Eyre*, *Villette*, *The Professor*, *Shirley*, *Agnes Grey*, and *The Tenant of Wildfell Hall*, Charlotte and Anne explored areas of human conduct partly in terms of their own religious views. Emily in her poetry devises her own religion using conventional ideas rather as metaphors than substance.

Madness and the Mind

Concepts of the mind and its disorders are relevant to the Brontës' writings not only because of the particular example of the mad Mrs Rochester in Charlotte's *Jane Eyre* but also because central to all their fiction is the psychological development of individual characters. Many well-known Victorians, however, had family members affected by what was regularly called 'madness'. Tennyson notoriously came from a family with 'black blood' and members who were mad; Thackeray's wife was confined to an asylum after developing a mental disorder that began as post-natal depression. The Brontës themselves were not untouched: Branwell's alcohol and opium addiction led to delirium tremens, described in Patrick's annotated copy of *Domestic Medicine* by Thomas John Graham as a state in which the patient 'thinks himself haunted; by demons, sees luminous substans [*sic*], in his imagination, has frequent tremors of the limbs'.[17] Both Charlotte and Emily suffered from serious depressions (then called hypochondria) and it is possible that Emily was anorexic. George, the brother of Charlotte's close friend, Ellen Nussey, evidently developed what would now be called a psychotic illness and was confined in an asylum in York.

The understanding of madness and attitudes to it were not regarded in the eighteenth century as medical matters since there was no real knowledge of the human brain or psyche, though philosophers discussed the nature of selfhood. The mad were not seen as a discrete group but as part of a set of deviants cut off in various ways from mainstream society, along with paupers and criminals. On the whole, those thought mad remained within their families and communities as burdens to be borne. There were very few asylums: a small number of charitable institutions for the mad poor existed and a few private places for the wealthy with mad relatives whom they did not choose to seclude in their own houses. Thus Rochester in *Jane Eyre* confines his mad first wife to an attic at Thornfield with a keeper, Grace Poole, to keep watch over her. The choicest of the private asylums was Ticehurst, a de luxe institution, which by the nineteenth century allowed rich mad men and women to enjoy 300 acres of grounds, an aviary, bowling green, summerhouse, and music room. All asylums were, as the name implies, places of containment and there was, until the mid-nineteenth century, no state provision.

In the eighteenth century also madness itself was not seen as a variety of disorders but as a state in which whatever symptoms there were resulted from the overthrow of reason by passion. This meant that the only known treatment for the symptoms either at home or in asylums was restraint by chains, fetters, gyves, or whips—hence the first Mrs Rochester is chained when she gets out of hand. In workhouses where lunatics were a nuisance to others, naturally they were restrained. Nor were the rich exempt from physical control: John Perceval, for instance, was the son of an assassinated prime minister and had been educated at Harrow and Oxford but later he became a religious fanatic who saw visions and heard voices predicting the future and in 1830 he was taken into an asylum and strapped to a bed for two weeks. Even a king could be subjected to such treatment: the mad George III (1760–1820) was treated in this way as his doctor, George Willis, controlled the king's insanity, now thought to have been caused by the rare disease porphyria, by violent means when necessary. Believing that madness was caused by a form of emotional overexcitement which needed to be reduced, Willis mainly used force of personality to subdue the king. When this failed he resorted to restraint: 'When therefore my gracious sovereign became violent, I felt it my duty to subject him to the same system of restraint as I should have adopted with one of his own gardeners at Kew. In plain words, I put a strait waistcoat on him.'[18]

Willis was able to claim credit for George's recovery but if the cause of his madness was porphyria, the 'cure' must have been spontaneous.

CHANGES IN ORGANIZATION: ASYLUMS AND DOCTORS

Attitudes began to change as industrialization took firm hold in the early decades of the nineteenth century. Once the aim of all politicians was the furtherance of a capitalist economy, the running of society became what has been called 'an adjunct to the market';[19] the single grouping of paupers, criminals, and the mad as 'deviants' was reconsidered in the light of their differing relationships to the marketplace. For both politicians who espoused laissez-faire economics and Utilitarians bent on the greatest happiness of the greatest number, paupers for instance were now definable as a separate and distinct category. They were potential workers who, if given the dole or poor relief at home, would be enabled to sponge on the state by staying unemployed in their native places. If the state were only to give them relief in harshly run workhouses, they would seek work elsewhere and fill an economic need, as the 1834 Poor Law Amendment Act implied. The insane were by definition not potential workers but burdens on families which usually needed all available hands to earn enough for them to live on. In economic terms, the most efficient way to deal with the mad, therefore, was to place them in communal institutions where they could be more easily and more cheaply managed.

Consequently there developed a demand for the state provision of asylums across the country, a movement reinforced by two social groups: evangelicals and doctors. For evangelicals, the mad, like the rest of society, had souls to be saved: they too needed the conversion which would save them from damnation. Grouping them together in asylums would make it easier for the enlightened to set about the work of converting them. At the same time sects like the Quakers and others, concerned to find more humane treatment, lauded the idea of 'moral management', a vague term referring to a pragmatic approach aimed at using the minimum of restraint or coercion, so that its absence became an incentive to self-control and a possible cure.

Those who treated the physically sick were doctors and one subgroup also began to see the merits of state asylums: those known as 'surgeons', a lower grade in the profession, contrasting with elite medical men called 'physicians'. The latter were highly trained and highly paid men who ministered to the wealthy and did not perform surgery. Surgeons, who had separated themselves only in 1745 from the Barbers and Surgeons Company of the City of London, were the rougher butchers: they performed amputations, extracted teeth, set bones, and treated wounds. They were already competing with lay proprietors for the ownership of the few profit-making institutions for the mad and, if they were able to take charge of state lunatic asylums, both their status and finances would be enhanced.

The consensus for state provision grew but those involved had to struggle hard and a series of Bills to introduce it failed until 1845 when two Lunacy Acts were passed. One of these set up a Lunacy Commission (with many doctors as members) to inspect all types of asylum; another made the erection of public asylums compulsory in boroughs and counties. Further, any asylum with more than 100 inmates was obliged to employ a medical superintendent. The passage of this radical Bill was made easier because by 1845 developments in diagnosis had taken place which lent credibility to the idea of madness as mental illness and so it clearly fell into the medical domain. By this time 'mad-doctors' were calling themselves alienists, a word first recorded by the *Oxford English Dictionary* in 1864 but in a context suggesting that it was already familiar. It derived easily from the phrase 'alienation of the mind' which had been regularly used for madness since the fifteenth century.

DIAGNOSIS AND TREATMENT

The diagnostic developments involved in transferring madness into the medical sphere relate to the spread from 1815 onwards of the pseudo-science of phrenology. Under the traditional description of madness as a state in which passion overcame reason it was not seen to have a physical basis but already in the early eighteenth century the pseudo-science of physiognomy existed: it assumed a link between facial features and the characters of individuals. The eyes and forehead, for instance, were said to indicate the intellectual powers of a person possessed whereas the features in the lower part of the face gave information about more 'animal' characteristics related to feelings. Elaborate distinctions, illustrated by drawings, were made in physiognomical textbooks which attributed traits and characteristics to groups as well as to single individuals.

Phrenology itself claimed that different aspects of character such as kindness or conscientiousness—up to thirty-five in number—were governed by organs in the brain, and that they were traceable by analysis of bumps on the skull. Phrenological theories aroused enormous public interest in Britain and attracted vast audiences for their exponents. Phrenology was seen as a medical advance, before which, as one phrenologist put it in 1828, 'all we knew about the brain was how to slice it'. Practitioners 'read' the bumps on the head with their hands and gave clients an account of their faculties and personalities. In 1851, for example, George Smith and Charlotte Brontë, posing as Mr and Miss Fraser, had their heads read by a phrenologist in London. Charlotte's reading begins,

Temperament for the most part nervous. Brain large the anterior and superior parts remarkably salient. In her domestic relations this lady will be warm and affectionate. In the care of children she will evince judicious kindness, but she is not pleased at seeing them spoiled by overindulgence . . . The Lady possesses a fine organ of language and can, if she has done her talents justice by exercise express her sentiments with clearness precision and force. (*Letters*, ii. 657–9)

With such phrenological interpretation of an individual, it seemed as though the particular disordered faculty could be recognized. The person in question could then be encouraged to control the deviant part of the brain by will-power when symptoms occurred so that sanity would be restored and the mad man or woman rehabilitated into society. This belief blurred the previously clear-cut frontier between the sane and the insane since insanity might now be seen as a temporary episode.

At a time in the mid-century when the paranormal was found fascinating by many, a 'treatment' grew out of phrenology which for a brief period proved popular. This was mesmerism, a combination of hypnosis and hands-on healing. Those gifted as healers were assumed to be capable of drawing on a curative invisible force which they could convey to the hypnotized patient. He or she would then awake cured from the hypnotic trance. Though mesmerism was a short-lived practice, it attracted many, including Charles Dickens who fancied himself as a practitioner. So too did Harriet Martineau who tried it on Charlotte, with inconclusive results. Apart from such dubious treatments, medical superintendents of asylums had, in addition to moral management, only the familiar medical practices of bleeding by leeches; blisters; purgatives; douches; and a limited range of drugs including opium as a tranquillizer, strychnine to brace the nerves, and arsenic to reinvigorate them.

In this primitive but analytical assessment of mental disorders, gender was an important factor. It could not be otherwise, since it followed from the account of women as more sensitive, more emotional, and less reasonable than men that they were more likely than men to cross the borderline from sanity to insanity. Since the basis of such accounts was women's reproductive function, they were seen as being at the mercy of their menstrual cycle and as one medical writer put it in 1848:

If corporeal agency is thus powerful in man, its tyrannic influence will more frequently cause the misery of the gentler sex. Woman, with her exalted spiritualism, is more forcibly under the control of matter; her sensations are more vivid and acute, her sympathies more irresistible. She is less under the influence of the brain than the uterine system . . . a hysteric predisposition is incessantly predominating from the dawn of puberty.[20]

The mental disorders to which women in particular were seen as predisposed in the first half of the nineteenth century included nervous collapse (later called neurasthenia), melancholia, neurosis, and moral insanity. Nervous collapse was manifested as fear, anxiety, despair, agitation, and insomnia. Melancholia was diagnosed as a state in which depression/melancholy persisted and became functionally disabling. The general term 'neurosis' was used for a disorder of the nervous system (which was only gradually being explored) which did not involve physical damage to it. By contrast monomania was seen as a physical disfunction of one part of the brain resulting in a pathological obsession in an otherwise healthy mind. Moral insanity was diagnosed when the patient seriously breached social rules: it was 'a want of self-government . . . an unusual expression of strong feeling in thoughtless and extravagant conduct'.[21]

As Sally Shuttleworth has definitively demonstrated in her *Charlotte Brontë and Victorian Psychology*, some of the textbooks on mental disorder were familiar to Charlotte, as was their terminology. Their accounts constituted the framework within which Charlotte explored the minds, motives, responses, and struggles of her fictional characters, particularly the women. These textbooks provided early nineteenth-century society with the equivalent of what Sigmund Freud bequeathed to the twentieth century with his account of the human psyche; and both Charlotte and Anne were influenced by them.

The Empire and the Orient

Despite the relative remoteness of Haworth from the wider world, the Empire and the Orient filtered through to the Brontë family as part of their consciousness—so too did fairly conventional attitudes to them, as is apparent in *Jane Eyre* and *Wuthering Heights*. Just before Charlotte was born, in 1815, imperial territory was enlarged further by the confirmation of British possession of some of the conquests won during the long struggle with the French. This left Britain as the most powerful empire in the world, but the relationships of foreign territories to the 'mother' country varied. The closest link existed between Britain and the 'white' colonies in North America, South Africa, and Australia which were visibly 'children' since they were populated largely by British emigrants. Charlotte's friend, Mary Taylor, was to become an emigrant to New Zealand, and the heroine of *Shirley* sees Canada as offering a peaceful life, close to nature, in North America.

The remainder of the Empire, peopled by black and oriental races, stood therefore in a very different relation to the centre of authority. The areas in question were India and the West Indian colonies. The Subcontinent was the enormous jewel in the imperial crown, later symbolically represented as such when in 1876 Disraeli had Victoria crowned empress of India. At first India was largely in the hands of the East India Company until 1857 when, after the crushing of the so-called Indian Mutiny, the British Crown took over their territories and properties and put in place a viceroy. Less dazzling but extremely profitable was the third section of the Empire in the West Indies to which the captured colonies of Trinidad and Mauritius were added in 1815.

The Empire was essentially a commercial enterprise wrapped in the flag. The so-called 'mother country' was nurturing only in so far as it supplied capital as well as maintaining control, if necessary, by military force. It expected and received profits in return in the shape of cheap timber from North America, wool from Australia, and sugar, tea, rice, cocoa, oil, tin, and rubber from the black colonies. For the first thirty years of the nineteenth century the cheapness of many of these products from the black colonies was ensured by slave labour. The 'mother country' also received profits from its role in transporting some 45,000 slaves per year. Ships from Liverpool and Bristol, loaded with firearms, gunpowder, alcohol, knives, mirrors, and beads, travelled to Africa where they exchanged their cargo for a human commodity—slaves. These captives had sometimes been seized especially for the slave trade or taken in battles. They were shipped to North America and the West Indies where they were sold and then employed to labour, producing cotton, tobacco, sugar cane, and coffee. The West Indian plantation owners were often British and able to build up large fortunes as Jane Eyre's relatives are said to have done. So Britain profited from the slave trade both by buying and selling slaves as well as by the importation of cheap products like sugar. Slaves were commodities and were treated as such, packed into the hold of ships, with little provision for their welfare. Captains of slave ships often took on board more potential slaves than they expected to sell to allow for deaths in transit. In one famous episode which took place in 1783, depicted by J. M. W. Turner in his painting *The Slave Ship*, a British captain, faced with an epidemic of illness, threw 133 sick slaves overboard so that he could claim that they had been lost at sea and be compensated by his insurers who would not insure against death on board.

A more respectable rationale for imperialism was the view that the Empire was an improving influence, bringing European civilization to the unenlightened. The enlightenment took the form of an organized bureaucracy in India and above all the passing on of Christianity and its values. The Anglican Church played its part by sending missionaries. This is the role Arthur Nicholls once aspired to and it was the fate of St John Rivers in *Jane Eyre*. In 1813 an Anglican diocese with its own bishop was set up in Calcutta; and in 1823, after a rebellion, in Jamaica and Barbados. Dissenters and evangelicals of all kinds took an interest in the process of spreading Christianity; and many with humane motives reinforced an anti-slavery campaign in Britain. Its badge was a ceramic made by Josiah Wedgwood, bearing the slogan 'Am I not a man and a brother?'. This became a famous and effective way of spreading the abolitionist message. The government withdrew from the slave trade in Britain in 1807; and in 1833 it abolished slavery in its West Indian colonies, providing £20,000,000 to compensate slave owners for the loss of their human property, rather as farmers in a foot-and-mouth epidemic might now be compensated for the loss of their cattle.

It has been argued that the government's motives for abolition were mixed: public pressure fronted by the crusading William Wilberforce; an acceptance of the humanitarian argument; and some belief in the earlier claim of Adam Smith that slavery was in strict terms the most uneconomic form of labour. An extra and important factor was a wish to claim the moral high ground for Britain and her empire. As the Lord Chancellor declared, ending the slave trade was 'our duty to God, and to our country which was the morning star that enlightened Europe, and whose boast and glory was to grant liberty and life, and administer humanity and justice to all nations'.[22] By 1846 the high ground was Britain's; and Palmerston was able to say of the slave trade in Zanzibar that it must be ended and that 'Great Britain is the main instrument in the hands of Providence for the accomplishment of this purpose'.[23]

The reaction to abolition was not entirely welcoming, a fact which is explicable in the light of long-standing assumptions about the inferiority of non-white races. This persisted even after the slave trade became illegal as, for instance, Thackeray's *Vanity Fair* (1848) shows. So deep-rooted was the belief that it is used as late as 1834 in Alexander Walker's textbook on physiognomy: when speaking of faces in general, he argues that the strength of the organs of feeling or sense is no prediction of the strength of the organs of intellect. To clinch the point he states that 'it often happens that the sensations, as in the negro, are strong while the mental operations . . . are weak'.[24] So his argument goes: negroes are already known to be sensual, stupid, and with little will-power; their features are of a certain kind; those whose organs of sense are also strong will, like negroes, be unintellectual and weak-willed.

The backlash against abolition was fed by these racist assumptions and affected those who focused on the damage to West Indian trade caused by the removal of cheap slave labour. The hostility this caused is expressed in an extreme form by Carlyle in his 1849 article in *Fraser's Magazine*, 'Occasional Discourse on the Negro Question', which was expanded and reprinted in 1853. He pictures the freed slaves in the West Indies as idle loungers, gorging themselves 'with their beautiful muzzles up to the ears in pumpkins, imbibing sweet pulps and juices'[25] while the sugar crops rot. All they do is clamour for ' "Higher wages, massa" . . . till no conceivable opulence of cane-crop will cover such wages!'[26] The remedy, he suggests, is compulsion: each of 'our beautiful Black darlings' has 'an indisputable and perpetual *right* to be compelled, by the real proprietors of said land, to do competent work for his living'.[27] Even Dickens, who devoted a whole chapter of his travelogue *American Notes* (1842) to condemnation of the physical ill-treatment of slaves and slavery in general, still regards them as innately inferior: 'The melancholy absurdity of giving these people votes . . . would glare at one out of every roll of their eyes, every chuckle in their mouths, and bump in their heads'.[28]

This belief in the inferiority of non-white races extends to orientals. Though they were seen as in a different category from blacks, like them they were thought closer to animals and, according to Alexander Walker the physiognomist, their features, though beautiful, showed much sensibility but not much intellect. Oriental women, in particular, were an object of interest to travellers: beautiful, indolent creatures, happy with the mindless lives Eastern society imposed on them. In Britain, tourists visited prisons and asylums to see the inmates as one might visit a zoo; travellers in the Middle East in the nineteenth century visited harems. Florence Nightingale inspected one at Alexandria in 1850 and writes of an occupant 'Oh, the *ennui*, of that magnificent palace, it will stand in my memory as a circle of hell! Not one thing was there lying about, to be done or be looked at. We almost longed to send her a cup and ball.'[29] Such women came to symbolize the decadence into which Western women could not afford to decline. The comparison is naturalized to the point where, like other expressions of racism, it becomes an unconscious assumption.

These were the events and assumptions of the society in which the Brontës wrote and, despite their remoteness from London, their novels engage with all these issues—class, gender, race, religion, the mind and the self—without becoming polemical or simplistic. Instead they capture the complexities and contradictions that marked the first half of the nineteenth century.

CHAPTER 3

THE LITERARY CONTEXT

Literary Resources

PERHAPS the most surprising feature of Patrick Brontë's treatment of his children was the freedom he gave them to read whatever was available, for the only known restriction that he placed on their reading was his prohibition on old copies of the *Lady's Magazine* which had either belonged to their mother or Aunt Branwell. The reason he gave was that they contained 'foolish love stories' (Alexander, p. 21), a complaint that sounds more literary than moral.

Like many other Victorian writers, the Brontës in their youth read the books most frequently found in such a household: the Bible, the Prayer Book, and that third 'sacred' text, John Bunyan's *Pilgrim's Progress*. To these were added commonplace textbooks such as Goldsmith's *Grammar of General Geography* which survives with marginalia scribbled by all the children (Alexander, p. 19). Even from these works they drew exotic elements such as the names of remote places and people: Dahomey, Gambia, Senegal, Ashantee. They also had the usual access to the delights of *Aesop's Fables* and the *Arabian Nights* but also, more unusually, to the poetry of Shakespeare, Milton, Ossian, Wordsworth, Southey, and Byron. They clearly already had a taste for stories of great men and were able to read biographies of Johnson, Sheridan, and Nelson amongst others, while nearer to home they devoured Gilbert White's *Natural History and Antiquities of Selborne* and Thomas Bewick's *History of British Birds*.

What evidently attracted them in all they read were works of the turn-of-the-century Romantics which fed their already excited imaginations: the poems of Wordsworth, Southey, Byron; Sir Walter Scott's works and Gothic novels. All of these captivated them and simultaneously legitimated the role of the imaginary in their lives. Romanticism stood in sharp contrast to the earlier eighteenth-century classicism in the arts, with its insistence on the supremacy of cool reason as manifested visually and verbally in order, symmetry, balance, and restraint. In literature this meant in particular the control of the emotions, whereas the Romantics gave primacy to the emotions and to the freedom to express them in a way foreshadowed superficially by the cult of sensibility. To Samuel Johnson and others in the mid-eighteenth century, to describe someone as 'zealous without enthusiasm' was to compliment him on his moderation. Conversely, to speak of the 'romantic notion' of building a bridge over the Thames at Putney was to discredit the idea as ridiculously fanciful. Later, for the Romantic writers like Wordsworth and Coleridge, imagination and fancy were faculties of great interest and value, needing to be carefully distinguished from one another. Fancy was a more superficial ability than imagination which totally transformed images that were merely remembered. Emily's poem 'To Imagination', published in 1846, captures this distinction and its basis in the contrast between imagination and reason:

> Reason, indeed, may oft complain
>   For Nature's sad reality,
> And tell the suffering heart how vain
>   Its cherished dreams must always be;
> And Truth may rudely trample down
>   The flowers of Fancy, newly-blown:
>
> But, thou are ever there, to bring
>   The hovering vision back, and breathe
> New glories o'er the blighted spring,
>   And call a lovelier Life from Death,
> And whisper, with a voice divine,
>   Of real worlds, as bright as thine.
>   (Gezari, pp. 19–20)

Since poetry was notoriously described as emotion recollected in tranquillity and transformed by the power of imagination, suppression of emotion was devalued and the natural and perfect expression of it sought, while nature itself was preferred in its wild, uncultivated state rather than when ordered into formally artistic shapes by landscape artists like Capability Brown. The appeal of all this to the temperaments of the Brontë children is evident in what they drew from their miscellany of reading.

  Charlotte, Branwell, Emily, and Anne took easily to the idea of becoming Romantic writers, concerning themselves freely with the expression of strong emotions of love, hate, and remorse, and they transformed these feelings into sensational narratives from which Emily later distilled her strange poems, combining passion with abstraction. All three sisters ransacked Romantic literature for exciting plots and strong feelings such as they would not have found in early nineteenth-century fiction when novels mainly belonged to one of two genres: the 'silver fork' type or the 'Newgate' novels. The former were stories of high-life with tepid plots; the latter used tales from the Newgate Calendar with its accounts of notorious criminals and their exploits.

As the intermixing of accounts of life at the Parsonage with goings-on in Angria and Gondal in the Diary Papers shows, the Brontës did not distinguish sharply between real and imagined worlds. Much of what they read in *Blackwood's Magazine* was news or information about actual events, people, and places and thus contemporary reportage seems to have appeared to them as on the same plane with what they absorbed from their reading in poetry and novels. Consequently their own writing mixed real people and events with the purely fictional. They began to read *Blackwood's* when the eldest child, Charlotte, was a mere 10 years old, and so were introduced to the contemporary political scene which within a year had begun to show through in the Islanders' Play which they composed and acted jointly. Charlotte used two stories involving her much-admired Duke of Wellington, both allegories of political events: one an attempt to poison him, the other a kidnapping attempt on his two sons, Arthur and Charles. Charlotte's account of how the Brontës received news of Catholic Emancipation is also found in this play and in 1830 another scene is set in Downing Street with Wellington, the Prime Minister, surrounded by his cabinet colleagues. It is evident that what was reported in *Blackwood's* provided the children with a prototype story: important aristocratic figures engaged in struggles over power. This pattern, with the addition of many tangled love affairs, forms the basis of the Angrian and Gondal sagas, and the virtual worlds that the Brontës created led ultimately to their published fiction and poetry.

What they drew chiefly from Romantic writers were sensational plots, exotic settings, large-scale characters, and intense emotions, which fleshed out their prototype narrative. Gothic novels and those of Scott offered exciting and even sensational plots. Byron's narrative poems added to these and also provided heroic figures in glamorous settings, consumed by powerful feelings of love, hate, jealousy, and lust for power.

GOTHIC PLOTS AND PLACES

The Gothic novels of the late eighteenth century were the equivalent of such mid-twentieth-century films as Alfred Hitchcock's *Psycho* or *Vertigo*: their purpose was to create a horrifying thrill from stories set in blatantly sinister locations—castles, abbeys, and ruins in isolated places often thought to be haunted. The tales involved a struggle between good and evil in a suspenseful and intricate plot in which malign beings or forces struggled for power and/or the life and/or chastity of a beautiful and virtuous heroine were increasingly threatened.

The imagination of the authors frequently stretched to the inclusion of the supernatural which is usually attached to a vague idea of poetic justice. In Horace Walpole's immensely popular *The Castle of Otranto*, an evil tyrant, Manfred, sees his son crushed to death, on the day he was to marry the beautiful Isabella, by a helmet which falls from the head of an enormous statue of Manfred's virtuous predecessor, Alfonso the Good. Manfred blames an innocent bystander, Theodore, for the death, though for no apparent reason. Eventually the statue comes to life to reveal all: Manfred's grandfather murdered Alfonso, and Theodore is the true heir who can then marry Isabella and take over the kingdom while a penitent Manfred retires to a monastery. But between these two interventions by the statue, many complications develop: Manfred decides to divorce this wife and marry Isabella; Theodore escapes from prison and wounds Manfred, who accidentally kills his own daughter.

Even this stripped-down account of the plot of Walpole's novel shows how typically sensational events which occur in rapid succession are only loosely linked together, so that it is not cause and effect but sheer effect which matters as in the Angrian and, presumably, the Gondal stories in which the narrators feel free to backtrack on events, introduce magical figures, or even reintroduce characters thought dead in an earlier story. Feelings in Gothic novels are invariably extreme and described or expressed melodramatically: when Isabella foils Manfred's evil designs by escaping through a 'subterraneous passage' which she suddenly recollects, her terror is acute. She imagines that she hears a noise: 'Her blood curdled; she concluded it was Manfred. Every suggestion that horror could inspire rushed into her mind. She condemned her rash flight which had thus exposed her to his rage' (*The Castle of Otranto*, chapter 1). These melodramatic accounts of emotion are also echoed in the juvenilia of the Brontës.

THE BYRONIC HERO

The life of Byron, Charlotte's hero, was itself a story suited to Angria and Gondal for he was a darkly handsome aristocrat, belonging to an ancient family, with the added attraction of being born with a disability, referred to as a club foot, suggestive of a satanic cloven hoof. He was well known for his heterosexual love affairs and, as it now appears, was bisexual. In 1815 he was married briefly to Annabella Milbanke, who within a year had given birth to a daughter and obtained a legal separation, allegedly because of an incestuous affair with his half-sister, Augusta Leigh. In any event he left the country in 1816 and later died in Greece where he had gone to help the fight for Greek independence. Though his life has more coherence than the stories devised by the Brontës, it had all their favourite ingredients; and they were able to read about his story in Patrick's copy of T. Moore's *Byron's Life and Works*.

Byron's poetry reflects his own public persona, a performance not even outdone by that of Oscar Wilde, and his personal pronouncements match the narrating voice in his poems for they are evidently designed to shock and thrill in a manner which suggests that there is something of the night about him: 'Every day confirms my opinion on the superiority of a vicious life—and if Virtue is not its own reward, I don't know any other stipend attached to it'. The central themes of his poems were: that passionate physical love was all-important; that it overrides social conventions such as marriage; and that the outside world exerts pressures to inhibit it which should be resisted. The poems are at the extreme of Romantic individualism.

The heroes of Byron's long narrative poems are in the main alter egos of each other and of his public persona, showing both his recklessness and his wit. The identikit for these heroes would resemble the appearance of 'the Corsair' in his poem of that name:

Sun-burnt his cheek, his forehead high and pale
The sable curls in wild profusion veil;
And oft perforce his rising lip reveals
The haughtier thought it curbs, but scarce conceals.
Though smooth his voice, and calm his general mien,
Still seems there something he would not have seen:
His features' deepening lines and varying hue
At times attracted, yet perplexed the view,
As if within that murkiness of mind
Worked feelings fearful, and yet undefined.

(McGann, p. 247)

The plots of Byron's verse narratives are all built around such a man, darkly seductive and mysterious and they follow a common pattern: in *Childe Harold's Pilgrimage*, *The Giaour*, *The Corsair*, and *Don Juan* an adulterous affair or affairs all end in confrontation with jealous husband or lover, as well as flights, battles, separations, and in extreme cases, violent death, shipwreck, and even cannibalism.

Like Gothic novels, the poems show extremes of feeling which are here vividly expressed, not merely reported, and the Giaour gives his definition of love as Byron saw it:

The cold in clime are cold in blood,
Their love can scarce deserve the name;
But mine was like the lava flood
That boils in Aetna's breast of flame.
I cannot prate in puling strain
Of ladye-love, and beauty's chain;
If changing cheek, and scorching vein—
Lips taught to writhe, but not complain—
If bursting heart, and madd'ning brain—
And daring deed and vengeful steel—
And all that I have felt—and feel—
Betoken love—that love was mine.

(McGann, p. 236)

The settings of Byron's poems vary as lovers move from place to place through Europe and love affairs have backgrounds such as the harems in *The Giaour* and *Don Juan*. They enlarged the Brontës' vision of the descriptions in *Blackwood's* and their geography book of regions like Africa and the Pacific. Charlotte in particular, with her taste for lush descriptions, was captivated by the glittering account of the rooms where Don Juan finds himself with his beautiful lover, Haidée. They sit with crimson satin at their feet and scarlet cushions embossed with a golden sun. In addition:

> There was no want of lofty mirrors, and
> The tables, most of ebony inlaid
> With mother of pearl or ivory, stood at hand,
> Or were of tortoise-shell or rare woods made,
> Fretted with gold or silver.
>
> (McGann, p. 505)

The women who live in this luxury and who are the object (for a time) of the Byronic hero's desire are languorous and sensual, as the long-standing convention about oriental women, particularly in harems, required. Byron puts it with witty irony in *Don Juan*:

> The Turks do well to shut—at least, sometimes—
> The women up—because in sad reality,
> Their chastity in these unhappy climes
> Is not a thing of that astringent quality,
> Which in the North prevents precocious crimes,
> And makes our snow less pure than our morality.
>
> (McGann, p. 587)

Angria and Gondal

The political saga at Westminster, as narrated by *Blackwood's*, metamorphoses into those of Angria and Gondal by the accretion of Gothic and Byronic elements which underlie the published writings of the Brontës, providing a subtext to the novels which are superficially constrained by the then current conventions about fiction.

Admiration for great men links Byron's narratives with Angria so that, at the beginning of *Don Juan*, Byron announces 'I want a hero' (McGann, p. 378) and centres all his long narrative poems on such a one. The words must have resonated especially with Charlotte whose desire for a hero persisted long after she had named her wooden soldier for the Duke of Wellington. At the Angrian stage of the Brontës' early fiction, the Duke of Wellington cedes the hero's place to his elder son, Arthur Wellesley, who becomes in rapid succession the Marquis of Douro, Duke of Zamorna, and finally King of Angria. The increasingly exalted titles figure Zamorna's rise to a

Zamorna, the Byronic hero of Angria, drawn by Branwell, 1835

Lord Byron, portrait by Thomas Phillips, 1835

dazzling status and power, accompanied by a rise in his dissoluteness in relation to women. He is plainly Byronic in appearance as an early description makes clear: 'his figure was toweringly, over-bearingly lofty, moulded in statue-like perfection, and invested with something which I cannot describe—something superb, impetuous, resistless. His hair was intensely black, curled luxuriantly, but the forehead underneath . . . looked white & smooth as ivory' (Gérin, p. 12). At a later stage, as Duke of Zamorna, his more vicious aspects are visible even as he lies asleep and the onlooker feels 'with startling force at the moment a conviction . . . that in the timber of this stately tree there was a flaw which would eat ere the lapse of many years to its heart' (Gérin, p. 67).

Byron cried in *Don Juan* 'I want a hero' but Emily seems to have read this as 'I want a heroine' for the Gondal poems show that Emily and Anne's saga replaced the central male figure with a larger-than-life queen with a name to match: Augusta Geraldine Almeda. She too probably appeared, like Arthur Wellesley, in the Angrian saga under other names: though originally a 'being whose very presence blessed, like gladsome summer day',[1] she later resembles him in her irresistible attractiveness and her ruthlessness towards those around her. The events in Gondal/Gaaldine can only be deduced from Emily's Gondal poems which are all that survive from the original multiple stories. The poems were passionate expressions of the feelings of individuals at crucial emotional moments in their lives. Sometimes in the manuscripts the names of the characters are indicated by initials such as A.G.A. for Augusta Geraldine Almeda. Hence the poems offer something equivalent to the major arias in an opera of which we lack the full libretto, though some inferences can be made from these arias: A.G.A. evidently had many lovers including a favoured one, Julius Brenzaida, who is victorious in battle but later dies; another lover, Alexander Lord Elbë, also dies; and a third, Fernando, is imprisoned by A.G.A. Another poem reveals that a mother (possibly A.G.A.) abandons her baby in the snow. Reactions to events such as these are operatically expressed, as when a man recalls his time of imprisonment:

> O God of heaven! The dream of horror
> The frightful dream is over now
> The sickened heart the blasting sorrow

> The ghastly night the ghastlier morrow
> The aching sense of utter woe
> (Gézari, p. 43)

Like Byron's narratives, the Angrian and Gondal stories are loosely held together by the presence of Zamorna or of A.G.A., and since in the Zamorna tales we have the full libretto, it is possible to see how events are handled by Charlotte, particularly Zamorna's many love affairs. He has three wives, all of whom he treats badly: the first, Lady Helen Victorine Gordon, who dies in childbirth; the second, Marian Hume, who dies neglected; the third, Mary Percy, is the daughter of his bitter rival, Alexander Percy, Duke of Northangerland. In addition to his favourite mistress Mina Laury, there is his wife's half-sister, Caroline Vernon, Northangerland's illegitimate daughter. Zamorna's treatment of all these and other women is ruthlessly Byronic: the desire of the moment is all that matters to him and loyalty goes for nothing. This is perhaps best illustrated by a scene where Mary, Zamorna's wife, comes to visit him in disguise, unwanted by him as he had plans to separate from her:

The Duke, gazing at her pale & sweet loveliness till he felt there was nothing in the world he loved half so well, & conscious that her delicate attenuation was for his sake . . . threw himself impetuously beside her & soon made her tremble as much with the ardour of his caresses as she had done with the dread of his wrath. (Gérin, p. 71)

The treatment of the scene indicates a degree of sexual frankness beyond the current conventions, as do many other scenes, particularly that recounting the treatment of Zamorna's seduction of Caroline Vernon, Northangerland's daughter. She is Zamorna's ward until the age of 15 when her father takes her off to Paris so that she may acquire her social 'finish'. On her return she runs away to Zamorna to prevent her father removing her from the social gaiety she loves. In an early scene, later rewritten, Charlotte had shown Zamorna grooming the girl for seduction and, when Caroline runs away to him, he fulfils his plan. She asks him if he is angry with her but his response is to seize her—'she found herself in his arms—He strained her to his heart a moment, kissed her forehead & instantly released her'. She asks him to take her with him to Verdopolis but when he hints at his desires she is 'struck with an agony of shame'. Zamorna is now said to reveal himself in his true colours and not to deny 'by one noble & moral act the character he had earned by a hundred infamous ones'. He tells her, 'If I were a bearded Turk, Caroline, I would take you to my Harem' and in fact he does the next best thing and promises to seclude her in his 'little retreat . . . hidden in a wood', a love-nest where her can visit her:

He smiled as Caroline looked at him with mixed wonder & fear—his face changed to an expression of tenderness more dangerous than the fiery excitement which had startled her before—he caressed her fondly & lifted with his fingers the heavy curls which were lying on her neck . . . She no longer wished to leave him, she clung to his side—infatuation was stealing over her . . .—She feared, she loved—Passion tempted, conscience warned her . . . & when Zamorna kissed her & said in that voice of fatal sweetness . . . 'Will you go with me to-morrow, Caroline?' she looked up in his face with a kind of wild devoted enthusiasm & answered 'Yes'. (Gérin, pp. 341–4)

This is *Jane Eyre* in Gothic mode, belonging to what Charlotte came to call the 'world beneath', and her fascination with the Gothic persisted until 1835 when, at the age of 19, she still found herself having realistic and seductive visions of Zamorna:

how distinctly I, sitting in the school-room at Roe-Head, saw the Duke of Zamorna leaning against that obelisk, with the mute marble Victory above him, the fern waving at his feet, his black horse turned loose grazing among the heather . . . I was quite gone. I had really utterly forgot where I was and all the gloom and cheerlessness of my situation . . . 'Miss Brontë, what are you thinking about?' said a voice that dissipated all the charm. (Alexander, p. 140)

By 1839 it becomes clear that she is distancing herself from the Angrian dream world when her narrator in *Caroline Vernon* takes a satirical perspective on its always sensational history. 'There's not always', she says,

> An Angrian campaign going on in the rain,
> Nor a Gentleman Squire lighting his fire
> Up on the moors with his blackguards & boors,
> Nor a duke & a lord drawing the sword,
> Hectoring & lying, the whole world defying.
> Then sitting down crying.

Nor is there always

A Death & a marriage—a Hearse & a Carriage,
A Bigamy cause—A King versus laws,
Nor a short Transportation for the good of the nation,
Nor a speedy returning mid national mourning,
While him & his father refuse to foregather
'Cause the earl hadn't rather.

(Gérin, p. 278)

In place of intricate plots and glamorous settings, *Caroline Vernon* unfolds a single story in locations which are often calculatedly mundane, a move away from the Angrian stories and many steps nearer to *Jane Eyre*. This mundanity is indicated in the opening of 'the novelette' where the narrator records how he was chased away by a gamekeeper after sitting down under a willow to picnic at the foot of a statue 'to eat cold fowl & drink a bottle of ginger-beer' (Gérin, p. 277). Zamorna is later mildly satirized as he performs the role of country squire in a histrionic way, standing in a hayfield in a broad-brimmed straw hat, wearing a plaid jacket and trousers while he discusses the quality of the crop with a dialect-speaking local. The satire persists when Northangerland visits his old enemy and derides this rural idyll. He has refused to correspond with Zamorna on the grounds that Zamorna 'smells so very strong of oat-cake & grouse' (Gérin, p. 281) and is disgusted by the fly-fishing tackle and agricultural magazines that he notices in Zamorna's home, Hawkscliffe Hall, which itself is described as blatantly unromantic, not a palace or a castle. When Northangerland tartly refuses dinner, he explains satirically 'I can't take porridge or fried bacon', plebeian dishes (Gérin, p. 291). Anne and Emily were to cling to Gondal for most of their lives but it is clear that already, some seven years before their first publication of the joint volume of poems, Charlotte is breaking free to some extent of her literary past, though it was to remain an influence on all she wrote.

Publishing, Publication, and Reviewing

When the Brontë sisters sent off their work to London publishers, they were entering a sphere of which they knew little, though they had played at publishing when creating the magazines in the juvenilia and seem to have been unfazed by the fact that they were now moving into a tightly organized and competitive industry. It is significant

Charlotte's romantic watercolour of 'Lake and Castle'

Emily Brontë's miniature writing in a diary paper with a sketch of Emily and Anne

that they first did so by offering a volume of poetry to which they had all contributed.

They sent their manuscript off at a time when a higher literary value was widely attributed to poetry than to novels, a long-standing view based on the importance of the genre in classical literature and reinforced by Romantic poets such as Wordsworth, Southey, and Keats, bent on high seriousness. This action implies that already in their first attempt at publication, as with their letters to Wordsworth and Southey, the Brontës reveal an ambition to achieve a place in the world of high culture. Consequently they were undeterred by the failure of the poems to sell since critics received them as 'genuine poetry' which it was possible to compare not unfavourably with poems of Wordsworth and Tennyson (Allott, pp. 59, 60). This mid-nineteenth-century view of poetry as a superior form had to be somehow justified in 'moral' terms. The rationale given was that, while novels offer an apparent replica of real life, poetry does not, because in poetry 'the wildest language of passion, though it may appeal to the feelings, is generally called forth in circumstances remote from the experience of the reader'. In fictional works which 'profess to paint real life', the reader may be led to identify with some character and so into erroneous ways of thinking: 'the novel-ist's pictures of real life are false, because necessarily covered with an unreal gloss. The object of the poet and artist is to embody their own lofty view of the truly beautiful'.[2] This argument satisfactorily explained away what might otherwise be thought of as immoral views of poets already long-established in the Pantheon—such as Shakespeare.

With the rare exception of works like those of Scott, whose plots were often historical and seen to endorse conventional morality, novels were regarded as part of popular culture. Novel-reading in general was still widely regarded as mere entertainment but this account of literary work as a whole had its opponents. The supposed hierarchy was dismissed by some who saw both poetry and novels as forms of fanciful self-indulgence. An extreme statement of this kind is found in the *Westminster Review*: 'Literature is a seducer; we had almost said a harlot'. Strict utilitarians like Thomas Love Peacock wrote ironically of the classical lineage of poetry: 'A poet in our times is a semi-barbarian in a civilized community. He lives in the days that are past. His ideas, thoughts, feelings, associations, are all

with barbarous manners, obsolete customs, and exploded super-
stitions.' Poetry is not 'what it was in the Homeric age, the all-in-all of
intellectual progression, and as if there were no such things in existence as mathematicians, astronomers, chemists, moralists, meta-
physicians, historians, politicians, and political economists, who have
built into the upper air of intelligence a pyramid from which they see
the modern Parnassus far beneath them'.[3]

But this view of literature did not prevail in a time of increasing
literacy and the cheap production in parts of works such as Dickens's
hugely popular novels, for by the time the Brontës published their
first novels, Dickens had already written *Pickwick Papers*, *Oliver
Twist*, *Nicholas Nickleby*, *The Old Curiosity Shop*, *Barnaby Rudge*,
and *Martin Chuzzlewit*. By the fifteenth instalment of the first of
these works, sales had reached 40,000 copies per issue (at one shilling
each, or one twentieth of a pound sterling). Furthermore, though
Paper Duty was not repealed until 1861, cheaper forms of printing
also created a wider middle-class readership.

Somehow, therefore, novels came to be acceptable when, like those
of Dickens, they did not breach standards of propriety: the ideal
novel was coded as a work which would not bring a blush to the
cheek of an unmarried and innocent young girl when read aloud by
the paterfamilias to his assembled family in the evening. The timing
and circumstances of reading were relevant to propriety: private
reading in the morning or even in the afternoon was more suspect.
Fortunately for the Brontë children, Patrick was somewhat of a
recluse and Charlotte even managed to read some dreaded 'French'
novels.

As the market grew, entrepreneurs grasped the possibilities of
financial gain in linking price and distribution, and a specific mechanism developed to exploit the growing taste for cheaply available
fiction. In many ways the mechanism devised, which lasted from the
1840s to the 1890s, resembled practices in publishing operating at
the end of the twentieth century. At this more recent date the control
of publication and circulation of books fell into fewer and fewer
hands: those of increasingly global companies who bought up
smaller firms. The practice was not always evident since these larger
firms often preserved the imprints of the smaller publishers that
they had swallowed up. Similarly in the first half of the nineteenth
century the control of circulation was the key in the hands of a small

number of individuals like Charles Edward Mudie and W(illiam) H(enry) Smith, which in the event gave them some control of publication. In both periods these external agents (global publishers or owners of circulating libraries) were able to affect the physical form and the content of work which they pushed into mass circulation by means of advertising. The global publishers do so by selecting writers who will produce a fairly standard commodity, 'the best-seller', according to the formula of the moment such as sex-and-shopping, sex-and-violence, documentary narratives. The requirements in the Victorian period, which will be discussed later, were used mainly retrospectively to select from what was on offer. It is likely, however, that the prospects for publication influenced the material of some authors. Global publishers work both prospectively and retrospectively in this matter. Now, as in the time of the Brontës, commercial pressures are effective in influencing the choice of subject matter and its treatment in many novels which reach a mass public. The source of pressure today is the lack of competition which allows large companies to select their future 'best-sellers' and market them with massive publicity in media other than print which sometimes they also own. The nineteenth-century entrepreneurs had more moderate assets but an equally efficient system in which those in control of circulation had the whip-hand over publishers and through them over authors. The crucial vehicle for circulation in a period of increasing speed of travel, thanks to the railways, was the circulating library.

Victorian readers were increasing in number and clearly had more stamina than their later counterparts. Thanks to the huge popularity of the novels of Sir Walter Scott, the three-volume hardback had become the standard format by the mid-nineteenth century. Such works sold for one and a half guineas or roughly £1.50, a large sum at a time when a labouring man might earn perhaps £15 or £20 a year. In 1842 the most well known of the circulating libraries was opened by Charles Edward Mudie and could order new works in large numbers of copies. By 1858 Mudie's had become virtually a national institution, offering to individual subscribers the loan of one volume at a time for just one guinea a year or four volumes for two guineas a year. Larger subscriptions could be taken out by clubs or libraries; volumes could be either collected or forwarded via the railway. From Mudie's point of view and that of his great rival W. H.

Smith, the three-decker format was ideal. With three volumes they could rapidly make available to several readers the new novels that, thanks to the library's publicity, they were eager to read. As Reader A passed on to volume two, Reader B could start on volume one; to be replaced in turn by Reader C; by which time Reader A was on to volume three. 'Mudie mania' set in, like 'railway mania', spawning visual cartoon jokes or verbal ones such as the rhyme:

> As children must have Punch and Judy
> So I can't do without my Mudie.[4]

Since the libraries bought large numbers of copies of new works, they were able to insist on three-deckers and to demand generous discounts. Part of the benefit to the author and publisher of such works was that, if they were accepted by a library owner, a reasonably large sale was ensured and the risk of publication for an unknown author was shared. By publishing a list of his new acquisitions in middle-class publications like the *Athenaeum* and the *Spectator*, the librarian was also able to offer effective publicity and a captive readership. So strong was the control exercised by the circulating libraries that they were able to require from the publishers not only a three-decker format and discounts but also an embargo on direct sales of books to the public for anything less than the artificially high price of one and a half guineas. Since at the end of a year the libraries sold their own three-deckers at a cheaper price, they left the publishers commercially hamstrung. Hence the significance of George Smith telling Charlotte, when he rejected *The Professor* (a work of one volume), that he would be interested in a three-volume narrative. Hence also the offer of *Wuthering Heights* and *Agnes Grey* jointly as a three-volume work of which Emily's novel formed two volumes and Anne's one.

In many instances the dominance of the three-volume format for much of the century influenced the narrative it contained. Everyone may have a novel in them but it is not necessarily a three-decker, though Charlotte produced one in a single year which fitted the form without strain. For other less talented authors the three-decker resulted in what was called 'stretching', discernible in many nineteenth-century novels. The publisher could help to stretch with wide margins and well-spaced type increasing the number of pages; and deliberate stretching by the author could also add length: padding of episodes, extra events, or characters not altogether relevant to the central storyline. Some, like Trollope, voiced their discontent with this pressure, seeing stretching in commercial terms as short-changing his readership:

I have always endeavored to give good measure to the public—The pages, as you propose to publish them, are so thin and desolated, and contain such a poor rate of type meandering thro' a desert of margin, as to make me ashamed of the idea of putting my name to the book. The stories were sold to you as one volume.[5]

Readers frequently grew impatient with the second volume of works stretched by the author since this was usually the weakest of the three. Each volume required a dramatic structure which the knotting-up of the plot provided for the first and its unravelling provided for the third. This left what was sometimes referred to as the 'sad second volume'.

Censorship and Public Taste

From what has been described it is evident that in the Victorian period it was the circulating libraries which were the prevailing manifestation of censorship. Their activities can be thought of like those of more recent publishers as a response to public taste or market forces but the narrowing of limits constitutes a form of censorship. The name of Mudie's concern, 'Mudie's Select Library', was pointedly chosen to indicate that the volumes listed in his advertisements had his sanction. The choice was indeed Mudie's own and, since he was a Nonconformist of strictly puritanical views, he took a sharp line on what he saw as propriety. He preferred to think of himself not as a censor but as a man responding to public taste. When accused of censorship he sprang to defend his own right to 'select': 'The title under which my library was established nearly twenty years ago implies this:—the public know it and subscribe accordingly and increasingly. They are evidently willing to have a barrier of some kind between themselves and the lower floods of literature.'[6] Mudie's claim that readers shared a common sense of literary propriety which required the exclusion of low literature from his library has a certain validity. Pornography flourished as a subterranean culture for men only; but Mudie is also excluding other non-pornographic works of which he disapproved. Still it is true that a kind of consensus as to appropriate standards in novels is apparent: from the nature of the fiction that middle-class periodicals chose to publicize; from critical reviews; and from public responses in the form of letters to the press, to libraries, and to publishers.

The criteria applied to literary works in order to assess their merit were also affected by the gender or presumed gender of the author at a time when fairly often female authors took masculine pseudonyms. As for the names that the Brontës took, it is often assumed that Emily's insistence on anonymity was the main reason but Charlotte, in 1850 in her 'Biographical Notice' prefacing her sisters' work, gives a different explanation. She asserts that 'the ambiguous choice' was dictated by

a sort of conscientious scruple at assuming Christian names positively masculine, while we did not like to declare ourselves women, because— without at that time suspecting that our mode of writing and thinking was not what is called 'feminine'—we had a vague impression that authoresses are liable to be looked on with prejudice; we had noticed how critics sometimes use for their chastisement the weapon of personality, and for their reward, a flattery, which is not true praise. (*Letters*, ii. 743)

The difference in standards as applied to female as opposed to male authors was in part a matter of degree. Some breaches of propriety would be unacceptable in both; some accepted in male authors would be castigated as 'masculine' and coarse if made by a woman. The force of Charlotte's comment on using personality as a weapon is illustrated by Elizabeth Rigby's view that if the author of *Jane Eyre* was a woman she must be one who had 'for some sufficient reason, long forfeited the society of her own sex' (Allott, p. 111). Similarly, G. H. Lewes, in reviewing *Shirley*, prefaces his review, now that he knows Currer Bell to be a woman, with a dogmatic account of women's defectiveness as writers. He claims that 'The grand function of woman . . . is, and ever must be, Maternity'. He concludes that, since women are all designed to be mothers, it is impossible 'to know who are to escape that destiny, till it is too late to begin the training necessary for artists, scholars, or politicians'. Females need therefore, when they write, to write 'as women' instead of 'rivalling men' (Allott, pp. 161–2). Though earlier he had offered extreme praise of *Jane Eyre* when merely guessing at Currer Bell's gender, he now writes of that work disparagingly: 'A more masculine book, in the sense of vigour, was never written. Indeed that vigour often amounts to coarseness,—and is certainly the very antipode to "lady like" '. He adds that 'This same over-masculine vigour is even more prominent in *Shirley*' (Allott, p. 163).

The standards applied (with this modification for gender) to authors of either sex can be inferred from the reviews in which they are implicitly alluded to as common knowledge. The requirements are: circumspection in handling anything even distantly related to religion; extreme reticence in sexual matters which must be euphemistically treated; abstention from too close an examination of the seamy side of life (violence, cruelty, alcoholism, adultery, bigamy); and above all the inculcation of a moral lesson, preferably by a display of poetic justice for the sinner. These rules, it was hoped, would prevent the middle-class girl's blush but a perhaps more realistic view of such young women is that of a reviewer of *Wuthering Heights*:

If we did not know that this book has been read by thousands of young ladies in the country, we should esteem it our first duty to caution them against it simply on account of the coarseness of the style. (Allott, p. 236)

The application of these standards by individual reviewers is not always comprehensive or unintelligent. Sometimes, for instance, the Brontës' novels are compared favourably with the usual fodder provided by Mudie's and the rest. One reviewer of *Jane Eyre* writes that no one can call it 'weak or vapid':

It is anything but a fashionable novel . . . It has not a Lord Fanny for its hero, nor a Duchess for its pattern of nobility. The scene of action is never in Belgrave or Grosvenor Square. The pages are scant of French and void of Latin. We hear nothing of Madame de Maradan; we scent nothing of the bouquet de la Reine. (Allott, p. 77)

Other comparisons disparaging to more conventional novels can be found, such as the choice of a 'homely' name and a plain appearance for the heroine of *Jane Eyre* which distinguishes it from 'the sickly models of the Minerva Press' (Allott, p. 81)—a byword for cheap romances.

Those who disliked or at least disapproved of *Jane Eyre*, *Wuthering Heights*, and *The Tenant of Wildfell Hall* found in them all the features they most condemned. In terms of religion, *Wuthering Heights* displays a profanity of language which offends against 'both polite-ness and good morals'; *Jane Eyre* is 'pre-eminently an antichristian composition' because it questions God's providence (Allott, pp. 236, 109); and *The Tenant of Wildfell Hall* asserts a belief that salvation is universal so that even the dissolute Huntingdon will be saved. This latter view is seen as a heretical distortion of the idea of God as merciful.

In discussing sexual matters, reviewers are reticent even about mentioning the lack of reticence in novels. There are a few sug-gestive general comments: the scenes of passion in *Jane Eyre* are too 'hot' and 'emphatic' with too much attention paid to 'mere animal appetite, and to courtship after the manner of kangaroos'; and *The Tenant of Wildfell Hall* has a 'gross, physical, or profli-gate substratum' (Allott, pp. 99, 250). More usually the occur-rence of intended bigamy in *Jane Eyre*, adultery in *The Tenant of Wildfell Hall*, and Heathcliff's necrophiliac desires are subsumed under general condemnations of too much seediness in the authors' preoccupation with the unpleasant side of life, 'the con-templation of which taste rejects' (Allott, p. 218). These are 'bru-tal subjects' which are 'positively disgusting'; dragging them into the light of day reveals them as 'coarse and loathsome' (Allott, pp. 224, 222).

Most of the critiques discussed so far share the common assump-tion that a literary work should be in some simple sense didactic but such lessons appeared to hostile reviewers to be lacking in much of the Brontës' work: *Jane Eyre* hovers on the brink of being immoral and 'it wears a questionable aspect'; *Wuthering Heights* reveals 'a purposeless power' and 'What may be the moral which the author wishes the reader to deduce from his work, it is difficult to say; and we refrain from assigning any because . . . we have discovered none but mere glimpses of hidden morals' (Allott, pp. 81, 228). Even Acton Bell does no better: *The Tenant of Wildfell Hall* offers the reader 'no enlarged view of mankind, giving a healthy action to his sympathies' but instead forces him 'to witness the wolfish side of his nature' (Allott, p. 262).

It is to be expected that hostile critics should beat the Brontës with these particular moral sticks as their weapons. More surpris-ingly the approving critics find morals in these works which allow them to classify the novels as good literature. Many different morals are drawn from *Jane Eyre*: the story shows the reformation of a libertine through the influence of a virtuous woman; the novel makes the case that 'The obvious moral thought is, that laws, both human and divine, approved in our calmer moments, are not to be disobeyed when our time of trial comes' (Allott, p. 79). Jane is said to struggle against temptation with honesty, kindness, and perseverance which overcome every obstacle; or the novel expands human understanding. *Wuthering Heights* and *The Tenant of Wildfell Hall*, on the other hand, teach a lesson against the evils of cruelty, violence, and dissipation: they represent awful warnings. A more sophisticated defence of Anne's novel is mounted by Charles Kingsley who reads it as a critique of hypocrisy: 'There are foul and accursed undercurrents in plenty, in this same smug, respectable, whitewashed English society, which must be exposed now and then; and Society owes thanks, not sneers, to those who dare to show her the image of her own ugly, hypocritical visage' (Allott, p. 270). *Wuthering Heights*, strangely, is said to make the whole world kin by creating an empathy with the feelings of childhood, youth, manhood, and age, and all the passions which agitate the restless bosom of humanity. What both hostile and approving critics share, however, is a common recognition of the powerful impact of these three novels.

The Brontës on the Novel

Much is revealed about Charlotte's attitude to her own and her sisters' works by the literary judgements she makes on them and on other novelists. Of Anne's views we are told a little but there is no direct evidence of Emily's attitudes except by inference.

Anne appears to show some acceptance of prevailing critical standards in her published Preface to the second edition of *The Tenant of Wildfell Hall* where she endorses wholeheartedly the insistence that novels have a didactic function: 'I wished to tell the truth, for truth always conveys its own moral to those who are able to receive it. But as the priceless treasure too frequently hides at the bottom of a well, it needs some courage to dive for it'. She responds directly to the charge that in describing the 'coarse, if not brutal' scenes relating to Huntingdon and his fellow profligates, she took delight in doing so. On the contrary, she claims earnestly, they were as painful for her to describe as they were for others to read.

She sees the moral of the novel as consisting in the warning it provides to the young of the 'snares and pitfalls' they may encounter in life. She asks whether 'To represent a bad thing in its least offensive light' so as to please the reader is really 'the most honest or the safest' way to handle it.[7] To those who argue against this detailed account of what is to be avoided, she offers a conventional but evidently sincere response, not claiming that this dissipation is the norm of behaviour for such people but—relying on the conventional idea of literary 'truth'—that it exists because she has seen it. This is presumably a reference to Branwell's decline.

Charlotte, unlike Anne, offers a double standard when writing of her own and her sisters' novels: in public statements she accepts conventional views; but in letters, particularly in those to Williams, her literary confidant, her true beliefs break through. The public views appear in her 'Biographical Notice' prefacing the 1850 edition of *Wuthering Heights*, *Agnes Grey*, and some of her sisters' poems where she is apparently prepared to accept that the choice of subject in *The Tenant of Wildfell Hall* was 'an entire mistake'. In saying this, she is not so much defending the novel as defending Anne's character in terms that will free her from the charge of unwomanliness: 'Nothing less congruous with the writer's nature could be conceived. The motives which dictated this choice were pure'. She uses Anne's own argument that she had actually witnessed such scenes as she describes but draws from it a different conclusion, using the weapon she despised in critics—the account of 'personality'. What Anne saw 'did her harm' by affecting her sensitive and depressive nature: 'She brooded over it till she believed it to be a duty to reproduce every detail . . . as a warning to others . . . She was a very sincere and practical Christian, but the tinge of religious melancholy communicated a sad shade to her brief, blameless life' (*Letters*, ii. 745).

In her 1850 Preface to *Wuthering Heights* Charlotte also mounted a defence of Emily's novel but the nature of the extraordinary events it contained made it impossible to make the same case as for *The Tenant of Wildfell Hall*. Instead, concentrating again on personality, Charlotte asserted that Emily's isolated life and reclusive nature meant that she was ignorant of the human nature which was the stuff of novels and had listened to old wives' tales of 'tragic and terrible traits' in 'the secret annals of every rude vicinage'. In saying this Charlotte apparently accepts the mistaken belief that Haworth was a barbaric and remote place and implies that these tales fired Emily's vivid imagination and led her to create Heathcliff, Earnshaw, and Catherine in all their strangeness. Crucially, having 'formed these beings, she did not know what she had done'. Charlotte then chooses to avert her eyes from these abnormal creatures and to search for some moral role models in the text: 'the true benevolence and homely fidelity' of Nelly Dean and 'the constancy and tenderness' of Edgar Linton (*Letters*, ii. 749–50).

This Preface, however, reveals Charlotte's own standards which contradict her attempts to return her sisters, if not their writings, to the conventional model. Though she is prepared to acknowledge that Emily did not know what she had done in creating the 'Ghoul', the 'Afreet' that is Heathcliff, she ends with a contradictory conclusion. This is that Emily was in the grip of a powerful 'creative gift' of which she is 'not always the master', a gift which may be called 'Fate or Inspiration direct' and serves the purposes of removing the impression that Emily was an agent in the matter and of allowing Charlotte to eulogize the novel she has claimed to be a mistake. Making use, as often, of dazzling metaphors, she writes,

'Wuthering Heights' was hewn in a wild workshop, with simple tools, out of homely materials. The statuary found a granite block on a solitary moor; gazing thereon, he saw how from the crag might be elicited a head, savage, swart, sinister; a form moulded with at least one element of grandeur—power ... With time and labour, the crag took human shape; and there it stands colossal, dark, and frowning, half statue, half rock: in the former sense, terrible and goblin-like; in the latter, almost beautiful. (*Letters*, ii. 751)

This duality in the Preface shows Charlotte's profound belief in the idea that serious novelists strive for a deeper truth than that which lies in naturalistic fidelity to detail. It contradicts the view that 'reality' can be replicated by an exact account of what the novelist has observed in the world around her. Her conception of what she really believed a novel should do is evident not in such ad hoc and defensive remarks but in her discussion of writers other than her sisters. Just as she tends to deal with the criticism of reviewers in terms of their own criteria, similarly when asked by Ellen Nussey for recommended reading, she distinguishes those parts of her own reading that will not shock her conventional friend. In poetry Ellen should read Milton (safely religious), Shakespeare (with omissions), Thomson, Goldsmith, Pope (though he is trivial), Scott, Byron (with omissions), Campbell, Wordsworth, and Southey. She herself had read all of these freely and therefore is able to warn Ellen to omit the comedies of Shakespeare, presumably because of their sexual innuendos. Byron's *Don Juan*, the narrative of a philandering hero, is also judged unsuitable for Ellen, though Charlotte finds it 'a magnificent Poem'. She tells Ellen that only a 'depraved mind' will gather evil even from *Macbeth*, *Hamlet*, and *Julius Caesar* (*Letters*, i. 130). In brief she has one standard for her friend and another for herself, indicating the distinction she makes between public standards and her underlying convictions about works of literature.

These convictions are more clearly seen in the views she expresses in her letters to literary correspondents such as W. S. Williams and G. H. Lewes on other authors and on her own work. She admires several contemporary writers including Ruskin whom she praises for his 'pure and severe mind'; she shows some approval of *David Copperfield* which she describes as 'very good, admirable in some parts' (*Letters*, ii. 546, 251). But her response to Dickens is less enthusiastic than many others at the time: she finds fault with the much-admired *Bleak House*; she likes the Chancery section but adds that 'when it passes into the autobiographic form, and the young woman who announces she is not "bright", begins her history, it seems to me too often weak and twaddling' (*LFC* iii. 322). It is perhaps indicative of her assessment of Dickens's work that she declined to meet him when the opportunity arose.

By contrast, she admires Elizabeth Gaskell whose industrial novel, *North and South*, appeared in Dickens's periodical *Household Words* and she thought highly of *Ruth* which was much attacked for making a fallen woman its central figure and heroine. Such women appeared in novels, if at all, only as the marginal figures they are in Dickens's work such as little Emily in *David Copperfield*. Most significantly Charlotte is unwilling to accept the convention that Gaskell follows of making Ruth expiate her sin by dying as a result of her assiduous nursing of fever victims. Charlotte in her letter to Gaskell disapproves of this particular instance of poetic justice: 'Why should she die? Why are we to shut up the book weeping . . . I hold you a stern priestess in these matters' (*LFC* iii. 332). Even more shocking to contemporary view, if publicly expressed, would have been her reaction to Gaskell's daring handling in *North and South* of an Anglican clergyman who leaves the ministry because of (unspecified) religious doubts. The novel attached no blame to him and his dere- liction is largely passed over, a treatment which hardly constitutes a circumspect treatment of religion in the 1850s but Charlotte writes to Gaskell: 'I think I see the ground you are about to take as far as the Church is concerned; not that of attack on her, but of defence of those who conscientiously differ from her, and feel it a duty to leave her fold' (*LFC* iv. 153).

Charlotte's most frequent comments on other writers are those she makes on Jane Austen and Thackeray. Despite the fact that both are satirists dealing with the mores of their own societies, her views on them are very different. She had read *Pride and Prejudice* when she embarked on a lively debate with Lewes about Austen and wrote to him: 'Why do you like Miss Austen so very much? . . . What induced you to say that you would rather have written "Pride & Prejudice" . . . or "Tom Jones" than any of the Waverly [*sic*] novels?'. She herself sees Austen's novel only as a (supposed) replica of reality such as that she had dreaded finding in Balzac's enormously detailed works. She regards it as 'An accurate daguerreotyped portrait of a commonplace face; a carefully fenced, highly cultivated garden, with neat borders and delicate flowers—but no glance of a bright vivid physiognomy—no open country—no fresh air'. She concludes that she 'should hardly like to live with her ladies and gentlemen in their elegant but confined houses' (*Letters*, ii. 10).

Since she valued Lewes's judgement, Charlotte proceeded despite her initial distaste to read more of Austen's novels, including *Emma* and *Sense and Sensibility*, but still found what she regarded as a shallow account of the superficialities of life, laboriously detailed:

She does her business of delineating the surface of the lives of genteel English people curiously well; there is a Chinese fidelity, a miniature delicacy in the painting: . . . Her business not half so much with the human heart as with the human eyes, mouth, hands and feet; what sees keenly, speaks aptly, moves flexibly, it suits her to study. (*Letters*, ii. 383)

She notes tartly that she has read *Emma* 'with interest and with just the degree of admiration which Miss Austen herself would have thought sensible and suitable, anything like warmth or enthusiasm;

anything energetic, poignant, heartfelt . . . the authoress would have met with a well-bred sneer' (*Letters*, ii. 383).

This last comment indicates her real objection to Austen's work: the absence in them of a deeper truth about human nature such as she saw in her sister Emily's work: 'Passions are perfectly unknown to her; she rejects even a speaking acquaintance with that stormy Sisterhood'. She recognizes, as her reference to what Austen would have thought a 'sensible and suitable' response shows, the ironic intent behind these novels dealing with social surfaces. But she finds them lacking in the essential probing of human nature at its most emotional level: 'what throbs fast and full, though hidden, what the blood rushes through, what is the unseen seat of Life and the sentient target of Death—*this* Miss Austen ignores' (*Letters*, ii. 383).

Her dislike of Pope, mentioned in her recommended reading for Ellen Nussey, is presumably explicable on the same grounds. Similarly her taste for Swift's bitter satire, evident in her reaction to Thackeray's lecture on him, shows that she admires his engagement with the blacker side of human nature. She does not think such engagement incompatible with a preoccupation with social mores, for her greatest admiration is for Thackeray, 'the first of the Modern Masters . . . the legitimate High-Priest of Truth' (*Letters*, ii. 98). This is what she perceives in *Vanity Fair*, Thackeray's satire on his own society, which asserts its claim to a moral stance by the choice of a title taken from Bunyan's *Pilgrim's Progress*. The final instalment of the novel in *Cornhill* in March 1848 deals largely with Becky Sharp's fate after her downfall from good society and Charlotte finds this 'Forcible, exciting in its force, still more impressive than exciting . . . [with] parts of it that sound as solemn as a oracle' (*Letters*, ii. 45). She sees in this a depth, 'a "still profound" . . . which the discernment of one generation will not suffice to fathom' (*Letters*, ii. 98–9). More specifically she speaks of how Thackeray stands 'alone in his sagacity, alone in his truth, alone in his feeling—(his feeling, though he makes no noise about it, is about the most genuine that ever lived in a printed page)' (*Letters*, ii. 45).

What she seems to refer to here is Thackeray's ability to analyse and understand human emotion in all its complexity. It is evident from her incredulity when Jane Austen is described by Lewes as one of 'the greatest painters of human nature' (*Letters*, ii. 14) that this is what she means by Thackeray's 'truth'. *His* feeling in this context appears to refer to his strongly moral stance which raises, though it does not answer, moral questions: she means perhaps that he feels strongly about the moral issues of which he speaks in an ironically detached tone. Later, in *Henry Esmond* (1852), she sees his attitude as more complex:

> what bitter satire—what relentless dissection of diseased subjects! Well—and this too is right—or would be right, if the savage surgeon did not seem so fiercely pleased with his work. Thackeray likes to dissect an ulcer or an aneurism; he has pleasure in putting his cruel knife or probe into quivering living flesh. Thackeray would not like all the world to be good; no great satirist would like society to be perfect. (*LFC* iii. 314)

The preferences and dislikes which Charlotte evinces in private in relation to other writers throw light on her view of her own novel-writing. She too wants to handle human motivation and passions in a way that will reveal their nature in the individual; and not simply to provide poetic justice or a moral lesson. She always despises the naturalistic representation of 'reality' such as she perceives in Jane Austen's work and it is only when driven into a corner in defence of some detail in one of her novels that she will argue that what she describes is 'true' because she had actually seen it. For instance, she uses this shallow defence when writing to Williams about the review which announced that Helen Burns, the long-suffering saint at Lowood School, was too exaggerated in her pious forbearance to be real. Knowing that she had based this episode on her sister Maria's experiences at Cowan Bridge, she tells him, 'I could not but smile at the quiet, self-complacent dogmatism with which one of the journals lays it down that "such creations as Helen Burns are very beautiful but very untrue" ' (*Letters*, i. 553). Later she chides Williams himself for his objection to her account of the rumbustious curates at the opening of *Shirley* on the surprising ground that 'The curates and their ongoings are merely photographed from the life' (*Letters*, ii. 181).

Aside from these minor inconsistencies, her understanding of what a novel should do underpinned a sense of rightness in what she wrote that was with her from the beginning of her career as a novelist. Hence her resistance before the publication of *Jane Eyre* to Smith's suggestion (now lost) that she should revise it and her lofty comment that her engagements did not permit it. Though sensitive to critical opinion, she was confident that the novel would stand on its own merits: she alleges, in response to a hostile reviewer, that if *Jane Eyre* has 'any solid worth', it 'ought to weather a gust of unfavourable wind' (*Letters*, i. 563). When Lewes, whom she admired as a critic, finds the plot of this novel too sensational, she replies ironically, 'If I ever *do* write another book, I think I will have nothing of what you call "melodrame"; I *think* so, but I am not sure. I *think* too I will endeavour to follow the counsel which shines out of Miss Austen's "mild eyes"; "to finish more, and be more subdued"; but neither am I sure of that' (*Letters*, ii. 10).

She was always willing to admit that she was ignorant of the practice of publishing but not of the rightness of her own judgement of her work as true (in her sense) and powerful. Lewes, in urging her to follow Jane Austen, argued that the earlier novelist understood the paramount duty of a novelist to draw only on what she herself had experienced. Charlotte expresses her own belief that an author who relied on experience alone risked repeating herself and becoming egotistical: 'Then too, Imagination is a strong, restless faculty which claims to be heard and exercised'. When imagination is 'eloquent and speaks rapidly and urgently in our ear are we not to write to her dictation?' (*Letters*, i. 559). She here draws on the same ardent belief in her own power of inspiration as that which lies behind her final defence of Emily's in the *Wuthering Heights* Preface, though it does not seem that she attributed this particular gift to Anne.

Later in life she is even prepared to say, apropos *Villette*, that she cannot 'write a book for its moral' (*LFC* iv. 14) as convention would have it, for she had never been prepared to do this and she castigates novels which meet conventional standards in this and other respects:

The standard heroes and heroines of novels, are personages in whom I could never, from childhood upwards, believe to be natural, or wish to imitate: were I obliged to copy these characters, I would simply—not write at all. Were I obliged to copy any former novelist, even the greatest, even Scott, in anything, I would not write. Unless I have something of my own to say, and a way of my own to say it, I have no business to publish; unless I can look beyond the greatest Masters, and study Nature herself, I have no right to paint; unless I can have the courage to use the language of Truth in preference to the jargon of Conventionality, I ought to be silent. (*Letters*, ii. 118)

Charlotte, like her sisters, was convinced that she understood perfectly how she should write as a novelist and scorned conventional standards for the genre, though she deployed them defensively in her criticism. As she wrote in 1849 after the publication of *Jane Eyre*, in an injunction to critics, 'to you I am neither Man nor Woman—I come before you as an Author only—it is the sole standard by which you have a right to judge me—the sole ground on which I accept your judgement' (*Letters*, ii. 235). Paradoxically, in *Jane Eyre* and *Villette* she appears to conform to models of reticence; but in fact in both these novels she uses these conventions merely to convert the deepest levels of her work into a powerful subtext, creating, like Angria, 'a world beneath', utilizing to the full the power of understatement.

CHAPTER 4

THE BRONTËS' NOVELS AND
SOCIAL CLASS

Class Boundaries

I CANNOT write books handling the topics of the day', wrote
Charlotte Brontë in 1852 (*LFC* iv. 14). Whether Anne or Emily
would have agreed with her is uncertain but addressing contemporary issues relating to class is precisely what all three sisters do.
Between them they cover most of the significant issues: individuals
in the grey area between classes; conflict between upper classes and
lower classes; and the question of social mobility. Charlotte's perception of her own inability to handle such topics probably results from
a failure to recognize that in her novels class boundaries are questioned. Presumably this is because class distinctions are so deeply
embedded in the society she describes as to pass unnoticed by her.

In practice, characters and narrators in the Brontë novels regularly 'classify' those they encounter or meet, partly in order to establish their own relative status. In *Jane Eyre* the heroine is first
received at Thornfield by Mrs Fairfax whose friendly manner seems
at odds with Jane's assumption that she is mistress of the house.
Mrs Fairfax is 'less stately and milder looking' than she had
expected: 'there was no grandeur to overwhelm, no stateliness to
embarrass'. The discovery that this woman is merely the housekeeper, 'no great dame but a dependent like myself', comes as a relief
to Jane. The reason is that 'the equality between her and me was real
and not the mere result of condescension on her part': Jane is more
at ease because she no longer fears that in being treated as an equal
she is being patronized and she can cling to her own sense of status
as a lady (book 1, chapter 11). When later she turns up starving and
cold on their doorstep, the Rivers sisters' first reaction is to decide
whether she is one of their own class as they automatically assess her
for markers which would declare her to be middle class like themselves: 'She is not an uneducated person, I should think, by her

manner of speaking; her accent was quite pure; and the clothes she took off, though splashed and wet, were little worn and fine'. She is definitely placed for the sisters by their brother, St John Rivers, who decides that she is 'some young lady' (not a 'person') 'who has had a misunderstanding with her friends and has probably injudiciously left them' (book 3, chapter 3). It is only when the Rivers's servant Hannah accepts this diagnosis of her status that her treatment of Jane changes from a contemptuous to a deferential one.

In *Shirley* Charlotte refers to criteria which, like the accent and dress that the Rivers assess, are recognizable markers of class. Robert Moore's sister, Hortense, feels that her education, manners, and principles show that she is a lady, worthy of the social distinction she received when living in Belgium. There is also a fairly elaborate discussion by the narrator of *Shirley* about how a new acquaintance might 'classify' Hiram Yorke, a wealthy radical. His face is 'inelegant, unclassic, unaristocratic' to the extent that 'Fine people would perhaps have called it vulgar' (book 1, chapter 4). But, though he sometimes spoke 'broad Yorkshire' which might seem to confirm his lower-class status, at other times 'he expressed himself in very pure English', a sure sign of the educated gentleman. At times too his manners vary similarly: now they are 'blunt and rough' like those of the working class; now they are 'polite and affable' like those of the middle class. The narrator points out the baffling nature of these facts: 'His station then you could not easily determine by his speech or demeanour; perhaps the appearance of his residence may decide it' (book 1, chapter 3). So it does—since his house shows signs of intellectual pursuits, cultivated artistic tastes, and foreign travel.

Interestingly, Yorke's variations in speech and manner are signs of his radicalism and the implication seems to be that he adapts both of these to the workers whose cause he favours, since he is said to be benevolent 'to all who were beneath him'. The narrative makes clear that his status as a gentleman is unaffected and he still maintains a sense of his own superiority: 'at heart he was a proud man; very friendly to his workpeople, very good to all who were beneath him, and submitted quietly to be beneath him, but haughty as Beelzebub to whomsoever the world deemed (for he deemed no man), his superior' (book 1, chapter 4). The characterization of Yorke reveals the importance in this society for middle-class individuals to be secure in their sense of their own status no matter what their political views. It is inroads into this belief in their own superior social standing which are explored by Anne and Charlotte in their novels.

Condescension to the working classes and a paternal concern for their welfare are acceptable or even praiseworthy but they are not allowed to disturb the hierarchy. Shirley Keeldar, like Yorke, is kind to all who are 'beneath her', even to the extent of jokingly berating them for gossiping after the attack on Moore's mill. The narrator's attitude to this is captured in the equally patronizing comment on Shirley's behaviour here: 'There is nothing the lower orders like better than a little downright good-humoured rating. Flattery they scorn very much: honest abuse they enjoy' (book 2, chapter 9).

Both of Charlotte's first two novels establish an acceptance and approval of the immutability of a rigid class hierarchy. Emily's *Wuthering Heights*, which contemporaries thought of as a novel about families remote from society, shares the preoccupation with placing and classifying individuals: Lockwood regards Mrs Dean as an appendage which comes with the Grange when he rents it and he comments patronizingly on her bewilderment as to the time at which he, as a gentleman, wishes to have his dinner served. Once Heathcliff has become rich and has married the upper-class Isabella Linton, he has at least the appearance of 'a born and bred gentleman' (chapter 14). When Cathy Linton, Edgar's daughter, mistakes Hareton, the son of landowner Hindley Earnshaw, for a servant, she orders him to fetch her horse. In all but name he is treated by Heathcliff as a hireling but he asserts his social status by calling Cathy a 'saucy witch' (chapter 18). She in turn is affronted by what she takes as a servant's challenge to her standing as a Linton. So class awareness is found in Emily's novel but, as will be seen later, she confronts the subject of class in broader terms than her sisters. Charlotte addresses it from time to time but Anne deals with a class boundary and its policing in great detail in *Agnes Grey*.

Policing the Frontier: the Governess Problem

By the mid-nineteenth century there had arisen what was called 'the governess problem', though the problem was in practice twofold, depending on whether it was looked at from the point of view of the employer or that of the governess and her supporters. Both problems are rooted in the ambiguous position of the governess on the boundary between lower and middle classes: at the time the chief requirement or qualification for such a post was that the woman in question should be a lady. This was because she would live in the home of a family that was either middle or upper class and that as 'pro-mama', in Elizabeth Rigby's words, she would relieve the employing mother of many of her duties. Rigby makes the case for gentility as the very essential for such employment: 'Take a lady, in every meaning of the word, born and bred, and let her further pass through the Gazette, and she wants nothing more to suit our highest *beau ideal* of a guide and instructress to our children'.[1] Hence, presumably, the import-ance not only of being well brought up but also of being the daughter of the right father, i.e. a gentleman. There was an anxiety gaining currency when Anne Brontë wrote *Agnes Grey* about women of the wrong class, the daughters of farmers and tradesmen, attempting to become governesses as a way of advancing themselves socially. They hoped to find themselves moving into a position that would enable them to cross class boundaries. Such attempts were unlikely to suc-ceed since, if she already saw herself as a lady, the governess would assume that she was the social equal of the family with whom she lived. Instead they saw her not as one of themselves but as a paid employee, a woman who had stepped out of her class. To them she was a kind of upper servant; and also, that dangerous creature, an unmarried woman living in the same house as middle-class men to whom she was not related. In any event a paid employee was de facto a servant and servants were the subject of numerous complaints amongst the upper classes. Sarah Ellis, in her guidance manuals for women, for instance, warns against the pernicious influence of servants on the characters of children.

Charlotte and Anne illustrate this disparaging view of the govern-ess in order to express strong disapproval of it. Jane Eyre, summoned to the drawing room at Thornfield, has to listen to Rochester's aris-tocratic visitors abusing all who are governesses. Lady Ingram even suggests that it may be salutary for such a one as Jane to overhear how she 'suffered a martyrdom' from the 'incompetency and caprice' of her own governesses. Blanche Ingram, thought to be Rochester's intended bride, joins in to tell him that it would be better to send his ward, Adèle, to school: '—you men never do consider economy and common sense. You should hear mama on the chapter of govern-esses: Mary and I have had, I should think, a dozen at least in our day; half of them detestable and the rest ridiculous, and all incubi'. She alludes here to the supposed sexual predatoriness of such women when describing how her own teacher, Miss Wilson, and her brother's tutor 'took the liberty of falling in love with each other'. Fortunately 'Dear mama there, as soon as she got an inkling of the business, found out that it was of an immoral tendency'. She sarcastically enumerates the standard results of this immoral tendency: the bad example to children, distraction and neglect of duty, joint insolence; 'mutiny and general blow-up' (book 2, chapter 2).

Later, in *Shirley*, Charlotte describes Shirley's governess, Mrs Pryor, detailing her own experiences with employers to deter her as yet unwitting daughter, Caroline, from seeking work as a governess. The family make it clear 'that "as I was not their equal", so I could not expect "to have their sympathy" '. She continues citing, as here, an abusive article on the governesses in *Vanity Fair* and *Jane Eyre* which had particularly angered Charlotte. Mrs Pryor relates how she was told that as an outsider she was ' "a burden and a restraint in society" ': 'The ladies' in particular apparently made it plain that they thought her ' "a bore" '. On the other side, she found even the family's servants 'detested' her, though she did not know why. Worst of all, 'the gentlemen' of the house 'regarded me as "a tabooed woman" to whom "they were interdicted from granting the usual privileges of the sex", and yet who "annoyed them by frequently crossing their path" ' (book 2, chapter 10). 'Tabooed woman' is a strong expression, implying that such a woman is unsuitable for marriage with a member of the family, and that, like a prostitute, the only possible sexual relationship with her would be illicit. She is not so much a bore to the men of the house as a temptation; and to the women a threat.

Mrs Pryor also elaborates a rationale given to her by a female member of her employer's family for men's liaisons with their children's governesses which explains them as a kind of providential arrangement: ' "WE", she would say,—"WE need the imprudencies, extravagances, mistakes, and crimes of a certain number of fathers to sow the seed from which WE reap the harvest of governesses" '. Since such progeny have the right fathers, they are sufficiently ladies to tend their superiors' children and do away with the necessity of governesses from the lower orders: ' "The daughters of tradespeople, however well educated, must necessarily be underbred, and as such unfit to be the inmates of OUR dwellings, or guardians of OUR children's minds and persons" '. This nice extension of the double standard is seen as producing a crop of women suited to the ambiguous class position of the governess: a semi-lady—' "born and bred with somewhat of the same refinement as OURSELVES" ' (book 2, chapter 10). Though this mortally offends Mrs Pryor, she does not wish to speak ill of those she still regards as superiors: the hierarchy must remain intact so that she and others can maintain their place in it.

The only governess in the Brontë novels who justifies the Ingrams' complaints about governesses as immoral incubi is Miss Myers in *The Tenant of Wildfell Hall*. There are fairly strong indications that she is not a lady when she is brought into the novel to show the lasciviousness of Helen Huntingdon's husband. Helen is suspicious of her unladylike and sycophantic manner: 'There was a look of guile and subtlety in her face, a sound of it in her voice . . . In her behaviour, she was respectful and complaisant even to servility; she attempted to flatter and fawn upon me at first' (chapter 43). The narrator is here accepting the employer's view of governesses while implying through the signs of the woman's vulgarity that she is not really of the class to which governesses need to belong in order to be employed. Helen's suspicions prove well founded when Miss Myers turns out to be the replacement for Huntingdon's last mistress, presumably one with designs on securing him for herself.

The Sufferings of the Governess

The insistence in *Shirley* on the unchangeable nature of the class system is also central to *Agnes Grey* and *Jane Eyre* since all three novels also explore the feelings of a governess as she endures the humiliating discrepancy between her own and her employers' perception of her social standing. None of the texts suggests that a revolution is necessary: it is precisely because they accept a class-based society that Agnes Grey, Jane Eyre, and Mrs Pryor are so concerned with their own status. To have it questioned by others is not only deeply humiliating but disturbing to their sense of self.

Agnes Grey's mother shares Mrs Pryor's dislike of her daughter taking a governess's position since, as a squire's daughter, albeit one cut off by her family for marrying beneath her to a poor clergyman, she feels that Agnes inherits her superiority. Deprived of her own proper environment, she tries to recreate it for her daughters by secluding them from the lower-class neighbours who surround her. Agnes tells how not only was their entire education conducted by their mother—without the substitute of a governess or pro-mama— but also, since there was 'no society in the neighbourhood, our only intercourse with the world consisted in a stately tea-party, now and then, with the principal farmers and trades-people of the vicinity, just to avoid being stigmatised as too proud to consort with our neighbours' (chapter 1). Mrs Grey, determined not to see her daughter declassed, rejects various projected situations for her as a governess: 'These were low people; these were too exacting in their demands; and these too niggardly in their remunerations'. When she fixes £50 per annum as the minimum salary Agnes should accept, her main concern is not financial: she is thinking of the status likely to attach to an employer who paid this much, imagining he would be a well-bred gentleman 'far more likely to treat you with proper respect and consideration than those purse-proud trades-people and arrogant upstarts' (chapter 6).

Mrs Grey presumably imagines the owner of some estate such as Thornfield where Jane's circumstances are extremely comfortable but even Jane does not escape humiliating abuse from the Ingrams. She is fortunate, however, to the extent that the household consists only of a bachelor (as it appears), his ward, and plenty of servants from whom she suffers no disagreeable treatment. The only unpleasantness arises when Mrs Fairfax sees her and Rochester kissing and assumes that one or other is bent on seduction. Like Mrs Pryor and Agnes Grey, Jane Eyre accepts the class hierarchy and is concerned only with her own status in it, as becomes evident in her reaction to Rochester's apology for his peremptory treatment of her which is indeed condescending. Her gratification at his stooping to apologize rules out any sense of humiliation. Instead she thinks to herself with a smile that 'Mr Rochester *is* peculiar—he seems to forget that he pays me £30 per annum for receiving his orders'. She even tells him that 'very few masters would trouble themselves to inquire whether or not their paid subordinates were piqued or hurt by their orders' (book 1, chapter 14).

Jane's fate may be seen as a rewriting of that of the sexually predatory governess in that she too, like Miss Myers, wishes to marry her employer; but the situation is unusual in that strangely he wishes to marry her and only decides to make her his mistress when that becomes impossible. 'Reader, I married him' is not the triumphant cry of a sexual and social predator who has achieved her aim; rather it is a statement which implies that justice has been done to her. It is moral justice since she will not countenance an illicit relationship; and social justice because it stabilizes her class status. It is only belatedly that the position which her birth warrants is restored to her: like Agnes Grey she is the daughter of a lady who married a poor clergyman.

It is only *Agnes Grey* which describes in great detail the painfully humiliating treatment that a governess such as Agnes experiences in what are represented as typical middle-class households. The account matches in experiential terms the more general description given by Mrs Pryor as well as those in the many articles of the mid-nineteenth century which dealt at length with the trials of the average, underpaid, overworked governess. Not least among Agnes's privations is the lack of respect felt towards such a 'paid hireling' as herself. From the viewpoint of both sets of employers, the Bloomfields and the Murrays, she is a cuckoo in the nest and they are not prepared to treat her as an equal but only as a servant. It is clear from her experiences that 'inherent in the employment of a lady was a contradiction of the very values she was hired to fulfil': she must be a lady but she cannot be treated as one. Once Agnes's relationship to the family who employs her becomes ambivalent, she feels a strong sense of injustice and a recognition that her place in society at large is now at issue.

She is aware at all times of the social implications of the family's behaviour and the fact that in her first post Mrs Bloomfield greets her 'with frigid formality' sensitizes her to anything construable as a snub. She is instructed by Mrs Bloomfield to tell no one of her (pampered and unruly) children's faults except herself. This undermines her further, though it was evidently a common instruction to governesses and, with no sanctions other than spontaneous outbursts of force on her part, Agnes is unable to control Tom and Mary Ann. The arrival on the scene of the loudly arrogant master of the house makes matters worse as his first remark to her is delivered from horseback and is a rebuke: 'Miss Grey . . . (I suppose it is Miss Grey) I am surprised that you should allow them to dirty their clothes in that manner—Don't you see that Miss Bloomfield has

soiled her frock and that Master Bloomfield's socks are quite wet.'
Having ordered her to keep the children '*decent* at least', he ignores
her and rides on. She is affronted at the idea that she, a lady, is
expected to call children under 7 'Miss' and 'Master' and the command is made more offensive by the fact 'that he should speak so
uncivilly to me—their governess, and a perfect stranger to himself'
(chapter 3). Other visitors to the house also ignore her and she is
finally dismissed like a servant for lack of 'sufficient firmness and
diligent persevering care' (chapter 5).

Her arrival at her next post, with the Murrays, on a cold snowy
night meets with what she now perceives as the treatment handed
out to the lower ranks of servants. She finds only indifferent children
to receive her and encounters a well-dressed female who condescends
to help with a minor request 'with the air of one conferring an
unusual favour'. This individual turns out to be a lady's maid as the
lady herself does not make Agnes's acquaintance until late the next
morning—a fact experienced as stinging impoliteness to one who
sees herself as an equal to her employer and superior to any servant—and she comments tartly that Mrs Murray met her 'just as my
mother might step into the kitchen to see a new servant girl—yet not
so, either, for my mother would have seen her immediately after her
arrival . . . she would have addressed her in a more kindly and
friendly manner' (chapter 7). Again the governess is obliged to
address her troublesome charges in a formal manner as a servant
would.

By now Agnes is sensitive to the minutiae of her treatment by the
Murrays and every detail is recorded by her as she tells her own
story. Nothing goes unnoticed: she is aware that, when returning
from church with the Murrays, she is not consulted as to whether
she wishes to walk with some of the party or take up some of the
limited space in their carriage. The choice is left to the Murray girls
and she is schooled to refrain from enquiring as to 'the causes of
their varying whims' and from this she concludes bitterly that 'to
submit and oblige was the governess's part, to consult their own
pleasure was that of the pupils' (chapter 13). Since they ignore her
whenever she walks with the Murrays, she reacts by walking behind
them to prevent them from talking over and across her: as she
explains to the sympathetic curate Weston, 'they consider themselves
as moving in quite a different sphere from me!' (chapter 15).

Agnes in practice finds herself not only declassed into a group below her but unclassed since even the servants will not accept her. She becomes a solitary refugee, wandering frontiers and belonging nowhere. She perceives the reason for the servants' treatment of her to be that, 'seeing in what little estimation the governess was held by both parents and children', they 'regulated their behaviour by the same standard'. The loss of standing with the servants is felt as strongly by Agnes as the failure of the Murrays to treat her as an equal. Believing herself superior by birth and education, she describes the servants as 'ignorant' and unaccustomed to the 'reason and reflection' which would reveal her to be a lady (chapter 7).

Significantly it is only the Murrays' servants that she castigates in this way. Her hostility to them is a means of keeping them at a distance without which she will lose caste. With the local villagers or 'the cottagers' as she calls them, the case is different: since she comes from the local grand house, she can act the part of a lady bountiful and assert her rank. She is assiduous in the charitable duties that belong to the middle class but which her pupils neglect: she reads to the aged and partly blind, visits the dying labourer, and takes 'small donations' to those in need. Agnes reasserts her moral and therefore social superiority over the Murray daughters by showing their vulgarity: they 'watch the poor creatures' in the village at their meals and deride both what they eat and how they eat it; and call the villagers 'old fools and silly old blockheads to their faces' (chapter 11).

While oscillating between her sense that her class status is being undermined and asserting her social superiority, Agnes Grey is befriended by the curate Weston who is also morally superior and socially disparaged; and since she finally marries him and becomes independent, the conclusion of the plot underwrites the view that social (and moral) superiority will finally find its proper place in the hierarchy. Like Jane Eyre, Agnes Grey eventually floats back to the class she belongs to. Mrs Pryor's fate in *Shirley* points to a similar conclusion. She is introduced as Shirley's governess, though she is treated by that independent woman with the courtesy and kindness due to a friend. When it is finally revealed that she is Caroline Helstone's mother, she is transformed from the status of pro-mama to that of real mother that is properly hers. Hence both Charlotte and Anne Brontë address the issue of class boundaries by dealing with individuals whose class identity is threatened. The satisfactory outcomes for the three women involved are only achieved by narrative sleights of hand. It evades the wider issue of the necessity for and justice of a rigidly class-based society.

Class Conflict in *Shirley*

Because the governess is represented as a solitary victim of class discrimination, the focus in novels in which she appears is on individuals' subjective experiences to the exclusion of larger issues: these are the unjust nature of a class-based society and the question of class conflict, issues which had already established a literary genre, 'the industrial novel'. The clash between employers and workers is the basis of such works as Harriet Martineau's *A Manchester Strike* (1832); Frances Trollope's *Michael Armstrong, the Factory Boy* (1840); Charlotte Elizabeth Tonna's *Helen Fleetwood* (1841); Benjamin Disraeli's *Sybil or The Two Nations* (1845); and Elizabeth Gaskell's *Mary Barton* (1848). Each of these novels shows workers driven into conflict by starvation wages and/or harsh treatment but differs from those that deal with the problems of governesses because they are addressing the basic issue in a generic form: the events described are implicitly assumed to relate to class hostility in similar circumstances elsewhere.

The violence that usually results from the economic clash between different classes can take various forms: strikes, attacks on factories and property which may involve machine-breaking or assassination attempts, all assumed to be replicated throughout industry. It is specifically said of Robert Moore in *Shirley*, for instance, that his behaviour is the same as thousands of other 'masters' at the time: typical are the strike in Martineau's novella; the assault on Mowbray Castle in Disraeli's *Sybil*; and the assassination of an employer's son in Gaskell's *Mary Barton*. The significance attributed to such acts is also variable: potentially they can signal the conflicting interests of different sections of the industrial community; a testing of the relative power of employers as opposed to workers; an evocation of the latent threat to society as a whole of working-class unrest; or the rights of workers to combine and the limits that should be set on them. Depending on which of these meanings the novelist draws out and on their view of the desirability of the status quo, some kind of resolution of the conflict follows.

Though *Shirley* was published in 1849 and written late in the 'hungry forties' when Chartism was at its height, the narrative is not set in that period: instead of using Chartist demonstrations for voting rights as a route to changing society, Charlotte chooses to give an account of the history of the West Riding some forty years earlier. She reverts to the violence of a time when the Luddites were active in attacking machines and their owners, events which Patrick Brontë had experienced at close quarters and had evidently retailed to his children. But Charlotte did not rely on what would now be called oral history: using as sources the files of the *Leeds Mercury* for 1813 and 1814, the period in which the novel is set, she found stories which she linked in a narrative chain in *Shirley*: machine-breaking, an attack beaten off with the help of soldiers, and the assassination of a factory owner.

The violent events in *Shirley* are set in an economic context which is seen to explain the causes of the conflict: international circumstances brought about by the Napoleonic Wars. This struggle was then at its height and had had a disastrous effect on the trade in woollen manufacturing. Early in the novel a detailed account is given of how a slump in trade came about, as the narrative somewhat laboriously links the chain of events that led from the disastrous war to the workers' misery. The narrator explains how, after Napoleon had by his Milan and Berlin Decrees prohibited several European countries from receiving British goods, the government responded with the Orders in Council. These, by 'forbidding neutral powers to trade with France, had, by offending America, cut off the principal market of the Yorkshire woollen trade and brought it consequently to the verge of ruin. Minor foreign markets were glutted, and would receive no more' and America's retaliatory embargo on trade with both Britain and France was thus the trigger for the state Moore describes: 'I am very rich in cloth I cannot sell; you should step into my warehouse yonder, and observe how it is piled to the ceiling with pieces' (book 1, chapter 2).

Because of this stagnating market, the mill-owners in general introduce 'certain inventions in machinery' into the 'staple manufactures of the north, which, greatly reducing the number of hands necessary to be employed, threw thousands out of work, and left them without legitimate means of sustaining life'. These workers 'could not get work, and consequently could not get wages, and consequently could not get bread' (book 1, chapter 2). So an unbroken chain of events is apparently demonstrated leading inevitably from the war to the workers' starvation: war thus becomes the source of their condition and the employers are not culpable. Equally inevitably there follows violence as 'Distress reached its climax'. Significantly here the distress is no more than an abstraction without the kind of specific details found in Gaskell's comparable novels. Later Charlotte claimed in a letter of 1851 to her publisher, George Smith, to be unfamiliar with the details of urban workers' lives. Writing of Mayhew's documentary account of 'The London Poor', she tells how it opened her eyes to 'a new and strange world—very dark— very dreary—very noisome in some of its recesses'. She wrote this despite having Haworth on her doorstep with its cellar dwellings, poor water, and lack of sanitation. The ambivalence which appears in *Shirley* is confirmed by her addition to this comment: that what Mayhew describes is 'a world that is fostering such a future as I scarcely dare imagine—it awakens thoughts not to be touched on in this foolish letter' (*Letters*, ii. 573). The implication here of a threat to society as a whole is an anxiety that explains the urgent sense of a need for 'a solution' that lies behind the novel.

Previously the mill-owners have been exculpated from the charge of being responsible for the workers' misery: bringing in machines which need less workers has been shown as their only option since they cannot control economic conditions. The workers too are the victims of these circumstances but, unlike their employers, they fail to understand what is happening and erupt into violence: there are food riots, a mill is burnt, a mill-owner's house ransacked and the family terrified. In part these actions are inspired by agitators of anarchic tendencies, such as Moses Barraclough as, 'Endurance, over-goaded, stretched the hand of fraternity to sedition; the throes of a sort of moral earthquake were felt heaving under the hills of the northern counties'. Barraclough represents this 'sedition'—the threat of action against the state, seen as latent in all Luddite activities and used in the novel as a label for the workers' action (book 1, chapter 2).

So far the employers have been represented as struggling against a threat arising from a cause outside their control; the workers, on the other hand, in their naivety have been led into practices dangerous to social stability. A further argument is made for the ruling class in the description of their responses to the fires, riots, and assaults on property. They are shown in their capacity as magistrates to apply the law leniently: 'local measures were or were not taken by the local magistracy; a ringleader was detected, or more frequently suffered to elude detection'. The impression is given that what the rioters did was pointless, like the strike in Martineau's novella: 'the sufferers . . . were left to suffer on; perhaps inevitably left; it would not do to stop the progress of invention, to damage science by discouraging its improvements; the war could not be terminated, efficient relief could not be raised . . . so the unemployed underwent their destiny—ate the bread and drank the waters of affliction' (book 1, chapter 2). Their plight is destined; it is inevitable; fighting it only causes misery and creates a threat to society.

There is from time to time some reference to indicate that Moore is somewhat too hard-hearted in his face-to-face treatment of his workers, for it is said by the narrator that he 'did not sufficiently care when the new inventions threw the old workpeople out of employ: he never asked himself where those to whom he no longer paid weekly wages found daily bread'. This indifference to suffering, however, is attributed to the fact that he is a foreigner, resident in the neighbourhood for too short a time to feel for his workers. His dismissal of the deferential workman William Farren, however, is fraught not so much with indifference as with arrogance: to the man's mild suggestion that he should introduce machinery more gradually, Moore answers with a fierce sense of his own superior class: 'neither to your dictation—nor to that of any other, will I submit . . . I will have my own way' (book 1, chapter 8).

Each admission that Moore is at fault is quickly followed by the account of some mitigating factor, as when he privately persuades Hiram Yorke to employ Farren as a gardener. Or his personal circumstances are said to explain his ferocity since he is an honourable man determined to repay debts incurred when his family became bankrupt. He sees his own impoverishment for this reason as far more serious than 'the natural, habitual poverty of the working man' (book 1, chapter 5); yet he is even seen to recognize 'in flashes' that his and his fellow manufacturers' wish to stop a just war because it cuts their profit is wrong and selfish. These suggestions of another side to the ruthless Moore prepare the ground for a resolution of the conflict with his workers such as had become almost the norm in earlier novels and was to continue in works like Gaskell's *North and South* (1854).

What Deidre David calls 'the fiction of resolution'[2] involves an asymmetry between what has been represented as a broad conflict of classes and a solution that relates solely to individuals and to personal relations between them. Usually the mediating agent between master and men is a suitable middle-class woman, ideally placed to bring about reconciliation since by definition she is a nurturer, a moral agent, and a restorer of peace. While she is socially the master's equal and therefore able to influence him, she can also stand in as a representative of the workers for, like them, she stands in a subordinate position to him, as a member of the inferior sex. Before she can accomplish her mission of bringing him to take a more compassionate view, she has to be placed in a position of estrangement from the master to complete the parallel with the workpeople. Margaret Hale in *North and South* is in precisely this position: she is Thornton's social equal when she arrives from her life in the South to find herself faced with Northern mores and roughness. Her increasing feelings of attraction towards Thornton serve only to alienate her, since she is seeing industrial poverty close at hand for the first time and is moved to a pity at the plight of the poor which allows her to identify with them. Ultimately the discord between her and Thornton is resolved and she is able to bring about his conversion to a kinder attitude and agree to marry him, thereby rewarding him for this change.

This parallels the situation of Caroline Helstone in *Shirley*. She is the friend and intimate of Robert Moore and is also in love with him. At the same time she identifies with the suffering of his workers, particularly through her friendship with the unaggressive William Farren. Already, before the attack on Moore's mill, she has suggested to him that he resembles the arrogant Coriolanus in Shakespeare's play after he has read aloud from his speeches and she tells him only half-jokingly: 'There's a vicious point hit already . . . you sympathize with that proud patrician who does not sympathize with his famished fellow-men' (book 1, chapter 6). Her dual role as Moore's friend and that of the workers is visible in the attack on the mill. She and Shirley Keeldar view the event from a vantage point which leaves them physically detached from the fight so that, as Shirley puts it, they are like women in earlier times watching a joust. They are also like an audience in a theatre, a fact pressed home by Shirley's preventing Caroline from making 'a romantic rush on the stage' to help Moore when he appears to be alone. Her sympathies are all with him when the mob attacks with 'A crash—smash—shiver', hurling a volley of stones at the mill and uttering a maddened yell.

Significantly, the narrator now moves into the heraldic imagery which neatly removes the need for a gory description of the carnage that follows as concealed soldiers open fire on the crowd: 'Wrath wakens to the cry of Hate: the Lion shakes his mane, and rises to the howl of the Hyaena: Caste stands up, ireful, against Caste; and the indignant, wronged spirit of the Middle Rank bears down in zeal and scorn on the famished and furious mass of the Operative Class.' This is the pivotal centre of the novel when the nature of the clash between Moore and his workers is revealed as class conflict, yet the symbolic account is unqualified in its condemnation of that 'Hyaena', the 'operative' class, and in its admiration for the rightful majesty of the lion-like 'Middle Rank' avenging its 'wrongs' (book 2, chapter 8).

When the dramatic spectacle is over and the lights of dawn reveal the scene, the consequences for the 'operatives' are briefly summarized: 'a human body lay quiet on its face near the gates; and five or six wounded men writhed and groaned in the bloody dust' (book 2, chapter 8). Even in death the workers are numbers not individuals. Predictably, once the bloodshed is over, the narrator finds mitigating factors for the merciless tirade. It is pointed out that, though Moore pursues the ringleaders of the mob with 'relentless assiduity', he does not pursue the other participants in the same way. These ring-leaders are characterized as 'bankrupts, men always in debt and often in drink': they are strangers, 'emissaries from the large towns', and mostly 'not members of the operative class'. This retrospective account of agitators who had secured the trust of a group of workers, only to stir up trouble and anarchy, is a tactic often used in contemporary novels to divert attention from the economic causes of the workers' privation by blaming an unspecified group of trouble-makers. Moore's restraint in turn is seen as a thoughtful act caused by 'an innate sense of justice' on his part and he believes that 'men misled by false counsel, and goaded by privations are not fit objects of vengeance, and that he who would visit an even violent act on the bent head of suffering, is a tyrant' (book 2, chapter 11). The implication of this account is similar to the earlier implication that the workers did not understand the economic pressures bearing down on their employers. The 'operatives' are now represented as a set of gullible and childlike men evidently in need of a kind of parental guidance. Properly guided, they are useful members of the community; with the false counsel of evil men (of uncertain origin), they represent a threat to the peace and stability of society which the 'Middle Rank' are duty bound to suppress. This characterizing of the workpeople is a further preparation for a paternalistic resolution of the underlying conflict.

Caroline is to be the agent of this positive outcome and she, like the workers, is by now estranged from Robert Moore, an estrangement of his making and, like that of the workers, the consequence of his pursuit of profit. Though strongly attracted to her, he deliberately withdraws from Caroline because she cannot provide the money that his business needs. His hard-heartedness/hard-headedness causes the men to starve and Caroline to pine and literally waste away: one rejection figures the other; physical starvation mirrors emotional starvation; one equals the other. Caroline has already, before the estrangement, drawn a parallel between herself and those who work for Moore:

I know it would be better for you to be loved by your workpeople than to be hated by them, and I am sure that kindness is more likely to win their regard than pride. If you were proud and cold to me and Hortense, should we love you? When you are cold to me as you *are* sometimes, can I venture to be affectionate in return? (book I, chapter 6)

Such a conversion of the arrogant Coriolanus figure of Moore as she envisages seems unlikely but the concept was a familiar one at a period when forms of religious dissent such as Methodism were spreading a concern, shared by the Brontë sisters, with being morally born again from an earlier state of sinfulness.

Moore has sinned in both the industrial and domestic sides of his life. His most heinous act domestically is his proposal to Shirley in the hope of procuring her fortune. He has always been identified by himself and by others with his mill which he describes as his castle, calling himself 'a hard dog brought up to mill and market'. Shirley has described the mill jokingly as his 'lady-love' and his proposal shows her that this description is only too apt. Her instant rejection of him is made in didactic biblical terms as she castigates him directly for bringing the values of the marketplace into the sacred sphere of domestic love and morality. As he later tells Yorke, she sees him as making 'a speculation' of her: 'You would immolate me to that mill—your Moloch!' She is referring here to the heathen god, said in the Books of Kings and Jeremiah to have been worshipped with human sacrifice and she sees his assumption that her friendship was caused by love for him as a slur on her womanliness. He has assumed that she 'acted as no woman can act, without degrading herself and her sex'. In doing so, he has become 'Lucifer—Star of the Morning' in his fallen state. She will no more believe his protestations 'than she would have believed the ghost of Judas'. Her words, Moore says, were 'a mirror in which I saw myself'. What he sees is the murderer of Abel with whom he is forced to identify: 'A sense of Cain-like desolation made my breast ache' (book 3, chapter 7). As Judas, Moore is guilty of betraying love for money; as Cain, he is guilty of murdering his brother(s) in the workplace. The biblical symbolism serves to conflate his private and public offences: against the woman he loves and against his workers. It also sets the framework of sin and atonement in which the narrative crisis can be resolved.

Moore's period of atonement for sin, triggered by Shirley's sermon on his preference for money over his love for Caroline, takes place during a withdrawal from the scene. His deep humiliation leads him to punish himself by visiting the hells of Birmingham and London that Mayhew was to bring to Charlotte's own attention. There his conversion takes place and he describes it to Yorke in a manner that links the industrial and the domestic. First he goes to Birmingham:

I looked a little into reality, considered closely, and at their source, the causes of the present troubles of this country; I did the same in London . . . I went where there was want of food, of fuel, of clothing; where there was no occupation and no hope. I saw some, with naturally elevated tendencies and good feelings, kept down amongst sordid privations and harassing griefs. I saw many originally low, and to whom lack of education left scarcely anything but animal wants, disappointed in those wants, ahungered, athirst, and desperate as famished animals: I saw what taught my brain a new lesson, and filled my breast with fresh feelings. (book 3, chapter 7)

What he describes here is of course precisely what he might have seen at home amongst his own employees but a statutory period elsewhere is needed to constitute his personal road to Damascus.

The narrator then tries to square the circle by linking the new (converted) Moore with the old. Somewhat surprisingly the new Moore denies the possession of 'more softness or sentiment than I have hitherto professed', regarding 'mutiny and ambition' as he has always regarded them: 'I should resist a riotous mob just as heretofore: I should open on the scent of a runaway ringleader as eagerly as ever, and run him down as relentlessly'. What then has changed? one might ask. Ironically Moore's account of the change is an explicit statement of what has previously been implied by the narrator 'but I should do it now chiefly for the sake and the security of those he misled'. He will do the same as he has done previously but for a different reason. He adds, somewhat unnecessarily to his more liberal listener, 'Something there is to look to, Yorke, beyond a man's personal interest: beyond the advancement of well-laid schemes; beyond even the discharge of dishonouring debts'. He intends to be 'more considerate to ignorance, more forbearing to suffering'. This is the limit of his life-changing conversion. He is ready to let 'Credit and Commerce' take care of themselves but enough of the capitalist still remains for him to describe his current state of remorse in industrial terms: 'The machinery of all my nature; the whole enginery of this human mill: the boiler, which I take to be the heart, is fit to burst' (book 3, chapter 7). At this point the novel is impaled on the horns of a dilemma: how to mediate between hearts and boilers: how is an entrepreneur to achieve the economic success necessary for himself and his worker-children if he abandons commercial values for those of romantic love and paternalism?

As with the question of the causes of economic difficulties and the resultant unrest, the answer to this problem lies with history. Precisely at the point of Moore's enunciation of his new creed he is struck down (like the manufacturer Horsfall whose fate was revealed by the *Leeds Mercury*) by an assassin's bullet. Unlike Horsfall, he survives but only after a period of recovery paralleling Caroline's emergence from her wasting disease. Like her, he succumbs to the withdrawn and feminine world of illness, remote from the marketplace which, though not explicitly, serves as a form of punishment, an expiation of his sins, and returns him to the domestic and emotional sphere through a reconciliation with Caroline.

More important, the time needed for recovery from Moore's injury allows a period to pass during which the hated Orders in Council are repealed: trade flourishes and the economy looks up. He is now able to combine hearts and boilers since a healthy profit now becomes compatible with a more generous treatment of his employees. Though this is a fictional narrative, documented historical facts are bizarrely used to validate the idea that the outcome of emotional honesty to Caroline and fatherly concern for his workers will inevitably be solvency and a happy marriage. As Moore points out on the day when the Orders in Council are repealed,

now I shall no longer be poor; now I can pay my debts . . . this day lays for my fortunes a broad, firm foundation; on which for the first time in my life, I can securely build . . . Now, I can take more workmen; give better wages, lay wiser and more liberal plans; do some good; be less selfish . . . *now* I can seek a wife. (book 3, chapter 14)

In practice then, altruism is made easy for him. He understands well the nature of what is in effect the domestic bribe. His wife will bring him 'charity' and 'purity' but also 'solace' in the shape of creature comforts: 'she *will* care for me . . . these hands will be the gentle ministrants of every comfort I can taste'. Ironically the final chapter of the novel has the throwaway title 'The Winding-Up' which fits it perfectly, since it consists of a farcically neat tying up of loose ends (book 3, chapter 14). Moore marries love not money but, as his brother Louis marries the heiress Shirley, Capital becomes his sister-in-law and he becomes prosperous enough to follow the example of Robert Owen and build a model mill and workers' cottages. The asymmetry between the threat to society and this relatively modest improvement of the workers' lot can only be resolved by an assumption that all other employers could do as Moore does. But they would need, depending on economic cycles, an assurance of prosperity coinciding with a fatherly attitude to employees: repeal of the Orders in Council or similar beneficial events do not occur every day or at need.

In addition, two aspects of the novel's structure work against the argument that benign paternalism is the solution to social problems. As has been pointed out, the workers are not individualized nor is their suffering detailed, apart from the sketchy figure of William Farren, that model of deference in distress who is separately rewarded for his submissiveness with work as a gardener. The anonymity of the workers goes further than this by concealing gender as well as individuality: though there would certainly be women workers in a woollen mill like Moore's, none is mentioned. The 'mob', as Moore calls it (even though Caroline rebukes him for it), takes violent, collective action in the dark, in unknown numbers and unknown forms. The casualties of the attack on the mill are merely pathetic numbers and the one dead man is referred to as 'it'. When Eagleton writes that the attack is 'structurally central and curiously empty',[3] presumably he is referring to the lack of any experiential account of the actions of the workers and their reactions. But such an absence works against the narrator's viewpoint to enact the middle-class view of the 'hands' or 'operatives' as no more than that—necessary parts of the machine. It leaves the working class uninscribed and therefore finally uncontained, rendering the proposed resolution of class conflict problematic.

A further feature of the narrative that works against a 'paternalistic' solution lies in the contemporary construction of childhood and the relation in which children stand to those whom J. S. Mill describes as in 'loco parentis'. As contemporary believers in paternalism saw it, the relationship was far removed from the child-centred one now familiar. The historian Lawrence Stone characterizes it by citing *The English Matron* (1846) which lays down the then-prevailing view of the family structure: 'the government of a household, for the sake of all its inmates, should be a monarchy . . . of all forms a democracy is the most uncomfortable in domestic life'.[4] The subjects in this monarchy (alongside the second sex) are the children who, by this time, are seen as in need of redemption. Stone quotes Hannah More writing on children in 1835 and insisting that it is 'a fundamental error to consider children as innocent beings whose little weaknesses may, perhaps, want some correction, rather than as beings who bring into the world a corrupt nature and evil dispositions, which it should be the great end of education to rectify'.[5] So, when J. S. Mill derides paternalism, he is alluding to this construction of childhood which equates the working classes with the corrupt and evilly inclined young. He sees the practice as superimposing this onto the working-class adults and allowing the employers to guide and restrain them sufficiently to restrict them to doing their work and being 'moral and religious'.

The degree of restraint felt appropriate for children can be inferred from other Brontë novels. Agnes Grey wishes she were not prohibited by her employers, the Bloomfields, from a 'few sound boxes on the ear' or blows from 'a good birch rod' that might chasten their children. But she does, as was common at the time, control the unruly children physically, though inflicting a milder alternative to the salvo of gunfire that Moore uses on his childlike workers, as she carries or drags them to the table where they are to have their lessons and holds them there 'forcibly till the lesson was done'. When Tom Bloomfield refuses to write, she wrenches his fingers round the pen and compels him to do so. When his sister Mary Ann proves even more uncontrollable, Agnes uses yet more violent methods: 'I would shake her violently by the shoulders, or pull her long hair, or put her in a corner' (chapter 3).

There is no indication that the peaceable Agnes sees anything amiss in this treatment of her charges: though she has to observe the Bloomfield parents' prohibitions, Bloomfield himself bullies his children into submission. Mrs Reed in *Jane Eyre* similarly uses the common practice of locking children in a confined dark space to break their sinful wills when she imprisons Jane in the Red Room. It then appears that the punishments inflicted on Heathcliff and Hareton in *Wuthering Heights* are merely an increase in the physical penalties that were thought more widely acceptable. To argue for paternalism with this view of how to treat children in mind sounds less convincing than when it is merely thought of as 'fatherliness'. It is seen to depend on keeping the idea of superior and inferior intact—merely a way of rationalizing restraint of adult workers as a means of confining them to the role of 'hands', not individuals.

Social Mobility in *Wuthering Heights*

The initial reaction of some contemporaries to *Wuthering Heights* was to see it as so far removed from reality as to be only explicable as a work produced in a remote and barbaric region. Heathcliff, one claims, 'has doubtless had his prototype in those uncongenial and remote districts where human beings, like the trees, grow gnarled and dwarfed and distorted by the inclement climate' (Allott, p. 218). Charlotte, writing the Preface for the second edition of the novel in 1850, reinforces this idea. She claims a kind of authenticity in 'the unbridled aversions, and headlong partialities of unlettered moorland kinds and rugged moorland squires, who have grown up untaught and unchecked, except by mentors as harsh as themselves' (Allott, p. 284). Nobody could fail to notice also that it was a tale of a strange, wild, love between two extraordinary characters, a passion made all the stranger for readers by Catherine's incomprehensible assertions about her feelings for Heathcliff. No one seems to have connected it with more mundane social issues which now can be seen as underpinning the complicated plot.

Underlying every twist and turn in the narrative are money, property, and social status, which root the novel in the major issues of the day. It handles the subject of social mobility in terms far removed from Samuel Smiles's bland examples of diligence and talent rewarded. Remote though the setting may be, every individual in the novel is 'classified' as clearly as in Dickens's works. Lockwood's gentlemanly status is plain in his elaborate greeting to his landlord, 'I do myself the honour of calling as soon as possible, after my arrival, to express the hope that I have not inconvenienced you by my perseverance in soliciting the occupation of Thrushcross Grange' (chapter 1). His first encounter with Wuthering Heights involves him in trying to 'place' everyone from the second Cathy to the dialect-speaking servant Joseph, who is no more welcoming than the ferocious house dogs.

Once Lockwood's first traumatic visit to the Heights is over, Nelly Dean's account correctly places the individuals involved in the story in terms of social class. The original Earnshaw, Catherine and Hindley's father, is a substantial yeoman farmer, rich enough to send his son away to college for three years so that his children's status and respectability consequently makes them socially acceptable to the local gentry. Heathcliff, by contrast, is a waif picked up by Earnshaw on the streets of Liverpool, classified as a gypsy, a nomadic alien who is an outcast from society and referred to as 'nameless', an epithet which is literally accurate since his name is unknown and he is given that of an Earnshaw child who died. The single name serves in place of both first name and surname. He is also legally *nullius filius*, nobody's son, a child with no legitimate father, and although he is at first treated as a member of the family by Earnshaw, that ceases when Hindley succeeds to the ownership of the Heights on his father's death.

The relative status of the Earnshaw's family and that of the local landowning gentry, the Lintons, is spelt out by a vivid episode in the childhood of Catherine and Heathcliff when, driven by curiosity to see the high life close to, they peer through the window of the Lintons' drawing room at Thrushcross Grange to glimpse the unfamiliar splendour. It makes a vivid contrast to the rough and inhospitable appearance of Wuthering Heights, established in the opening chapters of the novel. As Heathcliff tells Mrs Dean, who later recounts it to Lockwood, 'and we saw—ah! it was beautiful—a splendid place carpeted with crimson, and crimson-covered chairs and tables, and a pure white ceiling bordered by gold, a shower of glass-drops hanging in silver chains from the centre, and shimmering with little soft tapers' (chapter 6).

Amid these signs of a superior class, clearly not earning a living, nor wearing muddy boots and rising at dawn, the Linton children, Edgar and Isabella, are visible quarrelling and weeping over a small dog. To Heathcliff the implication of the scene is clear: these are members of an effete race rendered feeble by idleness and self-indulgence. Catherine takes a more ambiguous view, not disagreeing about the comically feeble children and captivated by the luxury and refinement of their trappings. She is, however, attacked by a vicious guard dog which signals that the Lintons do not forget to protect their property from intruders.

As Heathcliff remembers bitterly, he and Catherine are treated quite differently because she is 'Miss' Earnshaw and, once so identified, is accepted socially as someone they can 'know' (in Charlotte Brontë's sense). Heathcliff is classified as a 'villain', a 'Frightful thing', a 'gypsy' unfit to associate with her: 'she was a young lady and they made a distinction between her treatment, and mine'. A servant was 'ordered to take me off' and, when Heathcliff refused to go, he was dragged from the house while Catherine, whose ankle has been bitten by the dog, is ministered to by all the Lintons: a servant washes her feet; Mr Linton serves her a tumbler of Negus, and Isabella feeds her cakes; her hair is washed, dried, and combed; she is placed by the fire; and remains a kind of pampered hostage for several weeks.

On her return home, Heathcliff finds her visibly changed, with all the appearance of a lady. Somehow Thrushcross Grange has made her look like a Linton, which is indeed what she is literally to become. She is no longer a 'wild, hatless little savage' but 'a very dignified person, with brown ringlets falling from the cover of a feathered beaver, and a long cloth habit which she was obliged to hold up with both hands that she might sail in'. She offends Heathcliff mortally, despite her show of attention, by seeing him as comic compared to the Lintons: 'Why, how very black and cross you look! and how—how funny and grim! But that's because I'm used to Edgar, and Isabella Linton' (chapter 7). Her taste for the Lintons' lifestyle persists and she begins to occupy herself with their society. Heathcliff is excluded, partly because Hindley's maltreatment grows worse and partly because Mr Linton wishes it. Seeing Catherine become more and more overtly a fine lady, Heathcliff wallows in his own degradation, becoming surlier and dirtier: a perceived difference of class has been created between Catherine and him and he recognizes it.

Catherine, meanwhile, becomes a divided self: gratified by a life of luxury and refinement but still seeing herself and Heathcliff as indivisible. But she later agrees to marry Edgar—largely to consolidate her new status. Heathcliff overhears as she tells Mrs Dean that her motive is that Edgar will be rich, and 'I shall like to be the greatest woman of the neighbourhood, and I shall be proud of having such a husband'. Her concern with Edgar's social standing has a consequence for her relationship with Heathcliff, yet she still regards her love for him as unaffected by her decision to marry: 'I've no more business to marry Edgar Linton than I have to be in heaven; and if the wicked man in there had not brought Heathcliff so low, I shouldn't have thought of it. It would degrade me to marry Heathcliff now' (chapter 9).

What Heathcliff hears therefore is that the source of his loss of Catherine is not a lack of feeling for him on her part but the difference in class between Edgar and himself: to marry him would declass or de-grade Catherine. Earlier he has resolved to take revenge on Hindley who has further de-graded/degraded him: 'I don't care how long I wait, if I can only do it, at last. I hope he will not die before I do!' (chapter 7). This violent need for vengeance on Hindley extends to Edgar and fuels the dynamism that Heathcliff now shows. It is no exaggeration to say that everything which happens in the narrative from here on is either wholly or partly caused by him. He disappears from the Heights and reappears only when he has successfully made himself into a typical entrepreneur, a self-made rich man, secretive about the source of his wealth but always with an eye for the opportunity that he might profitably use. His career and Edgar's ironically offer examples of Samuel Smiles's gospel of *Self-Help*: 'The spirit of self-help is the root of all genuine growth in the individual; and, exhibited in the lives of many, it constitutes the true source of national vigour and strength.' So far Smiles describes Heathcliff perfectly; and he then goes on to characterize men who, the reader might think, resemble Edgar: 'Help from without is often enfeebling in its effects, but help from within invariably invigorates'.[6]

As Mrs Dean describes him to Lockwood, Heathcliff has also by the time he returns transformed himself into someone who at least looks like a gentleman:

He had grown a tall, athletic, well-formed man . . . His upright carriage suggested the idea of his having been in the army. His countenance was much older in expression and decision of feature than Mr [Edgar] Linton's; it looked intelligent and retained no marks of former degradation. A half-civilized ferocity lurked yet in the depressed brows; and eyes full of black fire, but it was subdued; and his manner was even dignified, quite divested of roughness though too stern for grace. (chapter 10)

But Heathcliff has no real aspirations to gentility for its own sake and he shows no interest in a luxurious lifestyle nor signs of rejoicing at his improved social standing—his new wealth and acceptability are merely weapons in his vengeful armoury. Since he has come to connect status and property and he now has money, he chooses to seize the opportunity to create a possible revenge on Hindley for treating him as a non-person. He knows of Hindley's taste for gambling and uses this as his entrée to the Heights, basing all his actions on careful calculations in the pursuit of money and property which will achieve his ends. He is not interested in using his wealth to buy the luxury and self-indulgence first glimpsed by him and Catherine at Thrushcross Grange where she is now installed as Edgar's wife. Since he now at least looks socially acceptable, his first move is to encourage Hindley to gamble recklessly. Once Hindley had absolute power over him when he was a child; now he secures power in his turn by offering Earnshaw liberal payment for permission to lodge at the Heights. Soon he is living in the property he intends ultimately to own by becoming Hindley's creditor for his gambling debts.

When Hindley dies, his lawyer sums up the financial position at the Heights and that of his heir Hareton: 'the whole property is mortgaged, and the sole chance for the natural heir is to allow him an opportunity of creating some interest in the creditor's heart that he may be inclined to deal leniently towards him' (chapter 17). Since the creditor to whom the estate is mortgaged is now Heathcliff, Hareton's prospects of softening him into generosity are bleak and Heathcliff systematically degrades Hareton as Hindley once degraded him.

Heathcliff's new appearance, demeanour, and evident wealth allow him before Hindley's death to charm Edgar's sister, Isabella, as a kind of quid pro quo for Edgar's marriage to Catherine but also as a move in Heathcliff's long game. Edgar recognizes clearly Heathcliff's real objects: to degrade a Linton in the shape of Isabella and also to raise the possibility that, as her husband, he might inherit the Linton property in default of 'heirs male' (chapter 9). This is in fact the reason why Heathcliff elopes with the infatuated heir to Linton's wealth, Isabella, who soon understands a 'diabolical prudence' in his marrying her to obtain power over Edgar and runs away to London where she bears Heathcliff's child, a son.

Heathcliff's opportunity comes when Isabella dies and he is able to reclaim his son, Linton Heathcliff. The child's name combines the proud name of his enemy and superior with that of the man whom the Lintons called 'nameless'. By a series of cunning manoeuvres, once Linton and the second Catherine are just of marriageable age, Heathcliff manipulates his weakling of a son and the girl into marriage. Heathcliff is now in line, in spite of his 'nameless' condition and his absence of a legitimate father, to inherit a great deal through his son. As Catherine's husband, Linton will automatically own any property that accrues to her as a result of her father's death. Again luck apparently favours Heathcliff as the enfeebled Edgar dies before he can change his will, as he apparently intends to do, to prevent his estate falling into Heathcliff's control. It later emerges that the latter has given luck a helping hand by bribing the lawyer that Edgar summoned to delay his arrival until after the man had died. The Linton estate now belongs legally to Linton Heathcliff and therefore de facto to Heathcliff himself, producing checkmate after the event, since both his enemies are dead and he has avenged himself on them only when they are finally out of reach.

It takes merely the death of his unloved son to complete his success. What has been demonstrated by his brilliant chess game is a less positive construction of social mobility than was usual at the time. Heathcliff has shown that upward mobility is available not only through a combination of high-minded diligence and talent but through low-mindedness, ruthlessness, and opportunism at the expense of others. But this is not a moralistic tale: Heathcliff's rise is emblematic of the power of the ruthless entrepreneur to rise in contemporary society. By focusing on a single object and making pragmatic use of every change in circumstance, he has mastered the traditional middle and upper classes. The account is a dark rewriting of Smiles's exemplary tales of upward social mobility effected by a combination of talent and perseverance. Yet this is represented neither as tragedy nor comedy and the narrative offers no hero: the Lintons are too effete as well as too inturned to defend their fortune and Heathcliff is too violently cruel and gratuitously malicious to suggest heroic status. Lockwood is manifestly not a narrator who can interpret these savage events and so the text remains ambiguously non-judgemental.

By a final irony, Heathcliff's belated revenge serves a purpose unthought of by him when—after his death, a kind of fugitive suicide—Cathy and the now refurbished Hareton marry. This means not only that the degradation inflicted on Hareton by Heathcliff is nullified but that Cathy inherits the Linton estate and the Earnshaws and the Lintons are united, as is their property. As Terry Eagleton puts it in his seminal study of these issues, Heathcliff's relation to the two classes represented by the Grange and the Heights is complex: 'Heathcliff is subjectively a Heights figure opposing the Grange and objectively a Grange figure undermining the Heights'. By bestriding both for a time 'he focuses acutely the contradiction between the two worlds. His rise to power symbolizes at once the triumph of the oppressed over capitalism and the triumph of capitalism over the oppressed'.[7] How the reader is to view the ultimate consequences of his revenge for the two classes is, however, something that Emily Brontë left, like so much else, unsaid.

CHAPTER 5

GENDER, NATIONALITY, AND RACE IN THE BRONTËS' NOVELS

English Femininity and Domestic Life

IN *Shirley* Caroline Helstone repeatedly asks herself a significant question: 'I have to live perhaps till seventy years . . . half a century of existence may lie before me. How am I to occupy it? What am I to do to fill the interval of time which spreads between me and the grave?' (book 1, chapter 10). This female dilemma becomes an issue as central to the narrative as that of the class conflict with which it is entwined. The answer which contemporary society had readily available was one which Caroline knows only too well: women were destined to fill their lives with domestic and nurturing duties to their families. As the author of one popular writer of conduct manuals for women, Sarah Stickney Ellis, put it in 1839: 'there is an appropriate sphere for women to move in, from which those of the middle class in England seldom deviate very widely. This sphere has duties and occupations of its own, from which no woman can shrink without culpability and disgrace'. Those who best fulfil this womanly role are those whose essential characteristic is 'disinterested kindness', an ability to adapt ceaselessly to the needs of others, a quality which leaves no room for self. Hence Dickens's portrayal of Little Dorrit whose ministrations to her father and siblings virtually erase her identity as well as her name, while involving her in lying and deceit. Ellis argues that 'a selfish woman may not improperly be regarded as a monster, especially in that sphere of life where there is a constant demand made upon her services'.[1]

This standard construction of femininity/womanliness informed not only explicit directives like Ellis's but also those implicit in the organization of society: the defined nature of women's educational needs—domestic skills and 'accomplishments'—reinforced the idea of what their futures should rightly be. All three self-educated and widely read Brontë sisters to some extent resisted these predetermined limits, as their attempts at self-sufficiency and their ultimate determination to succeed as authors confirm. Anne's novels depict women bent on some independence and Emily disregards the contemporary views of womanliness in *Wuthering Heights*, offering neither positive nor negative role models. Charlotte reveals a fluctuating viewpoint as she pays lip-service to the mores associated with womanly behaviour, alternating with resistance to more significant aspects of contemporary femininity. Charlotte's wavering captures the expected ambivalence of women struggling with values they had internalized that conflicted with the dissatisfactions of their daily lives.

It is precisely through the experiential account of women's everyday lives that Charlotte and, to a lesser extent, Anne capture this conflict. Complicating the experience they describe is their own first-hand knowledge that the prescription of domesticity and maternity as women's destiny fails to take account of the 'leftover' or 'odd', the unmarried and those without financial support. To raise the issue of what should be done about them was to ask awkward questions about the limits of work for women. The easiest course therefore was to argue from demographics that, since statistics in the 1851 census suggested that there were hundreds of thousands more women than men, these women were 'redundant' in Great Britain. Emigration to the colonies, however, could remedy this since there the demand for wives exceeded the supply, or as Greg put it later, if these women were to emigrate, it 'could not fail to augment the value, and the demand for, the remainder'.[2] The concept of redundancy was necessary if it were not to appear that God had got his sums wrong or that those who insisted on separate spheres had misunderstood his purpose.

These arguments and the practice of emigration failed to take note of the fact that there was likely to be a mismatch between women who happened to be unmarried and the requirement for a colonist's wife. They did not take account of the age of the 'redundant' women who might be not only genteel but also elderly. This is another question which, unusually, Charlotte chooses to address in the persons of the two 'old maids' (or elderly virgins), Miss Mann and Miss Ainley, in *Shirley*. Even Robert Moore derides these two women as useless and ugly; while Caroline Helstone, dreading the same fate, decides to look more closely at them as individuals. Both are 'ladies' but impoverished, and Caroline discovers that by contemporary standards they are, despite their unpromising exteriors, truly womanly. Both have spent their lives caring for others: Miss Mann has been a devoted daughter and sister whose life is now poisoned by a malady brought on by her nursing of the sick and dying, including one (shades of Branwell) whose desperate state was self-inflicted. The other spinster, Miss Ainley, also dedicates herself to nursing the sick, however dangerous the disease, while herself remaining 'serene, humble, kind and equable' (book 1, chapter 10).

Having tried to imitate their lives, Caroline finds the practice only efficacious enough to 'stun and keep down anguish' and no more; and this leads her to conclude, as suggested here, that avoidance of the problem is deliberate: 'People hate to be reminded of what they are unable to remedy'. The parallel between such women and the working classes comes home to her: 'Old maids, like the houseless and unemployed poor, should not ask for a place in the world: the demand disturbs the happy and rich: it disturbs parents'. Just as there is no work for some operatives, there are no husbands for some women since the 'matrimonial market' like the labour market is 'overstocked' (book 2, chapter 11).

Even Jane Eyre, living in comfort at Thornfield, expresses the same frustration at the emptiness of her life if it is to be filled with 'making puddings, and knitting stockings . . . playing on the piano and embroidering bags' (book 1, chapter 12). She has singled out here the two major activities with which middle-class women were expected to fill their lives: preparation and overseeing of meals; and functional or decorative needlework. Women and food were closely associated in the Victorian mind, as is shown by the many books of cookery and household management which, like the conduct manuals of Ellis and others, lay down prescriptive domestic rules. Since precision is required in the observance of these, *Beeton's Book of Household Management* opens with an appropriately militaristic image: 'As with the Commander of an Army, or the leader of any enterprise, so it is with the mistress of a house'.[3] Naturally in a period without modern gadgets, the preparation of food and its consumption in middle-class homes was a long-drawn-out matter. Isabella Beeton lays down the dogma in her first chapter that, even in preparing a family dinner, it is necessary to cook and serve the meal 'and to lay the tablecloth and sideboard with the same cleanliness, neatness, and scrupulous exactness as when there is company'.[4]

Given the necessary involvement of women with food in the course of their everyday lives, it is not surprising that food soon takes on a metaphorical significance in fiction. Dickens is the novelist who carries this to extremes as one reviewer noticed in regard to scenes involving women: 'all beauty, all that he thinks loveable is apt to be treated by him as if it were a pot of raspberry jam, something luscious to the palette, instead of something fascinating to the imagination'.[5] Examples of what this reviewer means are frequent. Ruth Pinch in *Martin Chuzzlewit* (1844) demonstrates her womanly value by her skill in preparing 'an unalloyed and perfect meat pudding' (to a recipe taken straight from a contemporary cookery book). Ruth merges with her confection as her 'charming laugh of triumph' becomes the 'ideal seasoning for the pudding' (chapter 39). Women become consumables as, when the besotted Copperfield dines with the Spenlows, his impression is that he 'dined off Dora, entirely, and sent away half-a-dozen plates untouched' (chapter 26). The apotheosis of these images comes when Amy Dorrit is said metaphorically to suckle her imprisoned father like a 'classical daughter once . . . who ministered to her father in his prison as her mother had ministered to her'. Amy, the reader is told, did 'much more in comforting her father's wasted heart upon her innocent breast, and turning it to a fountain of love and fidelity that never ran dry or waned, through all his years of famine' (volume i, chapter 19).

In *Shirley*, Charlotte subverts the familiar association of woman and food by using it to express the burden it places on women in the novel who have to provide it, including even the wealthy Shirley Keeldar. The novel opens with an account (which her publishers wished Charlotte to omit) of the three curates' visits to each other's lodgings, loudly demanding food from their landladies and listing their requirements as beef, Yorkshire pudding, cheese, spice-cake, and small beer. This is the first of several such lists that lace the novel, capturing the recurrence of the demands. After the attack on the mill and ensuing battle, Moore sends to Shirley for refreshment for the soldiers who aided him and Shirley responds lavishly by sending the entire contents of her larder and wine-cellar to the Hollow and after that tells her servants to go to 'the butcher and baker, and desire them to send what they have' (book 2, chapter 9). Caroline is worried when the three curates descend unexpectedly on the rectory in case they decide to stay for a meal which she anxiously provides, while Miss Ainley nervously offers refreshment to the more uncouth curate during a visit, hoping it will be thought suitable.

In these and other instances, two features mark out the contrast between Dickens's and Charlotte Brontë's use of the women–food link. Brontë focuses on the felt necessity of getting the provision of food correct in accord with local mores; and also on the recognition that the outcome of what is placed on the table will be an evaluation of the provider. As Beeton puts it, 'a well-served table will be used to evaluate human ingenuity and resources'.[6] Such indices are widely used in *Shirley*: when Caroline learns that the exigent curates demand high tea, she runs through what protocol requires on this particular occasion, down to the smallest detail of layout and quantity:

It was essential to have a multitude of plates of bread and butter, varied in sorts and plentiful in quantity; *it was thought proper*, too, that on the centre-plate should stand a glass dish of marmalade; among the viands *was expected* to be found a small assortment of cheese-cakes and tarts. (book 1, chapter 7, emphases added)

Caroline sees these directives as a serious matter, as if the curates were food critics inspecting a restaurant—which indeed seems to be their main role in the narrative. In addition to harassing their own landladies and Caroline, one of them, Malone, does the same with the impoverished Miss Ainley who offers him only slices of sponge cake and glasses of cowslip wine from her frugal resources. He rejects her offering with 'such open scorn' of it and her that she never repeats it.

Seen from the perspective of Caroline, the provision of food is purely burdensome, partly because it is seen as an alternative to intellectual pursuits which are appropriate only to men. Ellis writes, apparently without irony, 'It may be all very well for a man of science now and then to boil a watch instead of an egg for breakfast; but a woman has no business to be so far absorbed in any intellectual pursuit as not to know whether the water is boiling on the fire'.[7] Such advice given by those like Ellis and Beeton is not only strongly prescriptive but also addressed specifically to English women as opposed to those of other (lesser) nationalities. The titles of Ellis's books make this as plain as her directive language does: *The Women of England: Their Social Duties and Domestic Habits* (1839); *The Wives of England: Their Relative Duties, Domestic Influence, and Social Obligations* (1843); *The Mothers of England: Their Influence and Responsibility* (1843); *The Daughters of England: Their Position in Society, Character, and Responsibilities* (1845). (Significantly there is no companion volume on spinsters.)

The stress on nationality explains the paradox that while *Shirley* questions the construction of (English) femininity as built on domestic drudgery, the standards of Ellis and others are applied to ridicule the domestic inadequacies of the Belgian woman, Hortense Moore. This demonstrates that what had come to be called 'the woman question' was for Charlotte and others really 'the *English* woman question' since, for her, other standards applied to Continental or oriental women. The device used to satirize Belgian women draws on the link between women and food by reporting the comments made by Hortense's English maid, Sara. The latter describes the food that her mistress serves as 'not fit for dogs' (book 1, chapter 6); she asserts that 'the bouillon was no better than greasy warm water'; and the choucroute 'a tub of hog-wash' (book 1, chapter 5). The narrator reinforces this contempt with a detailed description of 'a dish of meat—nature unknown, but supposed to be miscellaneous—singularly chopped up with crumbs of bread, seasoned uniquely though not unpleasantly . . . a queer, but by no means unpalatable dish'. It is accompanied by 'Greens, oddly bruised'; and followed by 'a pâté' which is sweetened not with good honest sugar but with 'mélasse' (book 1, chapter 6).

These foreign messes and Hortense's slovenly house-dress signal the unsatisfactory nature of Robert Moore's domestic life before his conversion to a better treatment for his workers and before his reward in the shape of the English Caroline. This is not the only instance in which Charlotte judges foreign women as though they belonged to a different species from English women for she does the same in *The Professor* and *Villette* when describing English impressions of young Belgian girls and women. As will be shown later, she also handles the subject of oriental women in a belittling manner. A significant figure in this respect is Frances Henri in *The Professor* who is, unfortunately, half-Swiss but fortunately derives her housewifery from her other half which is English. Consequently the food she offers to her prospective husband, Crimsworth is, though 'foreign', 'tasty' and 'served with nicety' (chapter 24).

Seen from the viewpoint of the wealthy and independent Shirley, the women–food connection is something that she, at least, can divert to ironic account by mimicking it. Before she will allow the greedy and exacting curates, whom she sees as children naively interested in food, to enter her house after striking her dog, Tartar, she allows him to terrify and chase them. Only when they have been brought, dog-like, to heel does she feed them with her titbits of 'cold chicken, ham, and tarts' (book 2, chapter 4). Earlier Caroline's uncle has described his niece's fluctuations by seeing her and her like as 'To-day . . . bouncing, buxom, red as cherries and round as apples; to-morrow they exhibit themselves effete as dead weeds' (book 1, chapter 11). Later, Shirley appropriates this masculine language by using it to taunt her snobbish uncle Sympson when telling him that she is to marry his son's tutor, Louis Moore: 'A while ago you wanted much to know whom I meant to marry: my intention was then formed, but not mature . . . now it is ripe, sun-mellowed, perfect: take the crimson peach—take Louis Moore!' (book 3, chapter 13).

The other domestic occupation thought appropriate for women to fill their time was referred to as their 'work', a term which from the seventeenth century onwards meant, when unqualified as here, needlework of various kinds including knitting. It is all that Caroline has to fall back on to fill what she foresees as her empty life. Her questioning of how to do this is effectively answered by her uncle and guardian when he tells her to 'stick to the needle—learn shirt-making and gown-making, and pie-crust making, and you'll be a clever woman some day' (book 1, chapter 7). There are frequent references to the sense of pointlessness that constant resort to such work produces, especially when done in the Belgian fashion. So Caroline is obliged to endure an afternoon of what Hortense sees as 'one of the "first duties" of women': darning stockings 'stitch by stitch so as exactly to imitate the fabric of the stocking itself' (book 1, chapter 6). Nonetheless Caroline tries assiduously to follow her uncle's advice: 'She did sew: she plied her needle continuously; ceaselessly; but her brain worked faster than her fingers. Again, and more intensely than ever, she desired a fixed occupation no matter how onerous' (book 2, chapter 2). On such occasions she falls into 'a sort of brain lethargy' (book 1, chapter 7). Society polices this 'work' by the institution of the 'Jew-basket' or the 'Missionary basket' which women of the neighbourhood are required to fill with 'a monster collection of pin-cushions, needle-books, card-racks, work bags, articles of infant-wear &.&.&c' as the basket moves inexorably from house to house in circular fashion. Items, many of them useless trivia, are then 'sold', i.e. used to exact donations for the conversion of the Jews and others (book 1, chapter 7).

Charlotte's technique to capture the mind-numbing boredom of these unnecessary occupations for women's hands is to produce repeated lists of things done or produced. Others at this time write equally vehemently on the same topic: Charlotte's friend, Mary Taylor, in her novel *Miss Miles* which she began in the 1840s, shows a woman in the same claustrophobic situation as Caroline Helstone, making futile attempts to use up her time: 'She would trail about, doing something, she knew and cared not what. When told, she would go and sit down in the breakfast room, now the living room of the whole family. There she fiddled with some work, which she seldom finished . . . and never gave a sign of caring whether the world was coming to an end or not'.[8] Similarly the heroine of Geraldine Jewsbury's *Marian Withers* (1851) tells the industrial reformer Cunningham: 'I have nothing to occupy me . . . I feel as if I were buried alive'.[9] Perhaps the most striking account of all is given by Florence Nightingale in her polemic *Cassandra*, written in 1852. In the professional life she achieved Nightingale was always careful to behave with conventional womanly decorum and deference but in *Cassandra* she reveals her deepest feelings: 'Society triumphs over many. They wish to regenerate the world with their institutions, with their moral philosophy, with their love. Then they sink from breakfast till dinner, from dinner to tea, with a little worsted work, looking forward to nothing but bed'.[10] Such women are living the life 'of a corpse which lies motionless in its narrow bed'.[11]

In *Shirley* it is left to the young girl Rose Yorke (who is based on Mary Taylor's younger sister) to translate the factual accounts of women's lives into vivid symbols of entrapment. Her life, she tells her mother, shall not be deposited in 'a broken-spouted tea-pot, and shut up in a china closet'. She will not 'commit it to your work-table to be smothered in piles of woollen hose' and 'will *not* prison it in a linen press to find shrouds among the sheets'. Referring pointedly to the idea of women as food, she asserts, 'least of all will I hide it in a tureen of cold potatoes, to be ranged with bread, butter, pasty and ham on the shelves of the larder' (book 2, chapter 12).

Escaping Feminine Stereotypes

Rose, as one of the bolder, coming generation, characterizes such a life in the familiar terms of entrapment and claustrophobia but adds her determination to escape: 'my life shall be a life', she decides; 'not a black trance like the toad's; buried in marble; nor a long, slow death like [Caroline's] at Briarfield Rectory, and a place that when I pass it reminds me of a windowed grave' (book 2, chapter 12). Jane Eyre and Lucy Snowe may be said to belong to a generation which precedes Rose's, but they too, though it is not clear how, wish to push against the limited life they are offered. Jane Eyre at Thornfield wishes for something beyond the domestic: 'women feel just as men feel; they need exercise for their faculties, and a field for their efforts as much as their brothers do; they suffer from too rigid a restraint, too absolute a stagnation, precisely as men would suffer' (book 1, chapter 12).

Lucy Snowe, always more extreme than Jane Eyre, gives vent to the same desire more theatrically when a thunderstorm strikes Villette. The pupils wake and offer panic-stricken prayers for their own safety; while Lucy, 'thoroughly roused and obliged to live', climbs on to the outside ledge of the dormitory window and sits there letting the 'too terribly glorious' storm take hold of her 'with tyranny'. She exults in a sense of power and freedom; and is left afterwards aching for 'something to fetch me out of my present existence, and lead me upwards and onwards' in the future (chapter 12). Both Jane and Lucy yearn for new scope, for work that stretches their minds, so that Lucy toys with the alien idea of Roman Catholicism as a way of varying her life. This is like Frances Henri telling Crimsworth in *The Professor* as they plan their future together: 'I like a contemplative life, but I like an active one better' (chapter 23).

The activity Frances needs is provided by the school she sets up and runs successfully after her marriage which is echoed by Lucy's equally successful school which she too controls on her own while M. Paul is away. Both do so with complete contentment since they are exercising their faculties and controlling their own lives. The difficulty for women like the more passive Caroline Helstone was that most serious occupations, other than teaching, were closed to middle-class females. Even envisaging a life different from those of the women around them was difficult. Caroline does express to Robert Moore a wish for a demanding occupation but can only imagine what she has seen close at hand: 'I should like an occupation; and if I were a boy it would not be so difficult to find one ... I could be apprenticed to your trade—the cloth trade ... I would do the counting-house work, keep the books and write the letters' (book 1, chapter 5). She recognizes that without such scope she and others will be reduced to a pair of serviceable 'hands' and nothing more. She is clear that she wants real work and, when Shirley suggests such work might make her 'masculine, coarse, unwomanly' and not happy, Caroline is prepared to settle for 'varieties of pain' (book 2, chapter 7).

This desperate idea which captures the agony of monotony and the wish to vary it at any price is echoed by Nightingale in *Cassandra*: 'Give us back our suffering, we cry to Heaven in our hearts—better suffering than indifferentism; for out of nothing comes nothing. But out of suffering may come the cure. Better have pain than paralysis'.[12] Nightingale also speaks of how women for want of anything else fill their minds with daydreams in which they can envisage alternative lives while 'singing Schubert' or 'reading the Review': 'Is not one fancying herself the nurse of some new friend in sickness; another engaging in romantic dangers with him, such as ... afford more food for sympathy than the monotonous events of domestic society; another undergoing unheard-of trials under the observation of someone she has chosen as the companion of her dream?'.[13]

Shirley and Caroline escape in their imagination from their own gendered time and place, as they reinterpret or rewrite the literary works that they both read and enjoy. This dreamwork allows them to speak under cover supposedly unthinkable thoughts and desires. The timid Caroline, for instance, is able to rebuke the domineering Moore for his arrogance by discussing his likeness to the tyrannical Coriolanus when he reads part of the play aloud to her. Later, she substitutes womankind for mankind as the category which subsumes human beings of both sexes by making Eve the representative of both. As the independent owner of a wealthy estate, Shirley reaches for freedom from masculine interference such as that perpetrated by her uncle Sympson and Robert Moore. She wishes always to make her own decisions and choices and therefore resists even the tutor, Louis Moore, whom she loves. He is only able to persuade her to marry him by joining in the game of imagining to describe his own projected future in the forests of North America. There he will find the freedom he has always longed for with 'such a deep passion to know her and to call her mine—such a day-desire and night-longing to win her and possess her'. Finally he laments that no woman he loves will accompany him 'but I am certain Liberty will await me' (book 3, chapter 13). By this neat identification of freedom as his future and Shirley as its embodiment he lures her into accepting him. The narrative leaves no doubt that marriage does not mean more freedom for Shirley: she is now Prometheus-like 'fettered to a fixed day' and lies 'conquered by love and bound with a vow' (book 3, chapter 14).

Caroline's projections for an alternative future take a more practical form than Shirley's as she reinterprets Solomon's account in the Book of Proverbs of the 'virtuous woman' with a price 'far above rubies' as a model of what she desires. Solomon's virtuous woman is an omnicompetent housewife providing for and feeding her household literally by night and day: preparing food; spinning; making clothing; selling the linen she makes; planting vineyards; and helping the needy. Proverbs 3 concludes with the prayer that 'her own works [shall] praise her in the gates'. This then is a safe model for a woman—approved by the highest authority, the Bible—but Caroline chooses perversely to read it selectively:

The 'virtuous woman,' again, had her household up as in the very middle of the night; she 'got breakfast over' (as Mrs Sykes says) before one o'clock A.M.; but *she* had something more to do than spin and give out portions: she was a manufacturer—she made fine linen and sold it: she was an agriculturist—she bought estates and planted vineyards. (book 2, chapter 11)

Alluding to her uncle's recommendation to become 'a clever woman' by honing her domestic skills, Caroline, released into an imaginary world, concludes ironically, '*That* woman was a manager; she was what matrons hereabouts call "a clever woman" ' (book 2, chapter 11). She is here making the point that the woman in Proverbs was clever in her uncle's sense of being a capable housekeeper, despite also engaging in productive occupations thought suitable only to men. In this way she goes so far as to question the underlying premiss of domestic ideology: 'Is there not a terrible hollowness, mockery, want, craving, in that existence which is given away to others?' (book 1, chapter 10).

Such a challenge to the idea of womanliness as selflessness raises the heretical possibility that marriage and a household to run do not represent the limit of what women need to use all their capacities, and there is much in the Brontës' novels to reinforce this possibility. To the Reverend Matthew Helstone, questioning the need for woman to be selfless would be anathema, but he himself takes a jaded view of marriage as something undertaken by men only in moments of madness. His behaviour towards unmarried and personable women suggests that by this he means in moments of powerful sexual attraction which overcome judgement. He believes that in less heated moments those in question would recognize, as he had done, that 'Millions of marriages are unhappy . . . perhaps all more or less so' (book 1, chapter 7). Mrs Pryor, Caroline's mother, shares his view despite her deference to others, as, remembering Caroline's father, a violent drunkard, she warns her that 'life is an illusion'; and that the conventional representations of what marriage is like for women 'are not like reality: they show only the green tempting surface of the marsh' (book 2, chapter 10).

Wuthering Heights implies a similarly disillusioned view of marriage in its depiction of brutal or otherwise disastrous unions: there is physical bullying in that of Isabella Linton and Heathcliff who marries to revenge himself on her brother; deep division between Catherine Earnshaw and Edgar Linton leading to her mental instability; and psychological torment and physical force in the union between Linton Heathcliff and Catherine Linton. Also, as the names of these ill-matched partners suggest, there is an insidious aura of incest about them. Furthermore, legitimate marriages are contrasted with the non-marital bond between Catherine and Heathcliff, though the depth of even their union seems to be measured by the extent to which each can inflict pain on the other in a kind of sadistic deadlock.

In *The Tenant of Wildfell Hall* it is the detailed description of the deterioration of the marriage of Helen and Arthur Huntingdon that is the central focus of the narrative, a union contracted when both parties have let sexual passion overcome reason; and it soon turns to disillusionment and regret on both sides. This story of marital disintegration is set amongst the unfortunate marriages of

Huntingdon's friends which are also marred by violence or infidelity. Even in *Jane Eyre* the threatening presence of the wretched Bertha Mason looms as a warning against marriage undertaken out of passion or avarice.

Yet the three novels which most effectively challenge the idea of marriage as a domestic idyll resort to a conventional closure, since they each predict happy marriages as a solution to all questions raised in the text: those of Caroline Helstone and Robert Moore, Shirley Keeldar and Louis Moore; Hareton Earnshaw and Catherine Heathcliff (née Linton); and Helen Huntingdon and Gilbert Markham. Caroline's recurrent beating against her cage subsides; Shirley's taste for freedom evaporates; Hareton and Catherine fail to take account of past experiences. But the Brontës' lip-service to this particular novelistic convention cannot silence the challenges evoked so powerfully in the rest of the narratives. The resistance to the limits on women's potential is subsumed into a notion of a desire for some superficial 'equality' between the spouses which appears to be merely nominal. Caroline is able as Moore's chosen partner to influence him towards a kinder treatment of his workers but this in no way conflicts with an ideology that partly justified itself by offering women influence in place of equal power. Catherine Heathcliff starts the marriage to Hareton with a semblance of superiority by schooling him where he is lacking but when she has brought him up to scratch there is nothing to prevent a reversion to the usual power-hierarchy; and, as will be demonstrated later in full, Gilbert Markham, though chastened, shows no signs of decreased sexism. The ending of *Jane Eyre* offers a less definitive, more complex form of closure: Jane speaks of perfect concord and of mutual confidence, while Rochester's physical dependence on her gives her a gratuitous control over him which may suggest that agency and power now reside with her.

The most complex ending, however, of all the Brontë novels is to be found in *Villette* when Lucy Snowe fails to reveal whether M. Paul does or does not return from his long absence overseas. Her refusal is the culmination of several instances in which she leads the reader on to expect a conventional event. Sometimes the means of doing this is an illusory account as when, leaving Bretton, she instructs the reader to conjecture that she returned 'to the bosom of [her] kindred' to live in 'halcyon weather' (chapter 4). She does so only to thwart that expectation by recounting her eight years of misery. Sometimes the mechanism is the structuring of the novel, as in the example of the early sections leading to an expectation that she and Graham Bretton will ultimately be united in marriage. Similarly the conclusion announced that M. Paul's return is fixed: 'It is Autumn; he is to be with me ere the mists of November come'. Again she urges the reader to foresee a happy outcome: 'the rapture of rescue from peril', only to leave unanswered the question of whether her lover really was saved from drowning. Significantly she describes her three years alone, turning her school into a success, as 'the three happiest years of my life' as if the withholding of the truth about M. Paul's fate signals that her serenity and sense of identity does not depend on whether he came back or not (chapter 42).

Eastern Femininity and *Jane Eyre*

Already on her arrival at Thornfield, Jane Eyre, viewing the upper storeys of the mansion, sees the part where Bertha, Rochester's first wife, is imprisoned 'with its two rows of small black doors all shut, like a corridor in some Bluebeard's castle' (book 1, chapter 11). This evokes a narrative which is to shape Jane Eyre's relationship with Rochester. Bluebeard is a recurrent character in many folk tales, including the *Arabian Nights* (so familiar to the Brontës) where he appears as a cruel sultan. Like other Bluebeard figures, he murders a succession of wives on the morning after the consummation of the marriage. Their bodies are kept, like Bertha, in a locked room out of sight of his new wife, Scheherazade, who is determined to avoid the fate of her predecessors. She does so by her wit and intelligence in telling him each night a fascinating story which she stops at a point so thrilling that he is obliged to wait for the next night to hear the outcome.

It becomes apparent that Rochester is the Bluebeard-sultan with Jane as the Scheherazade of this story. This is confirmed when Rochester literally takes on the role of sultan in the charade he acts out with Blanche Ingram: 'costumed in shawls, with a turban on his head. His dark eyes, swart skin and Paynim features suited the costume exactly. He looked the very model of an Eastern emir' (book 2, chapter 3). The previous wives are figured by the mad Bertha locked in her attic but she has had a long line of successors in the shape of the mistresses whom Rochester has discarded all over Europe: 'I sought my ideal of a woman amongst English ladies, French countesses, Italian signoras, and German Gräfinnen' (book 3, chapter 1). There he hoped to find 'the antipodes of the creole', the antithesis of the mixed-race Bertha who had succumbed to an inherited form of madness triggered by her intemperate, lustful excesses. She had become the animal to which races such as hers were supposed by the likes of Carlyle to be so close. Rochester reveals her to the onlookers after his failed wedding to Jane Eyre: 'whether beast or human being, one could not, at first sight, tell: it grovelled, seemingly, on all fours; it snatched and growled like some strange wild animal: but it was covered with clothing, and a quantity of dark grizzled hair, wild as a mane, hid its face' (book 2, chapter 11).

Rochester-Bluebeard believes that in Jane Eyre he has found his ideal—and she is, of course, English; but Jane does not succumb like Céline, Giacinta, and Clara; instead, like her alter ego, Scheherazade, she holds her 'master' at bay by charm and wit. From that very first encounter in the lane he is struck by her spirited display of independence and honesty in spite of her powerlessness as a mere governess. Their meetings all turn into sparring matches like those between Scheherazade and her sultan, or Beatrice and Benedick in _Much Ado_, since Jane soon recognizes Rochester as a potential threat, though she is yet to discover its nature. Whenever she encounters him she comments to herself on how their battle is going. After the summons to his drawing room she is put at ease by his 'harsh caprice' in ignoring her, seeing that it gives her an advantage. The point-scoring continues when he asks for her opinion of his appearance and she gives it frankly, assuming he is trying to tempt her into flattery. When he thanks her in 'a trembling voice' for saving him from Bertha's murderous attack, she claims superiority by telling him coolly: 'There is no debt, benefit, burden, obligation in the case' (book 1, chapter 15). Presumably this is designed to thwart any desire on his part to evoke a feminine flutter.

Even after she has accepted Rochester's proposal of marriage, Jane insists on keeping her distance as he sings to her and turns 'his face all kindled, and his full falcon-eye flashing, and tenderness and passion in every lineament'. Her response is to quail momentarily— then to rally: 'Soft scene, daring demonstration, I would not have . . . a weapon of defence must be prepared—I whetted my tongue . . . I asked with asperity "whom he was going to marry now" '. The song had spoken of his dying with his wife but she tells him bracingly that she has no intention of doing that nor of being 'hurried away in a suttee' on his funeral pyre (book 2, chapter 9).

The cause of this asperity and her continued defensiveness is that she feels from the day of his proposal that he is beginning to behave as an Eastern tyrant might towards a concubine from his seraglio. He wishes to load her with heirloom jewels unsuited to her Quakerish appearance; and he insists on taking her to a silk warehouse to buy her elaborate dresses. Once there, he chooses 'a rich silk of the most brilliant amethyst dye, and a superb pink satin' and, though she exchanges these for sober black and grey garments and threatens to wear her oldest frocks, he assumes this to be entirely feminine whimsicality. He takes her hand and gives her a smile 'such as a sultan might, in a blissful and fond moment, bestow on a slave his gold and gems had enriched'. She is incensed by the idea that he feels he is buying a blissful and fond sexual encounter with his evident wealth and power. This interpretation of his behaviour is reinforced by his next remark 'Oh, it is rich to see and hear her! . . . Is she original? Is she piquant? I would not exchange this one little English girl for the grand Turk's whole seraglio; gazelle eyes, houri forms and all!' (book 2, chapter 9).

The patronizing implication that her resistance is a prettily acted farce for his benefit is unendurable and Jane answers tartly to this 'eastern allusion': 'I'll not stand you an inch in the stead of a seraglio . . . so don't consider me an equivalent in that line'. If a seraglio of any sort is what he wants, she advises him to visit 'the bazaars of Stamboul' and 'lay out in extensive slave purchases some of the spare cash you seem at a loss to spend satisfactorily here'. She promises meanwhile to go out as a missionary to women in seraglios (including his) and 'stir up mutiny'. In fact from Gateshead Hall onwards she has shown that stirring mutiny is her special talent and she has rebelled successively against Mrs Reed and the authorities at Lowood as now against Rochester. Significantly she will 'preach liberty to them that are enslaved' until 'three-tailed bashaw' as he is, he will find himself 'fettered' instead of them (book 2, chapter 9).

The impact of this sultan–concubine scenario is dependent on the contrast it provides between the typical Eastern and Western women as represented here. The former are depicted, in keeping with current views, as naturally indolent and sensual, brought by easy luxury to be the mindless sexual slaves of their masters. They are assumed to want nothing more than the pleasures of the senses and idle self-indulgence so as to throw the diligent, selfless, and asexual English women into high relief. There is no evidence of an argument for a different treatment from this traditional one for the inhabitants of the harem. Rather, they are offered as warnings to Western women to be true to the ideals imposed on them by society. This use in literature of oriental women as models of what not to be is traced by the critic Joyce Zonana back to the early eighteenth century and, as she puts it, Charlotte Brontë's sultan–concubine parallel displaces the source of Western patriarchal oppression onto an 'oriental Mahometan' society in a 'conservative effort to slough off Orientalism and make the West more like itself'.[14]

Zonana makes a convincing case for this reading but others, reluctant to fault a text claiming more freedom for women, try to oppose it. They urge that Charlotte is arguing for independence and wider lives for women of all races, though the only evidence for this would be Jane's half-joking threat to create mutiny in the harem. Against such an argument is the totally heartless attitude taken by all concerned to Bertha Rochester—even Jane, like Rochester, can only see 'the creole' as a wild animal. True, at one point she wishes him to pity the woman but never challenges the idea of Bertha as subhuman since her race is allowed to erase gender issues just as for early Marxist critics these were erased by those of class. This fits with the lack of any attempt in the text to draw attention to the slave trade as the necessary foundation for Rochester's fortune and also for the legacy which gives Jane independence and the prospect of a secure future.

It is true, however, that in one respect Charlotte does reaccent or modify the traditional comparison of Western and Eastern femininity by transferring an Eastern characteristic to the modest English Jane Eyre. The purpose of the harem/seraglio was to provide its Bluebeard, sultan, or Rochester with concubines such as those the latter had sought all over Europe and bought with his slavery-based fortune. The traditional *Arabian Nights* stereotype accepted that the Eastern woman was capable of sexual passion and sensual indulgence. Noticeably Rochester is particularly shocked by this aspect of Bertha's madness and speaks with horror, despite his own promiscuity, of 'the agonies which must attend a man bound to a wife at once intemperate and unchaste' (book 3, chapter 1). She appears to him to be an instance of (perhaps racially induced) nymphomania that William Acton referred to as 'a form of insanity that those accustomed to visit lunatic asylums must be fully conversant with'.[15] Usually such a woman as Bertha would represent the opposite of Western femininity which, if not entirely asexual, is assumed to be limited to stirrings of passion only after marriage.

Here Jane Eyre differs from the stereotype of the ideal Englishwoman. Long before Rochester's proposal she reveals herself as physically attracted to him. Studying him silently during the houseparty, she finds his appearance 'full of an interest, an influence that quite mastered me,—that took my feelings from my own power and fettered them in his'. She feels physically akin to him and senses 'something in my brain and heart, in my blood and nerves that assimilates me mentally to him' (book 2, chapter 2). As yet Jane's yielding to Rochester is still in her mind but she is already an explicitly sexual Scheherazade, resembling in this Caroline Vernon of the Angrian saga, though Caroline responds to Zamorna's physical approaches and Jane merely to Rochester's presence.

Jane's passionate feelings increase the tension as the narrative develops, since they make her task of warding off Rochester ever more difficult, particularly after they have agreed to marry. As a modest and virtuous Englishwoman, she has now to restrain not only Rochester but herself. Strikingly when, after attempting bigamy, he tries to coerce her into becoming his mistress, she is not, as might be expected, deeply shocked. Instead she is moved to sympathy by the 'unchanged love in his whole look and mien' and she forgives him instantly 'not in words, not outwardly; only at my heart's core'. She feels that death would be preferable to 'the effort of cracking my heart strings in rending them from Mr Rochester': again translating what she feels into terms of physical pain. Though she is struggling not to succumb to his pleas, she still has to use the tactics of a Scheherazade: if she is too vehement in refusing, she enrages him; if she is milder, he is encouraged to press her harder. When he talks of his delight in their early days, she is reduced to tears; when he asks her whether it 'is better to drive a fellow creature to despair than to transgress a mere human law—no man being injured by the breach', he is uttering heresy since marriage was regarded as a divine covenant, not a 'human law'. But strangely, Jane accepts his account: 'This was true, and while he spoke my very Conscience and Reason turned traitors against me, and charged me with crime in resisting him' (book 3, chapter 1). This is the climax of the scene: Jane is conquered and she now equates her desire to succumb with the prompting of conscience, so that resisting becomes a heroic act as she persists in her refusal.

This is Charlotte Brontë's triumph: she has effectively represented sexual desire as a central feature of her heroine's character at a crucial moment in the text. In overcoming it, Jane appears as indomitable in her final speech: the stronger the passion she represses, the more impressive her morality, the more womanly her nature. Her final refusal has heroic overtones, uttered, as it is, when her veins are 'running fire' and her heart 'beating faster than I can count its throbs':

The more solitary, the more friendless, the more unsustained I am, the more I will respect myself. I will keep the law given by God; sanctioned by man. I will hold to the principles received by me when I was sane, and not mad—as I am now. Laws and principles are not for the times when there is no temptation: they are for such moments as this, when body and soul rise in mutiny against their rigour. (book 3, chapter 1)

Masculinity

At a time when men and women were allegedly to be naturally and neatly complementary to each other, it was inevitable that texts which challenged the idea of women's separate sphere should also represent men differently. In the construction of gender which prevailed in the nineteenth century, forms of rationality and emotionalism were, as though scientifically, redistributed to male and female respectively. Thus the complementary view attributed to men characteristics which gave them the edge over women in all matters outside the home and set required limits on what women could do in terms of education and work, as well as meaning women had to be kept clear of politics. Chiefly men were represented as more logical, more rational, and more in control of their emotions than (oversensitive) women. It followed that men were natural agents, capable—as women were not—of sound decision-making and effective action. This made them appropriately dominant, legally and as a matter of usage, while women meantime were sheltered in a safe environment under the guardianship of their more rational and intellectually powerful fathers or husbands. Their position at home then enabled them to channel their quick emotions, their power of nurturing into responding to the needs of those around them.

Challenging these accounts could raise a variety of issues—as the Brontës' novels do: Is the attribution of innate, gendered characteristics accurate? Are the qualities so attributed properly viewed separately without reference to questions of balance? Are the assumed differences an adequate justification for a society currently organized to ensure the power of one sex over the other?

In her earliest novel, *The Professor*, Charlotte originally accepts the idea of masculine rationality by making her narrator and central figure, William Crimsworth, a cool pragmatist who sizes up each situation logically and then makes a decision. He is a model hero in that he is born into the gentry, educated at Eton, and gifted with the confidence in his own superiority and his ability to succeed economically that such an upbringing bestows. He is a man who, through self-reliance and perseverance, provides an instance of the type that Samuel Smiles eulogizes in *Self-Help*: though penniless, he rejects the offer of financial provision from his wealthy maternal relatives rather than acquiesce in their snobbery over his 'tradesman' father and treatment of his dying mother. Instead he climbs the worldly ladder through his own efforts and with the networking assistance of the mill-owner Hunsden who helps him to his first teaching post in Belgium. Narrating his own rise, he records in detail the increasing size of his salary which finally enables him to settle back comfortably in his English home in Daisy Lane with a half-English wife.

Charlotte, however, builds into Crimsworth's account evidence of his need for more feminine qualities in which he is evidently lacking. His indifference to others, except as objects, is demonstrated by his assessment of his female Belgian pupils in terms of whether he regards them as attractive or not. He finds them uniformly lumpish and animal-like, whereas he is flattered greatly by the evident infatuation of the school's proprietress, Mlle Reuter, whom he also despises. Her sychophantic behaviour grows on him to the extent that he even envisages a possible liaison with her. His callousness is only melted by the appearance of a teacher who is a model (half-)English woman, Frances Henri, whom he describes in terms of a charm so modest that he virtually asks to be given credit for noticing it. The contrast between Frances and Mlle Reuter produces an epiphany for Crimsworth as softer feelings erode his self-centredness. It is as though feminine empathy is infectious and he sees now what he has been doing in reacting to the Belgian woman:

I had ever hated a tyrant; and, behold, the possession of a slave self-given, went near to transform me into what I abhorred! There was a sort of low gratification in receiving this luscious incense from an attractive and still young worshipper . . . When she stole about me with the soft step of a slave, I felt at once barbarous and sensual as a pasha. (chapter 20)

The implication here is that Frances has introduced him to sensitive insights and feelings of delicacy which women instinctively feel, so that he has become a better, more upright person—a kind of nineteenth-century 'new man'.

This narrative of the 'feminizing' of a callous man was to become a familiar strand in certain novels later but in *The Professor* it does not remain uncomplicated. Towards the conclusion of the novel it begins to lose its clarity, as the last chapters show Crimsworth and Frances living, after ten years of marriage, in a comfortable English setting, close to Hunsden's estate with their young son Victor. The boy is the locus of a struggle: Crimsworth sees the 'feminine' softness introduced into his upbringing by Frances as undesirable and wishes to turn Victor into a tougher, more masculine creature. While Frances sees Hunsden as a malign influence, Crimsworth wavers unhappily between the two, half-deploring, half-pleased by a streak of incipient aggressiveness in the boy. This leaves the novel finally ambivalent as to the necessary balance of 'masculine' and 'feminine' qualities in any personality. The ambivalence is increased by the curious representation of Hunsden himself who, on his first appearance, is described as 'feminine', looking now with 'the mien of a morose bull, and anon that of an arch and mischievous girl' (chapter 4). The images suggest that a mixture of masculine and feminine, as here, is something grotesque, a reading supported by the unease that Hunsden generates in his attachment to a young man he barely knows but constantly supports and assists while verbally deriding his own affection.

In later novels the issue of innate characteristics is directly challenged by Charlotte as well as by Emily and Anne. All three represent central male figures as blatantly emotional rather than rational in the persons of Heathcliff, Rochester, and Huntingdon. Heathcliff, given his poverty and humiliation as a child, can be said to make a logical decision when, after losing Catherine to the Lintons, he resolves to revenge himself on them and on the Earnshaws. His decision develops into a long-term plan effectively carried out to take away the wealth and property of both families by some legitimate means. Heathcliff resists the temptation to take revenge by the use of physical violence and instead chooses a method which leaves him socially dominant and financially secure. So far, so rational, but what fuels both Heathcliff's plan for revenge, and his long perseverance in pursuing it, is a passion for Catherine Earnshaw which he cannot control even when she willingly marries another man. Though their relationship is never consummated and she bears Edgar's child, Heathcliff continues his belief that she belongs to him by right and he is, leaving aside morality or happiness, as strictly logical as Macbeth in pursuing his objective. His passionate attachment leads at the same time to wildly erratic behaviour: he unearths Catherine's body on the day of her funeral and later persuades the sexton to remove the side of her coffin to facilitate a kind of necrophiliac reunion, when he is buried beside her.

It might be argued that, for all his gentlemanly appearance latterly, Heathcliff's murky origins mean that he does not meet the criteria for English masculinity and so can be left out of the equation. It is hinted, though neither confirmed nor discounted, that his moral blackness is matched by the blackness of his race. When bringing him to the Heights, Mr Earnshaw describes him as an object 'as dark almost as if it came from the devil' (chapter 4). The Lintons believe him to be a gypsy or 'a little lascar'—the child of an East Indian seaman. Isabella, after their marriage, hears him praying for Catherine to a God he confounds 'with his own black father' (chapter 17). If he were certainly a member of a black race, then contemporary accounts of that race would find his irrational passion only to be expected but the question of Heathcliff's origins is never resolved and he remains to cast doubts on the rationality of English masculinity.

Rochester, by contrast, is without doubt represented as the English ideal of a gentleman, who has inherited a large estate as a result of his elder brother's death. His is rich, travelled, cultivated, universally respected and accepted as a magisterial overlord. He is a man of decision, efficiency, and power, good at handling difficulties rationally since he has dealt with a mad wife neither by scandalously leaving her nor by publicly placing her in an asylum but by securing her secretly in a fashion which, as he sees it, allows him to behave like an unmarried man. He has similarly dealt with his ward Adèle, who may or may not be his illegitimate daughter, by secluding her in the country with a governess. He controls Jane's activities as Adèle's governess to the extent that he can summon her at will to entertain him with her spiky spiritedness to a superior. His sense of mastery is matched only by his assumption that this control over others is entirely appropriate to him. Equally he is at ease with his research on European mistresses which finally convinces him that no one can come up to the criteria necessary for his sexual partner except an Englishwoman like Jane Eyre.

A pivotal scene occurs, however, on the day after his attempted bigamy when his behaviour reveals another aspect and he becomes indignant that Jane will no longer kiss him because of what he sees as her mistaken belief that he is 'the husband of Bertha Mason'. He is outraged by the fact that she has 'as good as said' that he is 'a married man', though this would appear to be a reasonable judgement after Mason's intervention at the wedding. Despite all that has happened and the fact that Jane has remained till now locked in her room, he is confident of her intentions: 'You intend to make yourself a complete stranger to me; to live under this roof only as Adèle's governess' (book 3, chapter 1). Arbitrarily he proposes as the only alternative that he should bribe Grace Poole to keep Bertha safely locked away while he and Jane Eyre retire to his more secluded estate, Ferndean. He anticipates no refusal from her and regards 'that fearful hag' Bertha as no longer his wife, a view he thinks so rational that, once Jane fully understands the position, she will accept it. His argument, put at length with a detailed account of Bertha's misdemeanours, is that this wild, mad, lustful woman's behaviour has nullified their marriage. He can, he believes, now make Jane his wife without a legal ceremony.

Undoubtedly Rochester's pre-emptive decisions are all based on a passion as uncontrollable as Heathcliff's for Catherine, strengthened by an apparently invincible assumption of his own power to control events. Jane's restraining responses go unheard: he will not hear what he does not wish to know until her resistance eventually enrages him to a Heathcliff pitch: 'His fury was wrought to the highest: he must yield to it for a moment whatever followed; he crossed the floor and seized my arm, and grasped my waist. He seemed to devour me with his flaming glance'. Jane, despite her passion for him, is still rationally able to say 'mentally, I still possessed my soul, and with it the certainty of ultimate safety' (book 3, chapter 1). This central episode completes what was, in conventional terms, role reversal. Rochester as much as Heathcliff is at the mercy of his emotions since, blinded by his sense of power, he cannot accept that, in his position as a rich man and someone of rank, he cannot control events. This suggests that it is the mere possession of social mastery from which arguments for men as superior arose; men are powerful *because* they are superior.

A similar way of thinking is perhaps the most prominent characteristic that Arthur Huntingdon evinces in *The Tenant of Wildfell Hall*: for him, too, a position of power makes absolute control a right. He is a rich man, in control of a large estate, a wife, son, servants, and a circle of male friends who are his satellites and throughout the narrative it is not reasoned consideration that determines any of his decisions or actions but appetites impulsively gratified. Unlike Heathcliff and Rochester, he has had no long-term plan; he acts on his immediate wishes and gives no thought to the consequences or to the future. When Helen meets him, her aunt already describes him as 'deficient in sense' to the extent that he leads a life of excessive drinking, gambling, and sexual promiscuity. He is already a profligate but by no means what Rochester would call 'a plotting profligate', yet on the strength of a brief physical attraction, he marries a woman of strict religious principles and narrow experience even though she is, as one of his friends advises, someone with 'a will of her own' who 'could play the vixen' (chapter 25). The marriage interferes with his later liaisons and leaves him subject to lengthy admonishments as to his vices from a disenchanted wife until, as a form of provocation, he trains his infant son to develop a taste for alcohol and induces would-be repenting friends to return to drinking and gambling. Throughout all this dissolute existence he maintains absolute confidence in his own invincible charm: he expects his wife to tolerate his mistresses and is convinced that she cannot hate him so long as he claims to love her. He attributes her anger to mere jealousy and is unmoved by Lowborough's fury at the seduction of his wife, showing his callous unawareness of the feeling of others as an almost psychopathic egotism.

These critiques of supposed complementarity between men and women take on a wider significance when they are considered as strands in the novels' structure because complementary spheres were supposed to produce domestic harmony in the middle-class home. On the contrary, *Wuthering Heights* and *The Tenant of Wildfell Hall* reveal the disastrous consequences of the imbalance of power that results from separate spheres. The very structuring of the two novels makes the point through the fact that each makes the narrators participants in the narrative, a practice that survives from the roles the Brontës adopted in their juvenilia, where the children took on the identity of specific individuals. This creates a story within a story and what looks like a frame around the events in the narrative. In both novels the structure is complex: in *Wuthering Heights* the auditor of Mrs Dean's account is Lockwood who is also the outer narrator. In both novels the predicted domestic harmony is replaced by horrors matching those in Gothic novels within the families represented, which are revealed by the two women. Both give accounts of unfettered male dominance resulting in aggression, mental cruelty, and violence: Hindley maltreats Heathcliff; Heathcliff in turn brutalizes Hindley's son, Hareton; Hareton strikes Cathy; and the servant Joseph is aggressive and abusive to all save his master. As Eagleton says, violence is 'endemic' to the Heights.[16] Similarly Huntingdon's cronies frequently become aggressively drunk; Hattersley seizes his mild-mannered wife, Millicent; her brother Walter Hargrave responds by knocking him down; Huntingdon seduces Lowborough's wife and laughs at his distress. Most crucially, Gilbert Markham in a fit of jealousy attacks Helen's brother with a riding whip and leaves him seriously injured, lying by the roadside.

This narrative structure provides a frame around the Gothic horrors of these domestic lives, inviting a contrast between the male and female narrators, as the latter describe the sensational events and the former participate in them. Lockwood appears at first to be an entirely innocent onlooker but his visit to his landlord, Heathcliff, disturbs this picture as he resolutely ignores the hostility and aggression evident from the moment he sets foot there. Hence his ludicrous assumption that Heathcliff is a hospitable host and the Heights a cosy refuge; and his avid taste for details of the feuds and violence that Mrs Dean is able to provide. His deliberate disengagement mirrors his own account of his behaviour to the woman with whom he fell in love before renting the Grange: when she responded to his advances he 'shrank icily into [him]self like a snail' and fled to this remote place. His apparent mildness gives place to indications of a capacity for violence as he dreams of the first Catherine's ghost and wrenches her wrist along broken glass until it bleeds. In this way he can be seen to collude with the violence he is so ready to ignore.

An even more extreme statement is made by the structuring of *The Tenant of Wildfell Hall* where the first-person narrator, Gilbert Markham, eventually replaces Huntingdon as Helen's husband. The interweaving of his long courtship with the story of her horrific first marriage and the death of her first husband invites a further comparison: that between the two men. An innocent reading would expect to see the two men as contrasted but, on the contrary, it is striking how similar they are since Markham shares many of Huntingdon's masculine characteristics, with his vain, arrogant, hot-tempered, and domineering habits. As his behaviour to other women such as Eliza Milward and her sister shows, he treats them as inferiors, there to serve and flatter him, while the violence he inflicts on Helen's brother in a jealous rage is more vicious than any physical cruelty in *Wuthering Heights*. His nature is the same as that which produced the domestic hell from which his future wife fled and she finally appears to marry a man as capable of mistreating her as her first husband.

Some have argued that Markham is softened and feminized *à la* Crimsworth by reading Helen's diary but there is no real evidence of this. As Tess O'Toole points out, however, the contrast provided by the structure of the novel is not that between first and second husband but that between relationships with sexual partners and with a male sibling.[17] The only benign relation that Helen enjoys with a man is that with her brother Frederick. It is he who provides her with shelter and support when she flees from her husband with their son and assumes a family name. Compared with the drunken and unfaithful Huntingdon or the jealous, mistrustful, and violent Markham, Frederick is resolutely helpful and calm. Not even Markham's unprovoked attack moves him to bitterness or desire for revenge. This does not imply that the brother–sister relationship is a panacea for the ills that undermine marital happiness: it merely indicates how men like Huntingdon and Markham relate to women with whom they are already, or hope to be, in sexual partnership.

It is perhaps superficially surprising that Charlotte (who, in *Shirley* particularly, makes such a strong case against the idea of the limits that the dogma of complementarity sets on women) should not also attack so forcefully the contemporary construction of masculinity. But the answer surely lies in her taste for masterful Byronic heroes such as Zamorna and his surrogate Rochester, and in Rochester's surrogate M. Paul. Throughout Jane's sparring with the former and the similar teasing of the latter by Lucy Snowe, the women take pleasure in the dominance of the two men. As N. M. Jacobs has accurately put it, Brontë 'eroticized the very dominance/submission dynamic from which she longed to escape'.[18] In all her novels she equivocates finally on the question of male–female equality in a marriage. It is even possible to read the end of *Jane Eyre* as suggesting that such equality is only made possible by the mutilation of the masculine which Rochester's injuries may seem to signify. A relevant image is offered by the incident in *Villette* where Lucy Snowe takes the part of a man in the school play. In doing so, she finds a sense of freedom which, while distorting the play, allows her to vent her real feelings about Graham Britton by outshining him as Ginevra's second suitor: 'Retaining the letter . . . I recklessly altered the spirit of the *role*' (chapter 14). The equivocation comes with her attitude to her dress for the part, for playing a man gives her the freedom she wants but when asked to dress completely as a man she refuses. She keeps her woman's dress but clothes the upper part of her body as a man with vest, collar, and cravat. The symbol catches perfectly Charlotte's ambivalence on the question of male–female equality which underpins the contemporary view of women.

CHAPTER 6

THE BRONTËS AND THE PSYCHE:
MIND AND BODY

Reading the Mind

THE aspect of science which most engaged the Brontës was that which related to the health of body and mind. At a time when mortality rates were so high in industrial areas it is not surprising that their father, who claimed to have given much attention to medicine while at Cambridge, was preoccupied—if not obsessed—with physical and mental health. This, along with the death of his wife and two eldest children within thirteen years of his marriage, explains his concern for the health of his four remaining offspring and his much-used copy of Thomas John Graham's *Modern Domestic Medicine* (1826). This volume included notes by Patrick indicating the use of some of the recommended remedies for his children and showing also his fears for their mental health.[1] Such concern proved well justified by the depressions and other disturbances suffered by Charlotte, Emily, and Branwell. Patrick signalled concern for his own physical health by the white silk cravat which, wrapped round and round his rather long neck, gave him such a distinctive appearance.

As has been shown, the first half of the nineteenth century was a time of great interest in mental health and consequently in mental disturbance or madness: protopsychiatry/alienism was developing and so too was serious work on the nervous system and its connections with the brain. In the process of examining links between mind and body, there was more at stake than the question of bringing mental disturbance under the control of medical doctors. In the eighteenth century it had been understood that mind and body were related by reciprocal influences: that much was evident to the naked eye since, clearly, injury to the head, or drunkenness, showed body affecting mind: and grief at bereavement, loss, or disaster clearly could produce visible effects on the body. The tradition of Ophelia turning mad for love never faded, though it went through many transformations. Caroline Helstone in *Shirley* is such an Ophelia when, grieved by Robert Moore's apparent indifference, she goes home 'in good health' but awakes 'oppressed with unwonted languor' and develops first a fever, then prostration, and finally a puzzling debility (book 1, chapter 1).

Such a connection between body and mind had implications beyond the medical which included matters of gender, class, and hence politics. In the eighteenth century the mind–body link had consequences for the contemporary construction of sanity and insanity, deriving from a belief that the power of reasoning and given knowledge were gifts from God. When in proper control therefore, reason—made of these two components—acted as a conscience separating right from wrong. But by the early nineteenth century the process of reasoning had for many replaced the idea of given knowledge as the supreme faculty of the mind and essential guide to conduct.

Since men were supposed to be endowed by nature with more reasoning power than women (who made up for the lack with more sensibility and quicker emotions), it was derogatory to describe any aspect of a man's personality as 'feminine'. When Crimsworth says of Hunsden in *The Professor* that he seems in part like a girl, he is being singularly insulting in suggesting a weak emotionalism. This defect in women was attributed by doctors to their reproductive function: their less-than-benign uterine system left them at the mercy of their menstrual cycles and its mental repercussions.

Further, the 'paternal' relationship supposedly existing between men and women was thought to parallel that between upper and lower classes in a newly industrialized society. Like women, the working classes had less intellectual and more volatile passions than their betters. For their own good and that of society, those like Luddites, rioters, and Chartists, who were capable of collective madness such as had been witnessed in the French Revolution, needed to be restrained or, as Roy Porter puts it, 'Just as the mob threatened the breakdown of law and order, so madness would shatter the individual when inflamed appetite, fanned by imagination, rebelled, usurped Reason's office, and became ruling passions'.[2]

Hence the progression in society towards bringing mental disturbance under medical control in asylums and hence also the ambiguous role of imagination for Charlotte Brontë. The extension of medical practice to mental as well as physical health was prefaced by the development of the two pseudosciences which, from 1770 onwards, claimed to make specific the link between body and mind and to provide diagnostic tools: physiognomy and phrenology. Physiognomical science, as has been said, claimed to read character through detailed examination of facial features according to a pre-determined list of types of nose, mouth, eyes, brow, etc., to each of which a value was attached. Value was attributed in general terms which distinguished between upper and lower parts of the face: upper features (eyes, forehead) were markers of intellectual faculties; lower features (mouth, nose, chin) were indicators of 'the organs of sense'. Within this broad division, varieties of individual features were listed and assigned an intellectual or emotional meaning. Since the method could be applied to groups such as male–female or black–white races, it could be used to justify accounts of men and whites as rational and women and blacks as more affected by emotion and the senses.

The use of facial detail as a medium for describing character naturally became part of the novelist's repertoire. By contrast, earlier novelists including Jane Austen rely more on action or narratorial comment. Austen, for instance, when introducing Marianne Dashwood in *Sense and Sensibility*, says plainly, 'She was sensible and clever; but eager in everything; her sorrows, her joys could have no moderation. She was generous, amiable, interesting: she was everything but prudent' (chapter 1). Such directness is very different from Charlotte Brontë's technique for indicating individual character. Her description of Hortense, Robert Moore's sister, in *Shirley* relies heavily on physiognomy: 'The lower part of her face was large in proportion to the upper; her forehead was small and rather corrugated' (book 1, chapter 5). Translated, this means she is a stupid woman with limited reasoning powers and is directed by feelings and emotions. Caroline Helstone, on the other hand, exudes more positive qualities, with her upper face prominent: 'her face was expressive and gentle; her eyes were handsome, and gifted at times with a winning beam that stole into the heart' (book 1, chapter 6). From this we are to infer that she is gifted with intellectual qualities including the important characteristic of 'benevolence'. Caroline's friend, Shirley Keeldar, is less transparent, with features 'whose changes were not to be understood all at once'. They are 'distinguished; by which I do not mean that they were high, bony, and Roman, being indeed rather small and rather slightly marked than otherwise but, . . . "fins, gracieux, spirituels" ' (book 1, chapter 11), i.e. delicate, benign, intellectual.

Evidently the Brontë sisters were up to scratch in how to read the face and both Charlotte and Anne make use of physiognomy as, in a general way, does Emily. Anne's most pointed use of it, however, is to ironic effect in *The Tenant of Wildfell Hall*, when the infatuated Helen Graham asserts that her own perception of the notoriously dissolute Arthur Huntingdon is more accurate than that of her worldly wise aunt. Claiming to be an excellent physiognomist, she says, 'I always judge of people's characters by their looks—not by whether they are handsome or ugly, but by the general cast of the countenance'. She illustrates her skill by adding, 'I should know by your countenance that you were not of a cheerful, sanguine disposition; and I should know by Mr Wilmot's that he was a worthless old reprobate, and by Mr Boarhams's that he was not an agreeable companion, and by Mr Huntingdon's that he was neither a fool nor a knave, though, possibly, neither a saint nor a sage' (chapter 16). In the event, after marrying him, she discovers that he is both fool and knave with an unquenchable thirst for wine, women, and gambling, and a habit of corrupting his infant son for the sake of entertainment. More unobtrusively in *The Professor* Charlotte slips in what proves to be a telling reference to the appearance of Mr Hunsden, Crimsworth's self-appointed mentor. At their first meeting, Crimsworth notices only Hunsden's general appearance apart from the fact that he has a very markedly 'retroussé' nose (chapter 3). This turns out to be a suggestive detail since, according to the physiognomical textbooks, a snub and turned-up nose is said to be a sign of a 'pert' or 'impudent' person which suits well a man whose entry into Crimsworth's life and subsequent reappearances are unprovoked and intrusive.

Though phrenology grew out of physiognomy, phrenologists did not claim the same legibility for the skull that physiognomists found in the face: they saw the external configuration of an individual head 'only as a system of signs to be decoded in order to determine what lay below'.[3] The decoding required expert knowledge of how to compare the size of bumps to each other and to the whole before an assessment of the faculties and a coherent interpretation of them, such as that for Miss Fraser, aka Charlotte Brontë, produced in 1851. Earlier the stomach and later the heart had been regarded as the seat of the emotions but the phrenological view firmly established the brain as the organ of the human mind. This was clearly put by the best-known British phrenologist George Combe, who saw as the core of the new science the fact that 'particular mental powers are indicated by particular configurations of the head', though from reading them it is not possible to produce a specific action.[4]

By examining the skull the phrenologist could identify various faculties, each defined as a mental power of reasoning or feeling in distinct ways. A 'mental organ' was said to be the mechanism for each faculty, 'a material instrument by means of which a faculty acts and is acted upon'.[5] This implies interaction between faculties which can affect each other in ways that are only speculatively predictable. Combe likened the brain to 'a musical instrument—a pianoforte, having various strings',[6] each string representing a faculty so that in different combinations they could produce different results. Such a system provides scope for the phrenological expert to describe several possibilities latent in each faculty or resulting from interaction with another. Quite how the mind and the body linked together to manifest the results of all this was a question which the new study of neurology sought to answer by the physical examination of the nervous system. For the Brontës and others one important consequence follows from the diversity of faculties: that they could be conflicting instead of harmonious and create the kind of psychological struggles which are central to the novels. This means that phrenology, unlike physiognomy, offered a flexible approach to the novelist.

Its terms and theory were as familiar in the discussion of individual psychology as expressions like depression, schizophrenia, and paranoia are today. It is in this language that the Brontës characterize people and their states of mind. In phrenology the terms used were placed in three different categories by theorists: Feelings, Intellectual Faculties, and Reflective Faculties. The names are somewhat misleading for Intellectual Faculties cover the five senses of taste, touch, hearing, smell, and sight, along with the capacity to perceive matters like form, size, weight, and colour. The Reflective Faculties listed by Combe are the ability to compare and make analogies. This leaves most of what we might think of as mental faculties under Feelings,

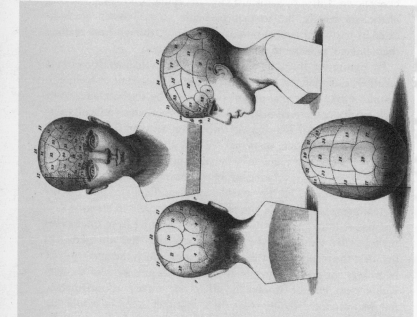

The rules of phrenology as Charlotte knew them, from Combe's *Elements of Phrenology*

NAMES
of the
PHRENOLOGICAL ORGANS
referring to the figures indicating their
RELATIVE POSITION.

I. Propensities.

1. Amativeness
2. Philoprogenitiveness
3. Concentrativeness
4. Adhesiveness
5. Combativeness
6. Destructiveness
7. Constructiveness
8. Acquisitiveness
9. Secretiveness

II. Sentiments.

10. Self esteem
11. Love of approbation
12. Cautiousness
13. Benevolence
14. Veneration
15. Hope
16. Ideality
17. Wonder
18. Conscientiousness
19. Firmness

III. Intellect.

19. Individuality { 1. or higher
                   2. or lower
20. Form
21. Size
22. Weight
23. Colouring
24. Locality
25. Order
26. Time
27. Number
28. Tune
29. Language
30. Comparison
31. Causality
32. Wit
33. Imitation

which are divided into Propensities, or impulses to action—like amativeness (which produces sexual feeling), destructiveness, and acquisitiveness—and Sentiments like benevolence, veneration, self-esteem, firmness, conscientiousness, hope, wit, cautiousness.[7] These are evidently so familiar to the Brontës that they can make casual use of them: in *Shirley* the Rector, taunting a curate for his credulity, accuses him of having 'an enormous organ of Wonder' (book 1, chapter 1) and Shirley is said to have too little of 'the Organ of Acquisitiveness' (book 2, chapter 11).

Charlotte, however, generally uses phrenological material more forcefully, though one can discount the idea that she saw in it a potentially dangerous theory, as apparently some others did. Shuttleworth quotes a contemporary who regards it as a form of social levelling and as a potential source of disruption aimed at 'rendering the great mass of this community discontented with the existing relations of society'.[8] Phrenologists like Combe, however, made it quite clear that they did not assume all human beings were equally endowed at birth. Yet Charlotte did use the technique to justify her own xenophobia towards Belgians by representing Crimsworth as noticing signs of vicious capability in the skulls of his pupils at the school in Brussels. One of them, Caroline, is said to have lips and eyes which reveal her sensuality: 'promise plain was written in her face of much future folly' (chapter 10). Another, Adèle, has 'Suspicion' and 'sullen ill-temper' marked on her forehead, 'vicious propensities in her eye', and 'envy and panther-like deceit' about her mouth. Mingled with such facial features are descriptions of the typical skulls of these girls and women: Adèle has a head which is 'so broad at the base, so narrow towards the top', with thus little space for the intellectual faculties which are located at the front of the crown; another pupil's skull has 'precisely the same shape as Pope Alexander the Sixth', a Borgia renowned for corruption and intrigue: 'her organs of benevolence, veneration, and conscientiousness, adhesiveness, were singularly small, those of self-esteem, firmness, destructiveness, combativeness, preposterously large' (chapter 12). This skull of 'penthouse shape ... contracted about the forehead and prominent behind' is evidently a characteristically Belgian shape and could hardly be worse. Benevolence is one of the most benign faculties which produces the desire of the happiness of others, disposes to compassion and active benevolence, and consequently to the smooth-running of society. Equally the lack of veneration bodes ill for a harmonious society since it represents 'the sentiment of respect and reverence' thought to glue together a hierarchical, class-based society dependent on deference to one's superiors. In lacking conscientiousness also the Belgians are seen to be without a proper sense of right and wrong.

Their lack of benevolence and veneration is shared by the Radical Hiram Yorke in *Shirley*, a fact which explains his total lack of warmth towards others, the result of an arrogant consciousness that no one is superior to him. It is also noticeable that the unlikeable and egotistical Mme Beck in *Villette* has a head which is very revealing to Lucy Snowe: 'her forehead was high but narrow; it expressed capacity and some benevolence but no expanse . . . Her mouth was hard . . . her lips were thin' (chapter 8). Her benevolence, as the narrative shows, extends no further than her own self-interest which is the origin of all she does.

The capacity to bend phrenology to support nationalistic prejudice in this way is equally illustrated by Crimsworth's reading of his English pupils and the half-English, half-Swiss Frances Henri who eventually becomes his wife. The English girls have 'more intellectual features' (as well as better posture) (chapter 12) than the Belgians and it is evident that Frances has superior qualities shown by a better head: 'The shape of the head too was different, the superior part more developed, the base considerably less' (chapter 14). The 'superior' part refers to the top of the head but it is also morally 'superior' as the site of intellectual abilities and benevolence. When Crimsworth praises Frances's character, however, he describes her as a model of 'discretion and forethought, of diligence and perseverance, of self-denial and self control', along with firmness, activity, and enterprise (chapter 19). These are essentially prudential rather than benign qualities and he evidently chooses to see them in the woman he loves because they are precisely those which he would like to possess himself, as the tools that Samuel Smiles recommends as the route to economic success.

Smiles's insistence on individuals as free agents crystallized a general social opinion and was at the same time particularly appropriate to the rise of the realist novel with its exploitation of the vicissitudes of the self of heroes/heroines, as they experienced a moral education. Such novels fitted phrenological accounts to the economic and political ideologies of capitalist society with '*homo economicus* as the sovereign individual producer-consumer pursuing his own private profit in the market'.[9] The qualities necessary for success as listed by Smiles—forethought, perseverance, and diligence—all required the exertion of overriding self-control of other faculties. Self-regulation at macro- and micro-level was a crucial underpinning to industrial society and fitted the established view that 'madness meant Reason ambushed by appetite'.[10] The moral management of lunatics as exemplified by the Quaker York Retreat, founded in the 1790s, was essentially an application of the idea of a common duty 'to lead a life of simple rational self-control'.[11] This was the treatment presumably meted out to Ellen Hussey's brother, George, at the Clifton House Asylum.

Crimsworth is a self-defined free agent, yearning to rise financially through his own diligence and perseverance but impeded at first by the 'cautiousness' for which Hunsden reproaches him on perceiving that the young man endures humiliation at the hands of his employer/brother merely to scrape a living. Caution in phreno-logical terms is a sentiment which, if overdeveloped, leads to 'doubt, irresolution, and wavering'.[12] In Crimsworth caution in the shape of prudential calculation at this point overrides other faculties until Hunsden's offer of a letter of recommendation to a source of employment in Belgium pushes him into leaving Edward's employ-ment and travelling to Brussels. Even there money remains his paramount concern when he falls in love with Frances Henri but is unwilling to marry her, even on his present adequate salary. Again later, after they have retired to England on their joint savings, his caution persists in the form of wavering as to whether to accept his wife's view of their son and his future or Hunsden's view.

It is on similarly prudential grounds that Crimsworth settles a minor moral dilemma over Mlle Reuter when she is about to marry his employer, Pelet. He is sexually attracted to her, rather as to some of his Belgian pupils, but decides to resign his post rather than risk anything by remaining a dependent dweller in a house which was soon to be hers. He is convinced that her feelings for him are unchanged: 'Decorum now repressed, and Policy masked it, but Opportunity would be too strong for either of these—Temptation would shiver their restraints'. Neither could *he* resist it since, as he says, he is 'no pope': 'if I stayed the probability was that, in three months' time, a practical modern French novel would be in full process of concoction'. Decoded, this indicates that despite his love for Frances he would not resist the opportunity of an affair with Mme Pelet. His grounds for avoiding this do not relate to Frances but are based on knowing that such affairs offered only 'a delusive and envenomed pleasure—its hollowness disappoints at the time, its poison cruelly tortures afterwards, its effects deprave for ever' (chapter 20).

This is as much of an internal struggle as he ever undergoes and is easily settled. In other novels by Charlotte and Emily struggles with madness take place in individuals which represent a characteristically nineteenth-century rewriting of the tradition of *psychomachia*, a battle between good and evil, virtue and vice, reason and passion, for possession of the mind or soul of a human being. In medieval times it was simplistically presented in the external terms of morality plays where a generic figure of Everyman or Mankind is fought over by vices and virtues, attempting to draw him into their power. Marlowe's *Faustus* shows the battle as both external in Mephistopheles and internal in Faustus' reactions. Significantly, divided selves already occur in the Angria tales, notably in Zamorna torn between strong affection and hatred for his rival Northangerland.

Phrenology was a convenient tool for Charlotte and Emily to depict the turbulent minds of Jane Eyre, Rochester, Lucy Snowe, Catherine Earnshaw, and Heathcliff in what Sir Thomas Browne earlier called the 'Theater of ourselves' or internal drama. Like Charlotte herself, whose mixture of passion and calm is revealed in her letters, Jane Eyre is a creature of extremes, of furious passions and unyielding self-control. As she herself says, 'I know no medium . . . between absolute submission and determined revolt. I have always faithfully observed the one, up to the very moment of bursting, sometimes with volcanic vehemence into the other'. She also realizes that, 'forced to keep the fire of my nature continually low, to compel it to burn inwardly and never utter a cry, though the imprisoned flame consumed vital after vital—*that* would be unendurable' (book 3 chapter 8).

The accuracy of this self-knowledge is borne out at every stage of her life resulting in a characteristic pattern. Her volcanic rebelliousness first breaks out in her stormy childhood at the Reeds where, after enduring bullying, abuse, and humiliation, she finally rebels

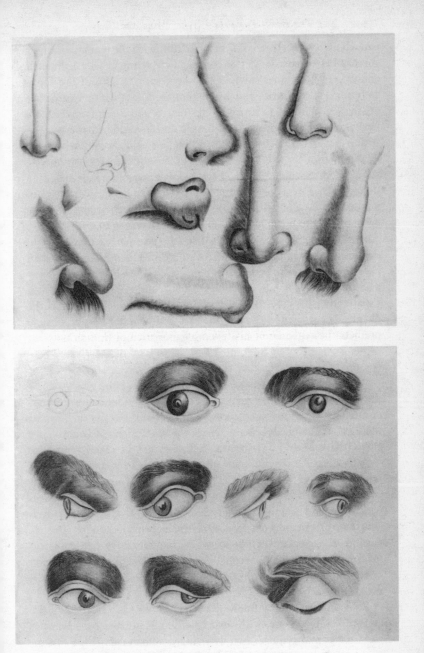

Charlotte as physiognomist: her studies of noses and eyes, c.1831

and, though powerless, confronts her aunt with the truth about how she has been treated. At Lowood her fury at the cruelty to herself and others is suppressed because she comes to admire the long-suffering Helen Burns and Miss Temple, a fact which causes her organ of veneration to expand. This new-found capacity gives her a new respect for fortitude in suffering and holds down the volcano within her. At Thornfield Hall, Rochester quickly recognizes the duality within her which he first sees in 'features and countenance—so much at variance'. Later, disguised as a gypsy fortune-teller, he describes it in detail. He points out that on her forehead (the site of intellectual organs) 'Reason sets firm and holds the reins, and she will not let the feelings burst away and hurry her to wild chasms. The passions may rage furiously, like true heathens as they are; and the desires may imagine all sorts of vain things, but judgement shall have the last word in every argument and the casting vote in every decision. Strong winds, earthquake-shock, and fire may pass by: but I shall follow the guiding of that still small voice which interprets the dictates of conscience' (book 2, chapter 4). Rochester here accurately predicts the outcome of his failed bigamy attempt though not that of her struggle with St John Rivers's proposal of marriage where emotion is given the casting vote.

Rochester himself is revealed as a divided self, as he points out by lifting the hair from his forehead: he shows Jane 'a solid enough mass of intellectual organs' on the crown of his head. But, as she notices, there is 'an abrupt deficiency where the suave signs of benevolence should have been'. This crucial lack does not necessarily produce 'cruelty or any bad sentiment', though it leads to 'regardlessness of others'. In response to Jane's comment that he is not a philanthropist, he argues, 'I bear a conscience' and points to the 'prominences which are said to indicate that faculty' (book 1, chapter 14). Evidently in practice his absence of benevolence proves more effective than his conscience when he shows no regard for the consequences for her if Jane agreed to become his mistress. His intellectual faculty of reasoning also deserts him so that he argues illogically that he is not really married.

Villette depicts Lucy Snowe (originally Frost) as a mixture of fire and ice like Jane Eyre, with sexual passion as fire and conscience as ice. Convention requires her, as a single woman compelled to support herself, to maintain a façade of calm rationality by the exertion of the vaunted self-control inspired by the dictates of conscience. Instead, driven by her passion for Dr John/Graham Bretton, she believes that 'Reason is vindictive as a devil' and claims 'for me, she was always envenomed as a step-mother. If I have obeyed her it has chiefly been with the obedience of fear, not of love. Long ago I should have died of her ill-usage . . . her savage, ceaseless blows' (chapter 21). Unlike Jane Eyre's, her fate is not ameliorated by providential intervention.

The internal conflict experienced by Catherine Earnshaw is in no sense moral. It results from a wish to reconcile the irreconcilable: an acceptance that Heathcliff is 'more myself than I am' and a belief that nothing will change if she marries another man. No resolution of this conflict is possible in either logical or emotional terms, so that the battle rages on with death as its only conclusion.

The Secret Self

Despite the accounts of the mind or psyche given by phrenologists, the self remained as mysterious when the Brontës wrote, as when the poet Thomas Traherne two centuries earlier asserted, 'I have a secret self enclos'd within, that was not bounded with my clothes or skin' (*OED*, self n.). The idea of self had in the intervening period been much contested and reconstructed by philosophers and poets as either a computer-like machine of a limited kind into which data was fed; or a supernatural being or soul; or variants on one of these.

In earlier periods, the inner reality of selfhood was believed to show itself, when normal, in socially acceptable, reasonable behaviour. For the Brontës such behaviour was the result of exercising control over mere feelings, a practice which, as Christians, they saw as the glue which kept the individual adhering to the moral principles laid down by the Church. When passion overtook reason, it was thought to result in abnormal behaviour that marked out the madman. There was a long literary tradition, dating back to Shakespeare at least, with Lear's ravings on the heath, Hamlet's real or feigned madness, and Ophelia going mad for love. For the next two hundred years 'Madness advertised itself in a proliferation of symptoms, in gait, in physiognomy, in weird demeanour and habits. It was synonymous with behaving crazy, looking crazy, acting crazy'.[13]

By the early nineteenth century Romantic poets like Wordsworth and Coleridge, whom the Brontës so admired, were preoccupied with the internal self, challenging reductive views of it. Their account of it laid stress on the creative quality and power of imagination. Coleridge, for instance, wrote a poem called 'To William Wordsworth' with the subtitle 'Composed on the Night after his Recitation of a Poem on the Growth of an Individual Mind'. For such writers the self and its development were 'inner, private and potent'.[14] These ideas, as well as those of the phrenologists, were tools deployed by Charlotte, strengthening her sense of the self as a citadel to be guarded. She at once admired imagination and was uncertain how to reconcile it with the common view of reason as the proper guide to conduct. The belief in a need to hide the self replaced an earlier superstition that to reveal your name to an enemy was to put yourself in his power. Ironically this self-guarding was precisely what the Brontës were doing by using pseudonyms.

They also make much use in the early writings of a literal concealment of identity: in *The Green Dwarf* the hero, St Clair, succeeds in an archery contest without revealing who he is, and later when treacherously imprisoned, is visited by an anonymous figure who turns out to be his judge, Zamorna. In *Mina Laury*, Zamorna's wife visits the house where his mistress, Mina, lives, using the identity of Mrs Irving, wife of a clergyman; Mina in turn cautiously misidentifies herself as the housekeeper and a distant relative of Zamorna; two men adopt false names and identities to visit a woman they have admired from a distance. Name-shifting is evidently routine in Angria and is practised even by the narrator, Charles Wellesley, with whom Charlotte identifies. Also recurrent is the concealment of intentions as Zamorna juggles his several mistresses. In one instance this leads to a deliberate deceit about the true self of Lofty Macara who assures Townshend, knowing it to be false, that 'You know me, Charles, I confess it, my character is at your mercy' (Gérin, p. 93).

Some relate the insistence on keeping the real self secret to what Foucault calls the period's obsession with 'panoptic' institutions like prisons, hospitals, military camps, and schools, which attempted to prevent such secrecy. The name derives from Jeremy Bentham's plan in the 1790s for a prison where the inmates would be under unceasing surveillance since the design contrives that there should not 'be anywhere a single foot square on which man or boy shall be able to plant himself . . . under an assurance of not being observed'.[15] Those in authority could literally survey and control the prisoners' activities by what became known as 'the gaze', an idea echoed in George Orwell's *Nineteen Eighty-four* by a kind of closed circuit television.

Certainly from the 1790s keepers/doctors of the mad controlled or claimed to control their patients by such a relatively humane procedure, presumably by inducing fear. It is reported that Edmund Burke questioned Francis Willis, the doctor treating the mad King George III, about his power of 'instantaneously terrifying [the king] into obedience'. Willis responded by facing Burke across a table lit by a single candle and replying ' "I'll give you an answer. There, Sir! By the EYE! I should have looked at him, *thus*, Sir"—thus Burke instantaneously averted his head and, making no reply, evidently acknowledged this *basiliskan* authority'.[16]

The practice of controlling by the gaze was readily accepted at a time when there was much interest in such techniques as mesmerism which spread to Britain in the 1830s. A pseudoscientific explanation was given for the claim that certain people had healing powers which they could activate by staring into the eyes of another person or by touching them. Even the atheist Harriet Martineau was sufficiently taken with the idea to try it on Charlotte Brontë; and Dickens caused a scandal by acting as mesmerist to Catherine La Rue, the wife of a friend. The nature of the scandal derived from the fact that the ability to control a woman was seen as a sexual threat to her. The power of the eyes to control others is referred to in several of Dickens's novels including *Dombey and Son* (1848) where Florence meets the eyes of the villain Carker, and recoils: 'Florence, meeting his eyes, saw, rather than heard him say, "There is no news of the ship!" ' She is 'Confused, frightened, shrinking from him, and not even sure that he had said those words, for he seemed to have shown them to her in some extraordinary manner instead of uttering them' (chapter 24). At about the same time, in *Mary Barton*, Elizabeth Gaskell, a devout Unitarian Christian, describes the reaction of Mary's aunt, the prostitute Esther, to a look from her innocent niece: 'As if, according to the believers in mesmerism, the intenseness of [Mary's] wish gave her power over another, although the wish was unexpressed. Esther felt herself unwelcome, and that her absence was desired' (chapter 21). This captures a kind of half-belief in the power of the gaze, possible even for Gaskell because mesmerists offered a supposedly scientific explanation of their technique.

Similarly but more emphatically, the power of the gaze is represented in *Villette* to a point where, as Sally Shuttleworth has shown, it dominates the text. Mme Beck's school is clearly a panoptic institution watched over by her sleepless eye as she 'rules by espionage'. Lucy Snowe details her methods: Mme Beck, remaining always mild and amiable, has a 'mass of machinery' to operate by ' "Surveillance", "espionage"—these were her watchwords'. So effective is Mme Beck's system that Lucy claims the school offered 'too limited a sphere: she should have been the leader of a turbulent legislative assembly . . . a first minister and a superintendent of police' (chapter 8). This comment draws attention to how the newly developing police force was seen as a panoptic institution for monitoring behaviour. Certainly this is how the first policemen in novels are represented: Sergeant Bucket in *Bleak House*, a novel published in the same year as *Villette*, intrudes upon and pries into the secrets of the central characters, disrupting their lives in the process.

It has been generally overlooked that Charlotte declares her own preoccupation with the self (rather as Wordsworth did) by adopting the 'I' pronoun for the narrators of three of her novels. In making a central character relate their own story in *The Professor*, *Jane Eyre*, and *Villette*, she appears to pledge that the text will give access to the narrator's interiority, a promise not always fulfilled. The first-person narrator is a device already used in the Brontës' earlier writings where Charlotte participates as Charles Wellesley/Townshend/ Townsend who takes a satirical view of events rather like the narrator in *Vanity Fair* which she so much admired. There Thackeray alternates a third-person narrator with one who participates in events in the novel, such as a dinner party at Pumpernickel where he overhears scandal he later reports.

Among Charlotte's novels it is *The Professor* which shows a central figure obsessed by warding off attempts to penetrate his inner self and who prides himself on the power to conceal it. Far from conducting a revelatory relationship with his readers, he seldom addresses them; and when he does so it is more in the tendentious spirit of Lucy Snowe than with a confessional voice. 'Now, reader,' he says, after meeting Frances Henri, 'though I have spent more than a page in describing Mademoiselle Henri, I know well enough I have left on your mind's eye no distinct picture of her . . . nor could I the first day, and it is not my intention to communicate to you at once a knowledge I myself gained by little and little' (chapter 14).

He conceals Frances's essential self and with his own he is even more protective, consciously seeing his social mask as a suit of armour such as that worn by anonymous and usually victorious knights in the *Morte D'Arthur*. When his brother, Edward, sets the chief clerk Steighton to watch like a prison-warder, he is confident of keeping his selfhood secret: 'I thought he was trying to read my character, but I felt as secure against his scrutiny as if I had had on a casque with the visor down—or rather I showed him my countenance with the confidence that one would show an unlearned man a letter written in Greek; he might see lines, and trace characters, but he could make nothing of them' (chapter 2). When Edward derides him, the sarcasm he utters meets 'a buckler of impenetrable indifference' until Crimsworth tires of 'wasting his ammunition on a statue' (chapter 3). Edward, for all his 'malignity' and 'prying' cannot 'baffle the lynx-eyes' of his brother's 'natural sentinels' of caution, observation, and tact. Instead, says Crimsworth, 'Day by day did his malice watch my tact, hoping it would sleep, and prepared to steal snake-like on its slumber; but tact, if it be genuine, never sleeps' (chapter 4). His armour reappears when he is faced by a class of Belgian girls: 'in less than five minutes I had buckled on a breast plate of steely indifference and let down a visor of impassable austerity' (chapter 10).

Everyone is a threat to Crimsworth, including his mentor, Hunsden, who comments on the fact that Edward has dismissed his brother. Hunsden takes it to be a misfortune and his friend, on 'the whim of the moment', allows him to think so since he is 'not disposed to show the satisfaction I felt on this point' (chapter 6). Crimsworth misleads the other man by not contradicting his erroneous assumptions, delighting in the fact that Hunsden, 'keen-sighted as he was', could not 'penetrate into my heart, search my brain, and read my peculiar sympathies and antipathies'. Instead he lets Hunsden think that Mlle Reuter's marriage to M. Pelet has devastated him and that his fiancée, Frances, is a rough, uneducated working-class girl, 'not feeling inclined to enter into an explanation of the real state of things' (chapter 22).

He contemplates marriage with Mlle Reuter and later thinks an affair possible but she is included in those whom he sees as bent on unlocking his secret self. He is convinced 'that she was feeling after my real character . . . and she wanted to know . . . by what feeling or opinion she could lead me' (chapter 10). He believes that 'she roved round me, baffled yet persevering' until 'her finger, essaying, proving every atom of the casket, touched its secret spring, and for a moment the lid sprung open; she laid her hand on the jewel within'. But characteristically Crimsworth temporarily withholds from the reader 'whether she stole and broke it, or whether the lid shut again with a snap on her fingers' (chapter 12).

The secret self he guards so obsessively is revealed only by his actions and these are not difficult to read since he follows a consistent course in his struggle to succeed. This is precisely the course recommended for the upwardly mobile by Samuel Smiles in the Preface to *Self-Help*: 'to apply themselves diligently to right pursuits—sparing neither labour, pains nor self-denial in prosecuting them'.[17] Perseverance or 'patient purpose' and 'resolute working' are also required.[18] The government must stand back and allow 'individual, action, economy and self-denial to drive a man on'.[19] These are the qualities that Crimsworth demonstrates as he tries first to work for his brother after rejecting 'the patronage' of his aristocratic uncles. Later he finds employment in Belgium as a teacher, first in a boys' school, then additionally in a girls' school until he moves to the top of his profession and can retire on the fruits of his toil and frugality. When he finally decides that Mlle Reuter is hostile to benevolence, devotedness, and enthusiasm, with a preference for dissimulation and self-interest, he appears to be describing the mirror image of himself. It does, indeed, seem to be admiration for her efficiency and prudence as much as her slave-like attachment which attracts him to her. His protection of his inner self appears to be a result not of vulnerability but of a cold unwillingness to engage with others. The values he invokes are those of the classic self-made man in a capitalist society. The narrative shows that the jewel he guards so jealously is composed of precisely the same faculties that he displays to the outside world: ironically, social mask and secret self are identical. The reader is allowed to see through him to his lack of positive qualities.

By contrast with Crimsworth, Jane Eyre lives up to the implicit promise of supposedly autobiographical narrative to reveal her inner self to the reader. From the early stages when describing her childhood, she is frank about the sense of liberation her rebellious fury against Aunt Reed gives her: 'my soul began to expand, to exult with the strangest sense of freedom, of triumph I ever felt. It seemed as if an invisible bond had burst'. But she is equally candid about the sense of guilt she feels afterwards at giving her fury free play, seeing her mind as 'a black and blasted ridge' razed by hatred (book 1, chapter 4). Confusing feelings recur when, after moving from Lowood in a search for 'life and movement', she goes to Thornfield Hall only to find that from the leads of the house she gazes at the skyline and longs 'for a power of vision which might overpass that limit, which might reach the busy world, towns, regions full of life' (book 1, chapter 12). These feelings are shared with the reader but not with those around her.

The same is true of her love for Rochester which long remains unspoken except in her thoughts which are revealed: 'I had not intended to love him: the reader knows. I had wrought hard to extirpate from my soul the germs of love there detected; and now at the first renewed view of him, they spontaneously revived green and strong! He made me love him without looking at me' (book 2, chapter 2). She explains her growing inability to recognize his faults: 'It had formerly been my endeavour to study all sides of his character, to take the bad with the good . . . Now I saw no bad' (book 2, chapter 3).

She records for the reader, as though to an intimate, her introspective and humiliating doubts during the house party with the Ingrams: when he asks for her opinion of himself, he is driven to say coaxingly, 'It would please me now to draw you out: to learn more of you—therefore speak' (book 1, chapter 14). Instead she smiles neither complacently nor submissively and when he again tells her to speak she still remains dumb. The banter that follows his attempts to grasp her true nature is a combination of teasing and evasiveness that deflects attention from her and provides a cover for her increasing attraction towards him. After she accepts his proposal, it becomes a refusal to act the role he tries to impose on her.

Her wariness grows greater after Mrs Fairfax's hint that he may attempt to seduce her before their wedding and she feels a need then to prevent him from perceiving the responsiveness she feels. Again her behaviour is calculated to keep him 'from the edge of the gulph' of seduction with the 'needle of repartee' which works him up to 'considerable irritation' (book 2, chapter 9). In this she colludes with the reader, saying, 'The system thus entered upon, I pursued during the whole period of probation . . . In other people's presence I was as formerly deferential and quiet . . . it was only in the evening conferences I thus thwarted and afflicted him' (book 2, chapter 10). By protecting her secret self she remains in control of her life. This conscious distancing becomes real when she leaves Thornfield after the abandoned wedding. Even at this point she is prepared to share with the reader her most intimate feelings. When she leaves to evade Rochester's proposal that she should become his mistress, Jane has done what she believes is morally right and obeyed the dictates of conscience as provided by reason. Yet, as she tells the reader, she is a conflicted self, torn by guilt for behaving virtuously: 'I abhorred myself. I had no solace from self-approbation: none even from self respect. I had injured, wounded—left my master' (book 3, chapter 1).

Lucy Snowe takes a different route from both Crimsworth and Jane Eyre in her dialogue with the reader, or rather produces something of each which conveys a different effect from either. Her attitude to the reader is strangely hostile, despite the implicit promise of confidences. She inscribes the reader in the text as one familiar with novelistic clichés and expectations of virtue rewarded. As Jane Eyre behaves to Rochester, Lucy behaves to the reader, whom she frequently addresses, by misleading and teasing. On leaving the Brettons she encourages the conjecture 'that I was of course glad to return to the bosom of my kindred . . . Far from saying nay, indeed, I will permit the reader to picture me, for the next eight years, as a bark slumbering through halcyon weather, in a harbour still as glass'. She urges the reader to picture her 'idle, basking, plump, and happy, stretched on a cushioned deck, warmed with constant sunshine'— only to reveal herself cast overboard and drowning with the 'rush and saltness of breezy waves' in her throat and 'icy pressure on my lungs'. Nor is the metaphor translated into the hard facts of eight years of misery but is merely elaborated into 'many days without sun and stars', 'a heavy tempest' with the ship lost, 'the crew perished'. She similarly tells of her visit to London en route to Belgium which 'tried to the utmost any powers of clear thought and steady self possession with which, in the absence of any more brilliant faculties, Nature might have gifted me' (chapter 5). Thus she withholds any positive statement about either her experience or faculties.

Lucy guards her inner self equally from those around her so that, when Dr John notices her careful scrutiny of him and attributes it to 'incautious admiration', she allows him 'to think what he chose and accuse me of what he would' (chapter 10). The reason why she does not confront Mme Beck, caught searching her locked drawers, is that if she were to do so 'there would be nothing for it then but a scene, and she and I would have had to come all at once, with a sudden clash, to a thorough knowledge of each other: down would have gone conventionalities, away swept disguises, and *I* should have looked into her eyes, and *she* into mine'. Left alone, this self-suppression troubles her mind and she weeps as she experiences 'an inward tumult' and 'Complicated disquieting thoughts'. But by the next day self-control takes over, the social mask is restored and 'I was again Lucy Snowe' (chapter 13). With the same caution she does not challenge Mlle St Pierre's and M. Paul's assumption that she has ignored his birthday. Like Crimsworth she feels 'too perverse' to defend herself from any imputation and sits 'insensate as any stone' (chapter 29).

Lucy's ability to conceal the essential nature which constitutes her identity is noticed even by Ginevra who raises the question that in a sense dominates the novel: 'Who *are* you Miss Snowe? . . . But *are* you anybody? . . . Do—*do* tell me who you are?' Ginevra seems to assume the name is an incognito for someone of a social rank that Lucy's humble position is at odds with. Lucy, however, gives her no satisfaction, explaining to the reader, 'As for me, it quite sufficed that I was known where it imported that I should be known'. She believes that self-worth is independent of 'pedigree, social position and recondite intellectual acquisition' (chapter 27).

Obviously it is significant that her true self is revealed to M. Paul whose love relieves what she has described as a state 'loveless and unexpectant of love'. But she refuses to let this be a reason for her finally to reveal the impact of whatever happened to her lover on the voyage home. She tells the reader to imagine their conventional happy ending:

There is enough said. Trouble no quiet, kind heart; leave sunny imaginations hope. Let it be theirs to conceive the delight of joy born again fresh out of great terror, the rapture of rescue from peril, the wondrous reprieve from dread, the fruition of return. Let them picture union and a happy succeeding life. (chapter 42)

The social mask is again intact and the readers, like those around Lucy Snowe, are excluded from her secret self.

Gothic States of Mind

Phrenology provides the Brontës with a framework within which they can indicate the psychological potential of characters who, as the plot unfolds, experience a sometimes conflicted interaction of temperament and events which determines how they develop. Such internal conflicts may in theory be hidden away in the secret self since they threaten the ability to keep within the limits of sanity by the exertion of will-power. But by the 1830s it was believed that sometimes signs of madness could break through the social mask to become as visible as Bertha Rochester's or Heathcliff's in the final stages of *Wuthering Heights*. Even if this did not happen, it was now thought that expert diagnosis could detect the inner disorder.

Both partial and complete insanity are on display in the Brontës' novels viewed together. In representing these states the authors drew, to powerful effect, on the Gothic novels they had devoured in their youth. In such earlier works the evil and supernatural powers which threaten men and women, usually in a grimly colluding landscape, actually exist. In *Jane Eyre*, *Villette*, *The Professor*, and possibly *Wuthering Heights* the terrors and apparently unnatural events are the perceptions of disturbed minds. Such depictions represent a shift in the Gothic from external to internal happenings. At a time when mental disorders were imperfectly understood, the Brontës managed to evoke them vividly by a process of displacement onto the outside world of the sufferer. The authors see the world 'unromantic as a Monday morning' transformed into a Gothic horror by troubled minds. They change the clinical diagnosis of contemporary mad-doctors into pictures of life as the temporarily- or permanently-mad see it.

The most frequent disorder that Charlotte depicts is a form known at the time as hypochondria; but not in our sense of excessive anxiety about one's health for she was evidently familiar with the description in her father's medical compendium:

Hypochondriasis, low spirits or vapours, is a certain state of the mind accompanied with indigestion, wherein the worst evils are apprehended upon the slightest grounds, and the worst consequences from any unusual feeling of even the slightest kind; and in respect to such apprehension and feelings there is always the most obstinate belief and persuasion.[20]

Already in 1846 Charlotte was attempting to see mental disorder from the sufferer's not an observer's viewpoint. In a letter to Margaret Wooler about her brother Thomas Wooler, she writes of him as a man who 'For ten years has felt the tyranny of Hypochondria—A most dreadful doom far worse than that of a man with healthy nerves buried for the same time in a subterranean dungeon'. Here she is evidently drawing on her own experience at Roe Head school when she described 'the concentrated anguish of certain insufferable moments and the heavy gloom of many long hours—besides the preternatural horror which seemed to clothe existence and Nature—and which made Life a continual waking nightmare . . . the morbid nerves can know neither peace nor enjoyment—whatever touches—pierces them' (*Letters*, i. 505).

In Charlotte's novels individuals several times diagnose, or misdiagnose, hypochondria. Rochester thinks that he discerns it in Jane Eyre the night before his intended bigamy when Jane, sensing something wrong, wishes that 'this present hour would never end'. Rochester, anxious for the marriage ceremony to be safely over, replies defensively, 'This is hypochondria, Jane. You have been over-excited and over-fatigued' (book 2, chapter 10). Another controlling man, Dr John, makes a similar misdiagnosis in *Villette* when Lucy tells him of the 'ghostly' nun she has seen in the attic. In fact the 'ghost' is Ginevra's lover de Hamal, but Dr John, the medical expert, is sure that 'This is all a matter of nerves . . . a case of spectral illusion: I fear, following on and resulting from long continued mental conflict'. He believes moreover that 'Happiness is the cure—a cheerful mind the preventive: cultivate both'. Lucy, looking back on this episode long afterwards, comments sardonically that 'No mockery in this world ever sounds to me so hollow as that of being told to *cultivate* happiness'. She reduces his suggestion to an image of happiness as a mere potato (chapter 22).

An accurate diagnosis of hypochondria is made in *Shirley* not by a medical expert but by the back-biting Mrs Yorke who sees 'hypochondriac fancies of the rich and idle' in Caroline Helstone after her rejection by Robert Moore. Caroline leaves him to return home 'in good health' only to wake next morning in a state which is 'as if a rock had rent, and in it a grave had opened, whence issues the body of one that slept'. She is like someone that has stood 'face to face with a shrouded and unthought of Calamity, a new Lazarus'. This invitation to, or threat of, death is a recurrent feature of the Gothic states of mind depicted in Charlotte's novels which is almost invariably accompanied by darkness and cold. Caroline's illness takes an icy form as she 'wasted like any snow-wreath in thaw'. She loses all control of her existence, in an absence of any sense of an object to live for, until she finds that her nurse Mrs Pryor is the mother who long ago abandoned her. Their affectionate reconciliation is an instance of Charlotte's remedy for hypochondriac depression: someone to love and be loved by. It works to restore Caroline to sanity and physical health (book 3, chapter 1).

Lucy Snowe makes a similarly accurate diagnosis of hypochondria simply from seeing the King of Labassecour at a concert. Gazing at 'the strong hieroglyphics' of his face, she reads 'those characters written without a hand'. In the 'silent sufferer' she discerns 'a nervous melancholy man' who is visited by 'the comings and goings of that strangest spectre, Hypochondria'. This account, like others in the novels, shows the disease embodied in the form of a powerful and threatening female, as life-destroying as any walking statue. She is either death or the threat of death and is characteristically pale and chill. Lucy reads terrors in the king's face 'dark as Doom, pale as Malady, and well-nigh strong as Death—she freezes the blood in his heart, and beclouds the light in his eye' (chapter 20).

The most revealing descriptions of the malady, however, come from the sufferers themselves—and perhaps most surprisingly from Crimsworth in *The Professor*. Despite his fierce control over his emotions, it snaps after his return to Frances Henri's presence after weeks of prudential absence. He explains it to the reader: 'Man is ever clogged with his mortality, and it was my mortal nature which now faltered and plained; my nerves which jarred and gave a false sound, because the soul, of late rushing headlong to an aim, had overstrained the body's comparative weakness'. It is at such moments as he describes here that Hypochondria comes to call and so she does now: 'A horror of great darkness fell upon me; I felt my chamber invaded by one I had known formerly, but had thought for ever departed. I was temporarily a prey to hypochondria'. Like a discarded mistress she seizes her unwilling victim 'with arms of bone' and takes him to 'her death-cold bosom' (chapter 23).

The familiar sense of darkness and chill descend upon him, enticing him to death:

How she would discourse to me of her own country—the grave—and again and again promise to conduct me there ere long; and drawing me to the very brink of a black, sullen river, show me, on the other side, shores unequal with mound, monument, and tablet, standing up in a glimmer more hoary than moonlight. 'Necropolis!' she would whisper, pointing to the pale piles, and add, 'It contains a mansion prepared for you'. (chapter 23)

He repulses her 'as one would a dreaded and ghastly concubine'. She leaves him but, as subsequent events back in England show, he is always, like the Belgian king, under threat from this demon lover.

Like Crimsworth and the king, Lucy Snowe also shares this experience when left alone in the long vacation after the departure of the child she calls 'the crétin'. At this moment of isolation she seems to see 'the well-loved dead, who had loved me well in life' now 'alienated' from her, 'galled was my inmost spirit with an unutterable sense of despair about the future'. As Caroline Helstone did, she feels 'motive there was none why I should try to recover or wish to live; and yet quite unendurable was the pitiless and haughty voice in which Death challenged me to engage his unknown terrors' (chapter 15). A Gothic horror takes over as a chill and fearful scene replaces the dormitory around her:

the ghostly white beds were turning into spectres—the coronal of each became a death's head, huge and snow-bleached—dead dreams of an elder world and mightier race lay frozen in their wide-gaping eye-holes. That evening more firmly than ever fastened into my soul the conviction that Fate was of stone, and Hope a false idol—blind, bloodless, and of granite core. (chapter 15)

The perception of a subterranean prison, referred to in Charlotte's letter to Margaret Wooler, recurs as Lucy feels compelled to escape 'from under this house-roof, which was crushing as the slab of a tomb' (chapter 15).

Lucy herself thinks she recognizes yet another mental disorder, particularly likely, it was said, to afflict women in erotic or religious forms, when she describes Polly Horne's extravagant love for her father shown by the child's prayers. These are like those of 'some precocious fanatic or untimely saint' and Lucy is confident as to its nature: 'This I perceived was a one-ideaed nature; betraying that monomaniac tendency I have ever thought the most unfortunate with which man or woman can be cursed' (chapter 2). Monomania was a disorder that had been identified as recently as 1839 by the Frenchman J. E. D. Esquirol, whose book describing it was only translated into English in 1845. Despite the name, 'monomania' was not a manic disorder in the extreme sense attaching to the noun 'maniac' at the time. It was said to be an obsessive preoccupation in which 'the understanding is partly disordered or under the influence of some particular illusion, referring to one subject and involving one train of ideas, while the intellectual powers appear, when exercised on other subjects, to be in a great measure unimpaired'.[21]

Ironically Lucy Snowe herself suffers for a time precisely from an erotic form of monomania, of which Dr John/Graham Bretton is the object. She matches in this exactly the contemporary description of those who 'vow a pure, and often secret devotion to the object of their love; make themselves slaves to it; execute its orders . . . and obey also the caprices that are connected with it'.[22] Hence her fetishizing of his friendly letters which, when one is dropped in the attic, she searches for, as she says, 'like a grovelling, groping monomaniac'. While she awaits the first of these letters she creates a torturing mental drama like that of a hypochondriac, in which Reason, the saner aspect of her thinking, appears as the twin sister of Hypochondria. This 'hag' is perceived to be 'laying on my shoulder a withered hand, and frostily touching my ear with the chill blue lips of eld'. Reason now appears in the light of her monomania, as it warns against a too affectionate response to a letter from Dr John, as a creature telling Lucy that 'According to her, I was born only to work for a piece of bread, to await the pains of death, and steadily through all life to despond . . . Long ago I should have died of her ill usage: her stint, her chill, her barren board, her icy bed, her savage ceaseless blows'. Often she turns Lucy out by night 'in mid-winter on cold snow, flinging for sustenance the gnawed bone dogs have forsaken' (chapter 21).

Lucy's monomania is cured by the recognition that Dr John's infatuation with Ginevra has shifted to Polly/Paulina and she conquers it by a burial of his letters. This is an end to the Gothic drama of her obsession as she accepts what Reason tells her and closes 'the eyes of my dead' so as to avoid the indulgence of being 'stabbed to the heart each moment by the sharp revival of regret' (chapter 26).

A factor strengthening her determination to do this has been the sight of the actress Vashti whose performance in a tragedy 'instead of merely irritating imagination with the thought of what *might* be done' (as Lucy has been doing) disclosed a resilience and power to control 'like a deep, swollen, winter river, thundering in cataract, and bearing the soul, like a leaf, on the steep and steely sweep of its descent' (chapter 23). This obscurely imaged sense of power, action, and release sustains Lucy Snowe through a prickly relationship with Paul Emanuel. In particular she survives the opium-induced hallucinations of the night of the fête to resolve the mystery of what is happening around her and finds its 'illusion unveiled' (chapter 38). She no longer sees her world in Gothic terms, even when tempted to do so.

Charlotte also handles the extremes of madness in *Jane Eyre* as well as temporarily disordered states of mind but does so without depicting the inner state of the sufferer. Writing of 'the Maniac' Bertha's derangement to W. S. Williams, she explains,

There is a phase of insanity which may be called moral madness, in which all that is good or even human seems to disappear from the mind and a fiend-nature replaces it. The sole aim and desire of the being thus possessed is to exasperate, to molest, to destroy, and preternatural ingenuity and energy are often exercised to that dreadful end. (*LFC* ii. 173)

So it is Bertha's behaviour that reveals her madness: the insane laughter, the attack on the sleeping Rochester, the bloody injury to Mason, and the tearing of Jane's wedding veil.

In the same letter Charlotte admits that she lapsed in not depicting Bertha as pitiful, and certainly this is true. She appears as a woman 'possessed' by demons, deprived of the precious faculty of speech, thought to distinguish humanity from the beast. Madness is the sole feature of her identity and she is ungendered, in a text sympathetic to women, by the allusions to her as 'it': 'whether beast or human being, one could not, at first sight, tell: it grovelled, seemingly, on all fours, it snatched and growled like some strange wild animal; but it was covered with clothing; and a quantity of dark, grizzled hair, wild as a mane, hid its head and face' (book 2, chapter

11). Like a dog 'the lunatic' tries to seize Rochester's throat until she is wrestled to the ground and pinioned with rope. The cause of her madness is allegedly the nymphomania said by contemporary doctors to be frequently observed in asylums.

Her death in the fire which destroys Thornfield is nonetheless an ambiguous event since she is often seen as Jane's alter ego, physically repressed in the attic as Jane's sexuality is repressed by both convention and self-control. On the other hand, the destruction of Bertha has been read as a catharsis, sweeping away the past, changing and subduing Rochester as well as clearing the way, in practical terms, for the union of Jane and her 'master'. The event can be variously interpreted as an endorsement of the conventional idea that female sexuality is dangerous or as a critique of that view.

But the most ambiguous treatment of extreme mental derangement is Emily's representation of Heathcliff in *Wuthering Heights*. Here the norms are different and, if Lockwood represents the conventional society outside this localized world, it is superficial and trivial-minded. He listens to Ellen Dean's narratives of violence and malevolence as though they were the latest gossip of which he cannot hear too much. In a final irony he is still able to imagine the tempestuous pair, Catherine and Heathcliff sleeping peacefully in a quiet grave. In this way the conventional standards from which most of the characters deviate are themselves undermined. Even Ellen Dean, who knows of Heathcliff's necrophiliac activities with Catherine's coffin and corpse, only sees his behaviour as showing 'a monomania on the subject of his departed idol' (chapter 33).

Emily's account of Heathcliff's final state and death is tantalizingly opaque. He is haunted by an 'unearthly vision' of Catherine beckoning him to join her beyond the grave as Hypochondria invited Crimsworth or Lucy Snowe to death and terror. But it is only through Heathcliff's reaction to Catherine's apparent presence that the vision is revealed and his reactions are difficult to interpret. The sight of her brings 'a strange joyful glitter' to his eyes but, as Ellen Dean describes it, the effect is unnatural: 'the same bloodless hue: and his teeth visible, now and then in a kind of smile, his frame shivering, not as one shivers with chill or weakness, but as a tight-stretched cord vibrates—a strong thrilling, rather than trembling' (chapter 34).

He himself describes his state as fluctuating: 'Last night, I was on the threshold of hell. Today, I am within sight of my Heaven'. The next time Ellen sees him she is terrified not by Catherine's 'ghost' but by him: 'Those deep black eyes! That smile and ghastly paleness! It appeared to me, not Mr Heathcliff, but a goblin'. Not only do pleasure and pain alternate but appear to result simultaneously from what he sees: 'he gazed at something within two yards distance. And whatever it was, it communicated, apparently both pleasure and pain, in exquisite extremes, at least, the anguished, yet raptured expression of his countenance suggested that idea' (chapter 34).

Heathcliff evidently dies as a result of self-starvation and it is not clear whether Catherine is distracting him or forbidding him to eat. On one occasion he dismisses food by saying 'I'm animated with hunger; and, seemingly, I must not eat'. At other times he prepares to do so and suddenly loses interest until Ellen finds him dead with a 'frightful, life-like gaze of exultation' (chapter 34). All this leaves open the question of whether what he sees is a hallucination or a real ghost. Once more an apparently sharp distinction is blurred as though to suggest that the difference between sanity and insanity is not distinguishable.

CHAPTER 7

RELIGION IN THE BRONTËS' WORKS

The Politics of Religion

THE Brontës were fascinated by the power games of political parties and were equally alive to the power struggles taking place between the different forms of Christianity, as these competed for congregations or souls—whichever way they chose to look at it. The competition is given physical form in *Shirley* where the Anglican Whitsun marchers meet those of the Dissenters head-on in a lane. With an irony reminiscent of her Angrian writing, Charlotte describes the clash. The Reverend Matthewson Helstone orders his accompanying band to play 'Rule Britannia': 'The enemy was sung and stormed down . . . as far as noise went, he was conquered'. Helstone then bellows 'follow me . . . not at a run, but at a firm, smart pace . . . keep together:—hold on by each others skirts, if necessary'. They obey with 'cool solid impetus' until the Dissenters in amazement and alarm are 'borne down and pressed back, and at last forced to turn tail and leave the outlet from Royd-lane free' (book 2, chapter 6).

The differing forms of belief existing at the time have already been described and bore a multiplicity of names: Anglicans, Dissenters, Methodists, Calvinists, Evangelicals, Unitarians, Baptists. Anglicans could be High, Broad, or Low Church; and evangelical (or not). Methodists could be Calvinists believing in predestination or not. In addition, individuals could change their views permanently or temporarily, as Charlotte did when she feared, at least, that it might be true that only those predestined by God would enjoy heaven for eternity. Patrick Brontë was of course an Anglican clergyman and a moderate evangelical, but he does not appear to have drummed a rigid orthodoxy into his children. As with their reading, he seems to have given them intellectual freedom; and each of them inflects her religious beliefs differently. His patriarchal dominance does not appear to have extended beyond practical matters until he became disabled in old age and forbade his only surviving child, Charlotte, to marry his curate Arthur Bell Nicholls.

The picture always before the eyes of evangelicals like Charlotte and Anne was the question of whether they were saved or not saved. It exercised both Charlotte and Anne quite strongly though Emily's preoccupations are less clear and certainly did not include this problem. Charlotte, in particular, underwent a period of religious doubt in the 1830s when she appeared to be troubled by a nervous anxiety about whether her life made her worthy of salvation. She tells Ellen Nussey how every New Year's Day presents to her 'a train of very solemn and important reflections and a question more easily asked than answered . . . How have I improved the past year and with [what] good intentions do I view the dawn of its successor' (*Letters*, i. 120). This suggests a focus on good works and proper states of mind that recurs repeatedly along with some questioning of whether she can stick to her good resolves. It is often feeling rather than actions which trouble her. Later she compares herself adversely with Ellen:

I could not help wishing that [my own] feelings more nearly resembled yours: but [un]happily all the good thoughts that enter [my mind] evaporate almost before I have had time to [as]certain their existence[,] every right resolution which I form is so transient, so fragile, and so easily broken that I sometimes feel I shall never be what I ought. (*Letters*, i. 122)

Three years later she is still anxious: 'I can *see* the Well of Life in all its clearness and brightness; but when I stoop down to drink of the pure waters they fly from my lips as if I were Tantalus' (*Letters*, i. 144).

These doubts occur in a framework of belief which allows her to feel that, difficult as it is, she can choose to pursue salvation. Worse than this anxiety, however, are the other doubts which less frequently cross her mind when it seems to her that according to the Calvinistic doctrine salvation is only for those predestined to it:

I keep trying to do right, checking wrong feelings, repressing wrong thoughts—but still—every instant I find—myself going astray . . . I have . . . a dread lest if I made the slightest profession, I should sink into Phariseeism . . . In writing at this moment I feel an irksome disgust at the idea of using a single phrase that sounds like religious cant—I abhor myself—I despise myself—if the Doctrine of Calvin be true, I am already an outcast. (*Letters*, i. 154)

Here she is interpreting her faults not just as lapses but as signs that she is predestined to damnation.

Anne for the most part seems to have been calmly confident of the individual's ability to choose and earn salvation. Some months before her peaceful death, however, she wishes to take an even more benign view. In a letter to a clergyman, David Thom, who articulated a third account of who was to be saved, she wrote:

I have seen so little of controversial Theology that I was not aware the doctrine of Universal Salvation had so able and ardent an advocate as yourself; but I have cherished it from my very childhood—with a trembling hope at first, and afterwards with a firm and glad conviction of its truth. I drew it secretly from my own heart and from the word of God before I knew that any other held it. (*Letters*, ii. 160)

This way out of the dilemma that haunted her sister was based on a theory that hell was a temporary clearing house and that all humanity will ultimately be saved. This win-win approach clearly suited Anne. Taken with Charlotte's reactions, it suggests that the varying views among evangelical Christians as to who would be saved depended on individual temperament.

One opinion of Patrick's that Charlotte in particular absorbed was intense suspicion of Roman Catholicism, though both he and she were in favour of Catholics having equal rights with other citizens. Charlotte's antipathy towards Rome does not seem to be doctrinal: it is the institution that she finds hateful and yet, it must be said, almost irresistible. She sees it as the British saw the Russian KGB during the Cold War but with more alluring trappings. It was felt that women were especially vulnerable to what it appeared to offer, often with the implication of a seductive power that was not entirely metaphorical. When *Villette* was written, there already existed a genre of novels portraying Catholic attempts to seduce women into the Roman Church. They included Elizabeth Sewell's *Margaret Percy* (1847) and Charlotte Elizabeth Tonna's *Falsehood and Truth* (1841). In both of these, the women in question recognize the Bible as a means of defence. In doing so they are alluding to the Catholic insistence that the interpretation of Scripture must come from priestly instructors while Anglicans held that the Bible as the Word of God was accessible to all conscientious individuals.

In life as well as fiction, Charlotte expressed her mixed feelings of loathing for and attraction to the Catholic Church and its clergy. In 1850 the Pope, for the first time since the Reformation, appointed a cardinal archbishop, Nicholas Wiseman, to be primate of England and thereby began to re-establish the organization of the institution in this country. Charlotte comments on a letter which would now be called his mission statement, in which he expresses his desire to have as his see 'nothing . . . but the back courts and dark alleys and all the human poverty and misery with which they teem'. She claims iron-ically that 'There is nothing jesuitical in this, nothing whatever of the wolf-in-sheep's-clothing'; and even 'the most carping heretic' will not quite dare to ask whether his church 'could not look after this quite as well in a curate's plain clothes as in a cardinal's robes and hat—whether the blaze and pomp of hierarchy is absolutely necessary to the instruction of ignorance and the relief of destitu-tion' (*Letters*, ii. 517). The Cardinal and his cortège were seen with horror by many as the spearhead of papal aggression and there were protests. One of these took the form of a meeting at Leeds where 250 clergymen, including Arthur Nicholls, signed a resolution 'con-demning the Pope for dishonouring the Queen, ignoring the exist-ence of the Church of England and sowing the seeds of strife throughout the land' (Barker, p. 662).

All Roman Catholic priests such as these, whether or not they were members of the Society of Jesus or Jesuits, were assumed to be, in Charlotte's term, 'jesuitical'. The epithet had long since acquired its highly pejorative sense of 'deceitful, dissembling', illustrated by Coleridge's use in *Biographia Literaria* (1817): 'The low, cunning and Jesuitical trick with which she deludes her husband' (*OED*, Jesuitical). Lucy Snowe makes a veiled allusion to Jesuitry in *Villette* when she says that Mme Beck should have been called 'Ignace'. The name is a feminized form of 'Ignatius' with reference to Ignatius Loyola, the sixteenth-century Spanish aristocrat who founded the Society of Jesus. The name is prompted by the revelation to Lucy that Mme Beck, like the Jesuits, controls her institution and those who enter it by surveillance or espionage or spying.

Nevertheless, it is to such a Jesuitical priest, Père Silas, that Lucy Snowe unburdens herself by a mysterious confession during her wretched solitude in the long vacation in *Villette*. There she feels 'the trial God had appointed me was gaining its climax'. Rushing out from the tomb-like school into the stormy streets she feels that 'Any solemn rite, any spectacle of sincere worship, any opening for appeal to God was as welcome to me then as bread to one in extremity of want'. As she enters first the Catholic church and then the confessional, it is evident that she is a woman now vulnerable to the lure of the priest and his practices. She is ripe for seduction in more senses than one since what she craves is the human affection that she perceives in this kindly man with a 'compassionate eye'. The secret nature of what passes between them charges the event with the force of a sexual seduction as she pours out her 'long accumulating long pent-up pain' and finds herself 'solaced'. At this point guilt or, as she sees it, common sense breaks in as the wily priest tells her that 'you have come and poured your heart out; a thing seldom done . . . Were you of our faith I should know what to say . . . It is my own conviction that these impressions under which you are smarting are messengers from God to bring you back to the true church . . . you must come to my house . . . Be there tomorrow morning'. With this revelation of the quest for power over her, Lucy awakes to the danger and silently scoffs at the idea of 'venturing again within that worthy priest's reach . . . As soon should I have thought of walking into a Babylonish furnace'. And yet and yet—she is not entirely free of his influence for she sees 'something of Fénelon about him'—the seventeenth-century archbishop noted for the benevolence and charity which enabled him to convert many to Roman Catholicism (chapter 15).

What was to be feared by a female victim of Jesuitical priests is represented in *The Professor* by the Belgian schoolgirl Sylvie, who is destined for the cloister. Unlike Lucy she has allowed control of her mind and body to pass into the hands of 'some despotic confessor':

She permitted herself no original opinion, no preference of companion or employment; in everything she was guided by another . . . she went about all day-long doing what she was bid; never what she liked, or what, from innate conviction she thought it right to do. The poor little future religieuse had been early taught to make the dictates of her own reason and conscience quite subordinate to the will of her spiritual director. (chapter 12)

Significantly, it is the fear of thought-control that is seen as crucial to the avoidance of the allure of Roman Catholicism and the loss of mental freedom that embracing it entails. Lucy Snowe's encounter with Père Silas enacts the crisis which Sylvie has undergone but with a different outcome: the two, Lucy and Sylvie, are opposite sides of the same coin.

While Mme Beck and Sylvie, Charlotte's two representations of female Roman Catholics, are perfect illustrations of the consequences of Jesuitry, the male figures who parallel them, Père Silas the exponent and Paul Emanuel the male subject, fare better. Père Silas has, unlike Mme Beck, his good side; and Paul Emanuel is almost wholly admirable apart from the flaw of his Catholicism. He reveals its nature when he tells Lucy Snowe how he enjoys spying from his window in the boys' school on the girls in Mme Beck's. His surveillance is not so comprehensive as the latter's, though secretly he does make a regular inspection of Lucy's desk. When this happens, Lucy finds the fact mildly amusing or even flattering, whereas Mme Beck's espionage enrages her. Furthermore she thinks of Paul Emanuel's guilt as lessened by the culpability of the Jesuits who taught him. When she protests that such spying is wrong, he cries 'By whose creed? Does some dogma of Calvin or Luther prevent it? What is that to me? I am no Protestant . . . My rich father . . . was a good Catholic, and he gave me a priest and a Jesuit for a tutor. I retain his lessons'. He insists that his Jesuit system works and that it has helped him to uncover Mme Beck's duplicity. In spite of this, Lucy manages to see him as mistaken rather than corrupt and finally compromises her position by telling him she wishes he were a Protestant (chapter 31).

Lucy does in fact herself become the victim of the kind of Jesuitical conspiracy she fears, plotted by Mme Beck, Père Silas, and Mme Walravens to whose house she is sent on a fictitious errand. The house becomes a metaphor for the Church of Rome with its 'churchlike windows of coloured glass' and its attendant old priest. Lucy finds herself a participant in a hallucinatory 'tale of magic' in an enchanted castle rife with the colour, ritual, and menace of Catholicism. The deformity of Mme Walravens is evidently an image for the Church to which she belongs with her head 'set not upon her shoulders but, before her breast'. She, like her Church presumably, is the Malevola or 'evil-wisher' of the chapter's title, with an appearance of rich pomp redolent of the Whore of Babylon. She wears 'a gown of brocade, dyed bright blue . . . and covered with satin foliage in a large pattern . . . a costly shawl gorgeously bordered, and so large for her, that its many-coloured fringe swept the floor'. She is bedecked with 'ear-rings, blazing with a lustre which could not be borrowed or false . . . rings . . . with thick gold hoops, and stones—purple, green, and blood-red. Hunch-backed, dwarfish and doting, she was adorned like a barbarian queen' (chapter 34).

Lucy is led to 'an oratory', the high altar of this sinister temple where the missal and rosary, emblematic of Catholicism, are surmounted by the portrait of a long-dead beloved of Paul Emanuel whose whole family he is said to support. Lucy is then told by Père Silas that, since the man she now loves gives three-quarters of his income to the surviving family of his last love, he will never be able to marry. This conspiracy, organized by the Roman Church, is designed to prevent Lucy from marrying Paul Emanuel by gaining control of her mind through this strange experience and presenting it as a Christian duty to forget him. It is an episode enacting in a more elaborate form the same kind of seduction as Père Silas tried to initiate in the confessional. Like that event, it reveals Lucy as vulnerable to the temptations of this alien form of religion which works on the senses to control the mind. It supports the suggestion that Charlotte's lifelong aversion to Catholicism was fuelled by a fear that she might succumb to the very forms she logically rejected.

The other contender for power in the religious arena, as the Brontës saw it, used very different tactics of a cruder kind of emotional terrorism. This at least is the impression given by their early writings in which they also scrutinize evangelical Methodist preachers of the fire and brimstone school. It is usually the preachers not the congregation who are their targets. A typical episode occurs in Charlotte's novelette *Passing Events*, written in 1836. A detached narrator reports what kind of sermon the Methodist preacher Bromley gives:

O Lord! A more infernal pack of defiled, depraved, bemired, besotted, bloody brutal wretches never knelt to worship in thy presence! . . . Filthy rags are we, potsherds were with [*sic*] the leper has scraped himself, bowls of the putrid blood of the sacrifices, sweepings of the court of thy temple, Straws of the dunghill, refuse of the kennel, Thieves, murderers, slanderers, false swearers. (Gérin, p. 52)

Sure enough the audience groans an 'Amen, Amen!' of agreement and Bromley then addresses God on their behalf: 'O shed thy grace upon us like a water-spout, wash us, scour us with sand & soap, heave us neck & heels into Nebuchadnezzar's furnace, bound in our coats & hosen, our garments, our shoes & our hat'. Carried away by his rhetoric, Bromley continues with his list adding household equipment such as pillow-slips, fish-kettles, soup ladle. Let all these things, he prays nonsensically, be burnt and, finally losing his thread entirely, he concludes with a meaningless prayer: 'When the fire is raked, let there be plenty of coke!' Even to this the congregation cry 'Amen!' Bromley appears, unlike Ashworth, to have forgotten the necessary plea for conversion. The implication is plain: that the congregation hear only the sound of the preacher's voice and know that they need to groan and cry Amen when it pauses or stops (Gérin, p. 52).

Bromley then introduces a visitor Brother Ashworth (alias Alexander Percy/the Earl of Northangerland, Zamorna's enemy) and Charlotte's alter ego, alias Charles Wellesley, brother of Zamorna, tells what Ashworth does next:

He took his text without opening the bible: 'I came not to save but to destroy . . .' A sermon followed, wandering & wild & terrible; now it was all curse & denunciation, then it diverged into a strange political harangue . . . he seemed to reserve his strength to the conclusion & then he poured it out in a powerful exhortation to a religious revival. (Gérin, pp. 53–4)

The pattern of such sermons is clear: first the congregation are brow-beaten into cursing themselves as miserable sinners; then their emotional state is channelled into an acceptance that they must save themselves by a conversion to 'the truth' as interpreted by the speaker. The psychological warfare proves effective in this instance and the sermon is followed by 'groans, & cries, & ejaculations' of the mass hysteria that Ashworth has worked for.

Unlike Roman Catholics, evangelical Methodists are not assumed in these early writings to be single-mindedly bent on control of their congregations. In *Julia* (1837), another of Charlotte's Angrian works, their pseudo-biblical language is again satirized when they are seen to have more material ends. A preacher, Barlow, breaks into the house of a wealthy opponent of the Methodists on the pretext of protesting at his refusal to allow a meeting in the warehouse he owns. Charlotte, in the guise of Charles Townshend, reveals Barlow's diary entry on the event. Since the owner Rhodes is at dinner, Barlow and his henchmen decide to wait in the servants' hall as they eat. Methodists were supposed to be open to divine guidance and Barlow receives a message from God: 'as I watched them bringing in first a tureen of soup and then a leg of pork & then a pie, vegetables &c, a voice came unto me "arise and eat"—"Thy will be done" I answered aloud'. Thereupon he seizes the soup ladle and helps himself, only to find further inspiration when he has finished the soup. He again hears the voice and feels 'in the situation of Elijah who, as he lay under the juniper tree, was again & again bidden to arise and eat— obeying the supernatural impulse, I cut into the pie, & helping myself to greens, took such sustinance as the body needed—Then whispered my inward monitor "Give unto the men that are with thee". So shaving a few slices off the leg of pork and adding turnips I passed it round' (Gérin, pp. 102–3).

He finally confronts Rhodes, the owner of this mansion, in a scene that anticipates the Reverend Brocklehurst's visit to Lowood School with his daughters, shortly after the arrival of Jane Eyre. Barlow finds Rhodes with his family and guests dining at a table loaded with decanters of wine, china, crystal, and gilt heaped with fruit. Mrs Rhodes is fashionably dressed in 'silks & satins & jewels & feathers'. Barlow sees the scene as a den of Satan where 'his worshippers' are pampered 'with magnificence here, ere he sends them to lament in the burning vaults of hell'. He then preaches a mini-evangelical sermon in the usual bastard-biblical language: 'Go to now ye rich men! Howl & cry for your miseries that are come upon you . . . you will not live long . . . you have nearly filled the measure of your iniquity—repent then while yet it is day . . . The crimes you have committed are black double-dyed—but the Lord's mercy knoweth no limits!' (Gérin, pp. 103–4).

In a similar scene in *Jane Eyre*, the hypocritical Calvinist Brocklehurst, who is based on the Reverend Carus Wilson of Cowan Bridge School, visits Lowood School and pillories Jane as a lost soul, 'not a member of the true flock'. This echoes Wilson's rationale for his treatment of children. Speaking in one of his writings as though to a child whose playmate has died, he gives an explanation of why God has spared his auditor: 'Why? That you may get ready to die. He has let you see a new year. Why? Because he wants you to seek a new heart and so be prepared for heaven'.[1] Brocklehurst also warns the teachers to punish the bodies of their pupils more severely than they are already doing; and to help save their souls by cutting off the girls' hair and even making them eat spoilt food. In this way, he says, they will no longer be feeding their pupils' bodies while starving their immortal souls and encouraging vanity. He is supported by his wife and daughters, 'splendidly attired in velvet, silk and furs' with 'a profusion of light tresses, elaborately curled' (book 1, chapter 7). In this scene Brocklehurst combines the hypocrisy of Barlow with the sins of Rhodes to create a blacker form of satire than in Charlotte's novelette.

A simpler episode reminiscent of the Angrian story is found in the shape of the 'joined Methody', Moses Barraclough in *Shirley*, who is presumably one of the products of the hellfire preachers and who leads the workmen's revolt against Moore's new machinery which will reduce their wages or throw some of them out of work. Like Barlow, he has a material objective but at the same time he is a stereotype of the political agitator who appears in later novels such as Dickens's *Hard Times* (1854) as a trade unionist. Clearly gain not religion is his aim and, like the Roman Catholics depicted in *Villette*, he is cunning and manipulative. Like Mme Walravens or some figure in medieval allegory, his appearance figures his nature: he is 'a broad-shouldered fellow, distinguished no less by his demure face and cat-like, trustless eyes, than by a wooden leg and a stout crutch'. The broad shoulders and stoutness of the crutch imply a threat masquerading as vulnerability, as he tells Moore that he needs to learn the 'unwisdom' of his behaviour over the machines. He adds characteristically that such destruction is 'the Looard's own purpose' (book 1, chapter 8).

Emily Brontë's explicit treatment of Calvinistic forms of Christianity in *Wuthering Heights* takes the extreme form of yet another ignorant working-class man adopting a blind and blundering view. Joseph, first Earnshaw's then Heathcliff's servant, has absorbed enough of Calvin's creed to regard himself as one of the elect, 'chozzen and piked out from the rubbidge' of those around him. This provides an excuse for him to give rein to his native misanthropy by despising his fellows and delighting in their misfortunes. He erupts into the narrative like a verbal Iago willing evil when, during an alarming storm, he prays that God will 'as in former times spare the righteous, though he smite the ungodly'. Later, when Heathcliff sets out to brutalize Hareton Earnshaw, the son of his old enemy Hindley, Joseph encourages him: 'It gave Joseph satisfaction, apparently to watch him go the worst lengths. He allowed that [Hareton] was ruined: that his soul was abandoned to perdition; but then, he reflected that Heathcliff must answer for it. Hareton's blood would be required at his hands; and there lay immense consolation in that thought' (chapter 18).

Like Charlotte, Emily satirizes extreme evangelism as a form of belief that takes a crude hold on the uneducated and unsophisticated by a kind of brainwashing. The more educated city-dweller Lockwood expresses his attitude to this form of religion in the dream he experiences when compelled to spend a night at the Heights. He finds himself in a 'chapel' or Methodist place of worship, forced to listen to the 'pious discourse' of the Reverend Jabes Branderham on the text in which Christ instructs his disciples to forgive the brother who sins against him not seven times but seventy times seven. Branderham subjects his congregation to an interminable account of each of the four hundred and ninety sins involved. At this point, bored beyond endurance, Lockwood imagines himself leaping up, before the preacher can describe the worst sin of all, the four hundred and ninety first (i.e. seventy times seven plus one), to denounce Branderham, urging the rest to 'crush him to atoms'. The latter counters this by crying blasphemously as Pilate is said to have done to Christ, 'Thou art the man!' He then proceeds to interpret Lockwood's act as the four hundred and ninety first which, by exceeding the limit laid down in the Gospel of four hundred and ninety to be forgiven, deserves punishment such as they can now all inflict virtuously. Lockwood, grappling with an imaginary Joseph, is wakened by the mysterious tapping on the window. This dream, though distanced from reality, captures what Lockwood sees as the damaging hostility to other Christians that Calvinism evokes and which is later demonstrated by Joseph's malignity (chapter 3).

The one form of Christianity which the Brontës did not represent as actively engaged in a political struggle for converts is the Anglican, even though the need for a personal form of conversion was preached by evangelical Anglicans like Patrick Brontë. Despite its hostility to the Church of Rome and what it saw as papal aggression, the Church of England did not seek conversions at home in Britain. Missionary work belonged overseas in the colonies such as India where St John Rivers hopes to acquire fame by his heroism as a missionary. The assumption that in this sense Anglicanism was apolitical does not mean that Anne and Charlotte deal lightly with the clergy in their novels.

Religion as Ethics

Though the Brontë sisters were plainly interested in the conflicts between different Christian groups, they were more deeply concerned with their moral teachings as they impinged on the lives of individuals. Charlotte and Anne unhesitatingly accepted the importance of trying to obey the Ten Commandments. But for both sisters Christianity was not simply a matter of signing up legalistically to a set of rules but rather of making choices like Jane Eyre's in the light of the New Testament emphasis on loving one's neighbour. They understood this as a matter of sympathetic emotion as much as of rational decisions.

Ever present in the background as a motivating force for action was the issue of salvation and a future beyond death in heaven or hell. The question of how far the redemption won by Christ's suffering and death extended was answered differently by the various Christian sects. Some believed that it belonged only to 'the elect', those predestined by God to achieve heaven as a reward. Some thought, by contrast, that it would be reached by all who committed themselves to the Christian faith and lived according to its ethical code. Others believed that by some act of divine mercy or perhaps through some painful period of probation in the afterlife, it might be available to the whole of humanity, good or bad. Ironically those who felt that they were among the elect were freer from constraints in their choices and actions than those who thought that they must earn the reward of eternal heaven by their efforts to live a Christian life.

As usual in religious matters, Charlotte, Emily, and Anne differed in their stance on the subject of the afterlife and its connection to the lived one. Emily as ever does not see things in black and white so that her handling of life after death is found in poems which fluctuate like the appearance of an opal. Often her poetry is categorized into two groups: those poems that are impersonal since they derive from the Gondal narrative; and those described as personal because they are independent of a matrix. This division is a mistake since all the poems imply a narrative act out of which they emerge as the voice of an individual in specific circumstances which are hinted at or sketched in. It is this particularity which matters: there is little difference, for instance, between a lament for a named Gondal figure and a similar elegy for anonymous kindred or friends. Each poem is best seen simply as a dramatic monologue or dialogue like those of Robert Browning: the voice of each is a constructed persona, not to be immediately identified as Emily's. Her treatment of redemption is therefore as variable as the speaker's character, mood, and relationship to whoever else is involved in each poem.

Both Gondal and non-Gondal poems cover the same topics of love, loss, suffering, imprisonment, death, desire for freedom, and the need for endurance. They display a spectrum of varying attitudes to belief or hopes about life after death, as they manifest themselves in the emotions of the speaker. Sometimes he/she takes a view that in the future life all will be well:

> But long or short though life may be
> 'Tis nothing to eternity.
> We part below to meet on high
> Where blissful ages never die.
>
> (Gezari, p. 59)

In other circumstances when the lover or friend has committed wicked deeds, the mourner dreads, as orthodoxy dictates, that damnation is to come to the lost one; and sees it as a hideous contrast to the joy felt by angels in heaven at the death of a virtuous Christian:

> Ah with no louder sound—
> The gold harp strings quiver
> When good men gain the happy ground
> Where they must dwell forever
>
> But he who slumbers there:
> His bark will strive no more
> Across the waters of despair
> To reach that glorious shore
>
> .   .   .   .   .   .
>
> Shut from his Maker's smile
> The accursed man shall be
> Compassion reigns a little while
> Revenge eternally—.
>
> (Gezari, p. 109)

A more ambiguous lament for a man who died for his 'idol queen' mingles resentment against the latter with pity for the dead who is damned:

> And this is she for whom he died!
> For whom his spirit unforgiven,
> Wanders unsheltered shut from heaven
> An outcast for eternity—
>
> Those eyes are dust—those lips are clay
> That form is mouldered all away
> Nor thoughts, nor sense, nor pulse, nor breath
> The whole devoured and lost in death!
>
> There is no worm however mean
> That living, is not nobler now
> Than she—Lord Alfred's idol queen
> So loved—so worshipped long ago—.
>
> (Gezari, p. 142)

In a poem thought to refer to the reprobate poet Shelley, there is a passionately willed hope in universal redemption:

> Deserted one thy corpse lies cold
> And mingled with a foreign mould—
> Year after year the grass grows green
> Above the dust where thou has been.
>
> I will not name thy blighted name
> Tarnished by unforgotten shame
> Though not because my bosom torn
> Joins the mad world in all its scorn
>
> .   .   .   .   .
>
> But God is not like human kind
> Man cannot read the Almighty mind
> Vengeance will never torture thee
> Nor hunt thy soul eternally
>
> Then do not in this night of grief
> This time of overwhelming fear
> O do not think that God can leave
> Forget forsake refuse to hear!
>
> (Gezari, pp. 123–4)

One of Emily's best-known poems ignores the question of future life for the lost one to focus instead on how to survive the kind of grief which, unknown to Emily, Charlotte was later to suffer after the death of her last three siblings within a year. The verses suggest not trust in God with prayer but self-generated stoicism:

> Riches I hold in light esteem
>   And Love I laugh to scorn
> And lust of fame was but a dream
>   That vanished with the morn:
>
> And if I pray, the only prayer
>   That moves my lips for me
> Is, 'Leave the heart that now I bear
>   And give me liberty!'
>
> Yes, as my swift days near their goal,
>   'Tis all that I implore;
> In life and death a chainless soul
>   With courage to endure.
>   (Gezari, pp. 30–1)

For Anne Brontë, on the other hand, belief was fixed and she embraces the prospect of universal redemption so strongly wished for by Emily in the 'Shelley' poem. Anne's conviction is not crystallized in lyric form but spelled out in the detailed account of Arthur Huntingdon's life in her second novel, *The Tenant of Wildfell Hall*. The narrative is devoted largely to his career of wild indulgence in alcohol and adultery, culminating in a slow and painful death as a result of his excesses. Consequently his wife, Helen, returning to nurse him, is in the position of the speaker in Emily's 'Shelley' poem and, as a result of her repeated pleas for him to repent his sins, they engage in a kind of doctrinal debate on the question of salvation.

From an early indifference to the subject he moves on to accuse Helen of priggish complacency about her own fate: 'when once you have secured your reward, and find yourself safe in Heaven, and me howling in hell-fire, catch you lifting a finger to serve me *then*!' But he proves not really to believe, as he has asserted, that talk of heaven and hell is all 'a fable' as he now begs her to rescue him, pleading that he wishes he had listened to her earlier. He admits to a fear that it is now too late and to wish that there were no life after death, a clear sign that he is accepting the orthodox view of the need to earn heaven. As though inviting Helen to tell him otherwise, he now argues that it would be hopeless for him to repent after a life of sin: 'Are we not to be judged according to the deeds done in the body? Where's the use of a probationary existence, if a man may spend it as he pleases, just contrary to God's decrees, and then go to heaven with the best . . . by merely saying "I repent"?' (chapter 49).

Since his last words are 'Pray for me', it is open to his wife to think he did repent. Whether he did or not, she believes he will reach heaven in the light of what she has seen him suffer:

How could I endure to think that that poor trembling soul was hurried away to everlasting torment? It would drive me mad! But thank God I have hope—not only from a vague dependence on the possibility that penitence and pardon might have reached him at the last, but from the blessed confidence that, through whatever fires the erring spirit may be doomed to pass—whatever fate awaits it, still, it is not lost, and God, who hateth nothing He hath made, will bless it in the end. (chapter 49)

This conclusion, reached by feelings of compassion rather than logic, matches the exultant tone of Anne's poem 'Music on Christmas Morning':

> A sinless God, for sinful men
> Descends to suffer and to bleed;
>   Hell *must* renounce its empire then;
> The price is paid the world is free,
>   And Satan's self must now confess
> That Christ has earned a *Right* to bless:
> Now holy Peace may smile from Heaven,
>   And heavenly Truth from earth shall spring:
> The captive's galling bonds are riven;
>   For our Redeemer is our King;
>   And He that gave His blood for men
> Will lead us home to God again.[2]

Charlotte is less explicit about who is to be saved and her poems focus on those who have earned heaven by their virtuous conduct, for instance in 'Stanza on the Death of a Christian':

> Calm on the bosom of thy God,
>   Fair spirit rest thee now;
> Even while with ours thy footsteps trod,
>   *His* soul was on thy brow.

Dust to the narrow house beneath
  Soul, to its place on high.
They that have seen thy face in death
  Will never fear to die.[3]

It is clear from their novels as well as their poems that both Anne
and Charlotte attach great value to living a Christian life, though
they position the value differently in relation to the question of
redemption. Each insists also that sympathy and action must combine since imagination or empathy is a necessary part of the make-up
of a Christian. It is seen as particularly desirable in the men like
Patrick who choose to undertake responsibility for the moral welfare
of other Christians. Threats of hellfire or religious duties coldly
performed were not in their view adequate for the clergy on whom
they focused as often (though more briefly) as on the moral choices
made by their central characters.

At the time when Anne and Charlotte were growing up, the
Anglican Church was seen to be in decline in terms not merely of the
size of congregations but also of its significance to the lives of many
of its members. One explanation attributed this decline to the
Church's place in an establishment riddled with privilege and
materialism. A movement grew up calling for the reform of church
endowments, an end to the holding of plural livings, absentee rec-
tors, and inequality of salaries as between vicars and curates or one
bishop and another, regardless of the size of bishoprics. The root of
the problem was evidently how the institution disposed of its wealth
but this was exacerbated by shifts in population which were left
unacknowledged. In effect the Church had become venal from the
centre as individuals with a living in their gift favoured relatives or
protégés looking only for a secure income. As the Earl of Rochester
put it in the eighteenth century, it was often true that such men
would 'hunt good Livings but abhor good Lives'.[4]

As this arrangement impacted on ordinary churchgoers, it meant
ill-kept churches, infrequent services, poorly paid or negligent curates, rich remote bishops living like aristocrats. For the urban poor it
meant either huge, ill-managed parishes or no churches at all. Eventually in the 1830s and 1840s a period of legislative reform began and
an Ecclesiastical Commission was set up to deal with some of these
problems. But Charlotte and Anne, though writing in the 1840s, deal
with the period before reform set in: *Shirley* is set in 1810 and 1811

before reform had sent 'an abundant shower of curates' to the area; Anne dates the events of *The Tenant of Wildfell Hall* to 1827. Though the deepest ethical concerns of the sisters are dealt with in the conflicted feelings of their central characters, they also dealt with the Church as an institution by showing the secularism, negligence, or other moral defects of its clergy.

Shirley, *Agnes Grey*, and *The Tenant of Wildfell Hall* all address the state of individual clerics, most of whom regard ordination as a gateway to a secure income and perform services as routine requirements while behaving in other respects as minor gentry. There are few who perform their duties with passionate conviction and, aside possibly from St John Rivers, only two clergymen take the care of their congregation's spiritual needs seriously: Edward Weston in *Agnes Grey* and Cyril Hall in *Shirley*.

Unlike their worldly fellows, however, these two good shepherds are shadowy figures, presented somewhat mechanically as paradigms of the ideal curate and vicar to set against the rest. The impeccable Weston is presented through the admiring eyes of Agnes Grey who eventually marries him and her admiration is cast in copybook terms: 'He read the lessons as if he were bent on giving full effect to every passage: it seemed as if the most careless person could not have helped attending, nor the most ignorant have failed to understand; and the prayers, he read as if he were not reading at all, but praying earnestly and sincerely from his own heart'. On another occasion she is priggishly pleased by 'the evangelical truth of his doctrine, as well the earnest simplicity of his manner, and the clearness and force of the style' (chapter 10). She records his virtuous behaviour to his flock as he visits the poor, the sick, and the old and backs this up by reporting the views of a blind parishioner and the wife of a man dying of consumption. All these accounts keep Weston as a generic figure and leave him with no characteristics other than unrelenting virtue.

The same kind of official testimonial, more briefly manifest, is used to represent the vicar Cyril Hall in *Shirley*, as the narrator transcribes for us: 'To men of every occupation and grace he was acceptable: the truth, simplicity, frankness of his manners, the nobleness of his integrity, the reality and elevation of his piety won him friends in every grade' (book 2, chapter 3). The only touch of humanity is his popularity with the local ladies who see him as their pope.

Both these men serve as foils to the more interestingly defective clergymen in the Brontë narratives. Both Hatfield in *Agnes Grey* and Millward in *The Tenant of Wildfell Hall* are entirely secularized and the particulars of their defects are vividly detailed. Hatfield is the flamboyant opposite of Weston and, when he conducts a service, gives a theatrical performance as he comes 'sailing up the aisle or rather sweeping along like a whirlwind, with his rich silk gown flying behind him and rustling against the pew doors' to 'mount the pulpit like a conqueror ascending his triumphal car; then sinking on the velvet cushion in an attitude of studied grace'. He removes a bright lavender glove to flash his 'sparkling rings' and 'lightly pass his fingers through his well-curled hair'. Once gracefully settled, unlike Weston, he is ready to 'mutter over a Collect, and gabble through the Lord's Prayer' and deliver a 'studied and artificial' sermon of which Agnes Grey disapproves (chapter 10).

His interest in church matters is restricted to the arid issues of 'church discipline, rites and ceremonies, apostolical succession, the duty of reverence and obedience to the clergy, the atrocious criminality of Dissent . . . and . . . the necessity of deferential obedience from the poor to the rich' (chapter 10). The morality enshrined in the New Testament is less familiar to him than patristic works which enable him to show off his erudition when he quotes them. He sees himself as upwardly mobile and aspires to marry into the local gentry by proposing to Rosalie Murray who contemptuously rejects him.

The Reverend Michael Millward in *The Tenant of Wildfell Hall* is a secularist of a different hue with the attributes of a yeoman farmer rather than a dandified gentleman. He looks the part with his 'tall, ponderous' figure, 'square massive-featured face', and 'powerful limbs' encased in knee breeches and he carries a 'stout walking stick'. This hint of aggression is borne out by a domineering manner since he acts 'under a firm conviction that *his* opinions were always right, and whoever differed from them, must be, either deplorably ignorant or wilfully blind'. His hearty appearance is matched by his appetite for plebeian food and drink: 'malt liquors, bacon and eggs, ham, hung beef, and other strong meats which agreed well enough with his digestive organs, and were therefore maintained by him to be wholesome for everybody' (chapter 1). He takes it as a personal affront that Helen Graham tries to instil a distaste for alcohol into her young son. He describes her action as criminal and, ironically, even finds spurious religious reference to back up his distaste for it: 'Not only is it making a fool of the boy, but it is despising the gifts of Providence, and teaching him to trample them under his feet' (chapter 4). His role as a vicar merely serves to give him a sense of power over those around him.

Far more subtle critiques of contemporary clergy are represented by Charlotte's extended account of Caroline Helstone's uncle in *Shirley* and St John Rivers in *Jane Eyre*. The force of her depiction of these two rests on the indications that in various ways they are apparently dutiful and effective clergymen. Matthewson Helstone's positive qualities ring true: he is a 'conscientious . . . brave . . . faithful little Man . . . true to principle,—honourable, sagacious, sincere' (book 1, chapter 3). There is nothing of the hypocrite about him as there is about Hatfield and Millward; and nothing negligent as there is with the light-headed local curates, Malone, Donne, and Sweeting. His conscientiousness is made clear at the same time as the inappropriateness of his profession: when Helstone comes to chide the frivolous curates he does so with 'more the air of a veteran officer chiding his subalterns, than of a venerable priest exhorting his sons in the faith'. In fact his mission is a military one since he has come to summon the cowardly Malone to help defend Moore's mill from attack by the workers. He chides the curates for their lack of discipline and general slackness and addresses them as their commander-in-chief: 'I come to see Malone—I have an errand unto thee, O captain!' (book 1, chapter 1). Similarly at the Whitsun march he prepares his congregation as for a battle as his company is divided into regiments with each of whom a band is stationed.

In this way Charlotte overlays the priest with the military man and confirms the narrator's statement that 'He was not diabolical at all. The evil simply was—he had missed his vocation: he should have been a soldier, and circumstances had made him a priest'. Interlaced with the account of his conscientious and principled nature are the characteristics that make him unsuitable ethically as a clergyman: he is 'hard-headed, hard-handed . . . stern, implacable . . . a man almost without sympathy, ungentle, prejudiced, and rigid' (book 1, chapter 3). As is evident elsewhere in Charlotte's novels, sympathy, compassion, Christian love for one's fellows are as important as conscientious observance of rules and duties. It is Helstone's lack of these which unfits him for the priesthood and the lack is amply demonstrated in his attitude to women. He cannot 'abide sense in women': he prefers them to be 'as silly, as light-headed, as vain, as open to ridicule as possible; because they were then in reality what he held them to be and wished them to be—inferior: toys to play with, to amuse a vacant hour and to be thrown away' (book 1, chapter 7). His own wife, snatched from his rival Hiram Yorke, was 'of no great importance' to him so that he failed to notice her decline and feels her death 'who shall say how little?' (book 1, chapter 4). This absence of what for Charlotte is a mainstay of Christian ethics cannot be compensated for even by a conscientious and militaristic attention to propriety and order.

There is a similarity between Helstone and the most complex figure of a clergyman in the Brontë novels, St John Rivers in *Jane Eyre*. On the surface he is a deeply conscientious clergyman but, unlike Weston and Hall, is not represented through others' reports but through his relationship with Jane Eyre after her flight from Thornfield. His first encounter with her sets the tone: she has already been turned away from his house by the servant Hannah when he finds her lying destitute on the doorstep. St John arrives to hear her pious words of trust in God and takes her in, telling Hannah 'You have done your duty in excluding her, now let me do mine in admitting her' (book 3, chapter 2). He and his sisters minister to the starving woman and Jane speaks of Diana as 'instinct both with power and goodness' and of both sisters as sharing 'spontaneous, genial compassion'. But she soon notices a difference between sisters and brother, recognizing that St John's kindly treatment, 'evangelical charity', is dictated not by natural human warmth but by a sense of Christian duty. The same is true of his insistence on visiting his parishioners despite distances and severe weather.

The overriding figure for Helstone is that of a military man, the image for Rivers is beautiful but cold as marble: 'Had he been a statue instead of a man he could not have been easier . . . his face riveted the eye; it was like a Greek face, very pure in outline; quite a straight classic nose; quite an Athenian mouth and chin' (book 3, chapter 3). The chill this suggests is reinforced by his cold, harsh sermons which lack 'consolatory gentleness' for they are fuelled by a belief in 'election, predestination, reprobation' (book 3, chapter 4). He himself recognizes this when he tells Jane in a confiding moment, 'I am simply, in my original state, stripped of that blood-bleached robe with which Christianity covers human deformity—a cold, hard, ambitious man . . . Reason and not Feeling is my guide' (book 3, chapter 6). His marble coldness suggests as always cold does for Jane, something which gives pain.

Beneath this chilly surface, however, Jane senses a lack of ease springing from 'a depth where lay turgid dregs of disappointment— where moved troubling impulses of insatiate yearnings and disquieting aspirations. I was sure St John Rivers—pure-lived, conscientious, zealous as he was—had not yet found that peace of God which passeth all understanding'. He is remote from his congregation, from Jane Eyre, and even from his sisters who speak of 'a fever in his vitals' and of how he is 'in some things . . . inexorable as death'. He creates a 'barrier to friendship with him: he seemed as of reserved, abstracted, and even of a brooding nature. Zealous in his ministerial favours, blameless in his life and habits, he yet did not appear to enjoy that mental serenity, that inward content, which should be the reward of every sincere Christian and practical philanthropist' (book 3, chapter 4).

The key to his restless unease is discovered by chance when Jane, asking him to help her find work, tells him she is not ambitious. Startled by her words, he reveals the monumental egocentricity which feeds a desire to make his mark in the world. He describes his present life as it seems to him: he cannot bear 'to live buried here in morass, pent in with mountain—my nature, that God gave me contravened; my faculties heaven-bestowed, paralyzed—made useless'. Later he admits that he made a mistake in entering the ministry: 'its uniform duties wearied me to death. I burnt for the more active life of the world . . . for the destiny of an artist, author, orator; anything rather than that of a priest'. He even confesses to being a 'votary of glory . . . a lover of renown, a luster after power'. Moreover he believes he has the abilities to achieve one of these goals: 'skill and strength, courage and eloquence' (book 3, chapter 5). He has managed to transform his ambition into a religious one by deciding that he is called to be a missionary in India, called by God to achieve greatness there.

In his pursuit of this ambition, St John reveals his ruthlessness, a quality made easier by his marble indifference to others which gives him a Napoleonic focus on his aim. Lucy Snowe in *Villette* believes herself to be the victim of a ruthless conspiracy but, if so, it is one which fails. Jane Eyre falls prey to an attempted manipulation more cunning than the crude play-acting of Père Silas and contrived not by a Catholic but by an Anglican priest who prepares to take over her life. He understands Jane Eyre well and it is he whose investigations bring to light her real name, her relationship with the Rivers family, and the legacy from her uncle. He recognizes her need for a wider sphere than that of a village schoolmistress and attributes to her a restlessness like his own. At the same time his plan depends on her dedication to what she perceives to be her moral duty as a Christian. Once she has divided her legacy and is safely installed as the owner of the family home with him and his sisters, he develops a careful strategy to ensnare her, far more carefully worked out than Rochester's botched attempt at bigamy. He first asks her to leave off her study of German in order to learn 'Hindustanee' with him. His pretext is that having a pupil will help him in learning the language as he will need to go over the elements and fix them in his mind. The real reason is that this is the language he will need as a missionary and the tutor–pupil relationship is a first step on the way to taking control gradually so that she will agree to go with him as his helper. For that purpose he believes it necessary to marry since a wife 'is the sole helpmeet I can influence efficiently in life, and retain absolutely till death' (book 3, chapter 8).

His strategy works to the extent that, as Jane says, 'By degrees, he acquired a certain influence over me that took away my liberty of mind' by requiring much of her and praising her achievement. She finds that she can no longer talk or laugh freely in his presence because she knows that vivacity is distasteful to him. She falls under his 'freezing spell' and 'When he said "go" I went, "come" I came, "do this" I did it'. But already she dislikes the increasing servitude and when he starts to give her also the nightly kiss he gives his sisters, she feels 'a seal affixed to my fetters'. As her sense of imprisonment grows worse, she finds herself wishing more and more to please him even though by doing so she must 'disown half my nature, . . . force myself to the adoption of pursuits for which I had no natural vocation' (book 3, chapter 8).

Having worked on her in this way and by pious exhortation to a life of duty, he reveals his plan and is met by a plea for mercy as though it were not within her power to refuse. But he knows 'neither mercy nor remorse' and mixes tyranny with flattery, telling her she is both very gentle and very heroic, until she feels an 'iron shroud' contracting around her. Jane is well aware that he is fascinated and attracted to the beautiful Rosamond Oliver but is crushing these feelings to procure a wife he does not love who can become the unpaid assistant he needs. When she continues to refuse marriage he subjects her skilfully to a silent disapproval he knows will disturb her. Or changing his approach, at evening prayers he prays for those (of whom she is presumably one) that have strayed from the fold by failing in their duty and who (like her) are brands to be saved from burning in the fires of hell (book 3, chapter 9).

His pursuit of her consent is unceasing and, like a skilled interrogator, he changes tactics to mild and earnest in the manner of 'a pastor recalling his wandering sheep—or . . . a guardian angel watching the soul for which he is responsible'. Jane bends under the ceaseless pressure and, as he embraces her, she almost feels he loves her: she was able to 'resist St John's wrath' but 'grew pliant as a reed under his kindness'. But before she can commit herself she hears Rochester's voice calling her, despite the distance between them, and recognizes it as 'the work of nature'. It is her 'time to assume ascendancy' and she leaves Rivers abruptly (book 3, chapter 9).

This emotionally icy episode, as compared with the fire of the relationship with Rochester, reveals St John as a man driven by ambition to attempt to convert Jane to his views by cunning manipulation. In Charlotte's terms his behaviour is deeply immoral and more culpable than Rochester's excess of passion. Rigour in performing clerical duties and austerity as regards material comfort do not atone for this warped attitude to his fellow Christians. St John is portrayed as more corrupt than any other clergymen in Charlotte's novels. The admiration for him and his martyr's death expressed by Jane at the end of the novel does not achieve the closure it claims to provide, for it leaves unanswered the major question of ethics posed by this strand in the narrative: St John is a martyr but is he a Christian?

Wuthering Heights and Christianity

Emily Brontë's poems, as has been shown, resist the attempt to extract from them a definitive answer to the contemporary question of who will achieve salvation and heaven in the afterlife and who, if anyone, will suffer an eternity in hell. Similarly *Wuthering Heights* does not provide any moral judgement on the cruel choices and violent actions that take place in the narrative. A major obstacle to such a judgement is created by the complex structure of the work with its two narrators providing a narration within a narration. Lockwood reports mainly at second hand what he has heard from Ellen Dean who, looking back, tells him what she remembers of the Earnshaws, the Lintons, and Heathcliff before he arrived; and later, when he has been away, what happened during his absence. Both narrators are somewhat discredited as reporters and their accounts undermined by what we learn of them as individuals.

Lockwood reveals his vanity and superficiality early on by explaining that his arrival at Thrushcross is the result of his hasty retreat from a woman to whom he was attracted once he perceived signs that she might reciprocate. He even toys with the egotistical notion that he sees a possible replacement for the woman he has deserted in the 'exquisite little face' of the second Catherine, Edgar Linton's daughter. On a later visit, piqued by the girl's evident indifference to him, he consoles himself with the thought that 'Living amongst clowns and misanthropists, she probably cannot appreciate a better class of people when she meets them' (chapter 31). Later still, her affectionate treatment of Hareton irks him still more: 'I bit my lip, in spite, in having thrown away the chance I might have had, of doing something else beside staring at its smiting beauty' (chapter 32).

His reaction to what Ellen tells him and also his obtuseness lead him to read the events of the narrative in a foppishly romantic way as one destined to have a sentimentally happy and peaceful end for the lovers reunited in death. Though Ellen Dean reports what she herself has seen at first hand, she is also an unreliable narrator who interprets events inconsistently, partly as a result of her own role in some of what takes place. She only momentarily realizes that her weakness in controlling Catherine allows Heathcliff to imprison them both at the Heights and to force the girl to marry his son, Linton: 'I seated myself in a chair, and rocked, to and fro, passing harsh judgement on my many derelictions of duty; from which it struck me then, all the misfortunes of my employers sprang'. But this self-knowledge does not last and she manages to suppress the unpleasant realization of her guilt: 'It was not the case, in reality, I am aware; but it was, in my imagination that dismal night' (chapter 27).

The unreliability of Lockwood and Ellen Dean as commentators on the violent events they observe is a contributory factor in the lack of an angle of vision, point of view, or fixed focus in the novel. The critic Lisa Wang, discussing the paucity of scriptural reference, writes tellingly of the absence of an 'underlying Christian and moral ideological framework', creating 'a sense of vagueness—a kind of moral silence in [Emily's] use of theological discourse'.[5] The phrase 'moral silence' is an apt description of a work from which God and Christian ethics are noticeably absent. Some have tried to replace God or to fill the moral silence with a single voice by equating him with the freedom of the moors and the permanence of the 'eternal rocks' beneath them. Wang, on the other hand, reads God back into the text by focusing on the idea that the Holy Spirit or Paraclete is represented by the many allusions to 'death', 'wind', and 'spirit'. She believes it possible to trace, in the use of these words, a manifestation of God as 'an eternal force which moves through all creation', which 'Changes, sustains, dissolves, creates and rears'[6] while others read the novel as a flat denial of the existence of a loving God. All these readings are suggestive of identifiable aspects of the novel but it remains an open and multi-layered narrative which does not privilege any one of these interpretations. In this way it resembles the variations in the poems.

Certainly there is very little in *Wuthering Heights* of the biblical quotation that Charlotte and Anne use so freely. There are only a dozen or so such allusions in all and they are mainly found in the servant Joseph's Calvinistic tirades and the hellfire sermon given by the preacher Branderham in Lockwood's dream. Consequently such references are associated with the extremes of mindless religious intolerance which the two represent. The absence of biblical references helps to make this a secular world in which the only recurring feature of Christian terminology and concepts which remains is the idea of hell (and, infrequently, heaven). The word 'hell' already possessed a non-religious sense of 'a place of extreme misery and suffering' and it is prominently used by all the main protagonists except Edgar. The characteristics attributed to hell in their usage have been plausibly linked to the horrors of the Gothic novels which so fascinated the Brontë children: haunted buildings, graveyards, ghosts, violent deaths, fierce cruelty, dark conspiracies. One nineteenth-century review speaks of how in the novel 'From beginning to end, terror is dominant and we witness a succession of scenes presented in a light resembling that of a coal-fire, some of which achieve the intense horror of Hoffmann's *Majorat*' (Allott, p. 376).

This intertextuality confirms a perception that in *Wuthering Heights* Emily replaces the supernatural framework that goes with Christianity with the preternatural or arbitrary magic world of prophetic dreams, visions, ghosts, and inexplicable events. Heathcliff's names, like Satan's, are legion: he is 'diabolical', 'a devil', 'a lying fiend', 'a hellish villain', 'a goblin', 'an incarnate goblin', and possibly 'a ghoul' that preys on corpses or 'a vampire' that sucks human blood. His uncertain origins and single name reminiscent of the one name for Gilmartin, the murderous devil in that other favourite novel of the Brontë siblings, *The Confessions of a Justified Sinner* (1824) by James Hogg, also suggest a satanic figure. He has 'kin beneath' in the infernal world and fights like 'a legion of imps'. Hareton is possibly 'witched' and Lockwood sees his chamber at the Heights 'swarming with ghosts and goblins'. He sees or thinks he sees the first Catherine's ghost and she haunts or appears to haunt Heathcliff. It is said by locals that she and Heathcliff 'walk' the moor as ghosts after their deaths. As has been shown, throughout the novel the preternatural phenomena are of uncertain authenticity, a fact which helps obscure any definitive reading.

The secularizing effect of substituting the preternatural for the Christian afterlife leaves the novel free to explore the nature of hell as human beings might experience it. In this it relates to Blake's exploration of the elements that constitute hell and heaven in his *Marriage of Heaven and Hell* where he contrasts the body, energy, desire, and freedom he associates with hell, with the soul, reason, restraint, and prohibition he attributes to heaven. But whereas Blake makes a case for the necessity of combining these opposing elements, Emily recreates human hell in experiential terms.

Wuthering Heights is hellish in the obvious sense that it is full of suffering, including the physical violence so often depicted in paintings of Doomsday or the Day of Judgement, but here the devils causing it are members of an extended family inflicting it on each other. Catherine Earnshaw as a child lashes out at those who displease her; so too does her brother Hindley who later cultivates ways of maltreating Heathcliff and even threatens the life of his infant son. Edgar Linton is himself prepared to exert physical violence by proxy through dogs and servants. There are also casual acts of cruelty such as Heathcliff hanging his wife's springer and Hareton killing a litter of puppies.

Against this backdrop of enough familial hatred to provide a Greek tragedy, there is displayed worse suffering of a mental and emotional kind inflicted by individuals upon one another. Heathcliff marries and torments Isabella Linton in order to revenge himself on her brother who now becomes alienated from her. The hanging of her pet dog is carried out deliberately by Heathcliff in order to see how far he can go without disgusting the infatuated woman. But it is the mental suffering created by the strange passion of Catherine and Heathcliff which is the central focus of the emotional torment. It can be read as a transposition of a traditional Christian view that the pains of hell are not the result of fire and pitchforks but solely caused by the absence of the loving God who created the souls now damned for eternity. This is a concept captured in the famous lines in Christopher Marlowe's play *Doctor Faustus* when Mephistopheles bargains with Faustus for his soul. When Faustus asks how is it that, if damned, Mephistopheles is now out of hell and present on earth, his seducer answers,

> Why, this is hell nor am I out of it.
> Think'st thou that I, who saw the face of God,
> And tasted the eternal joys of heaven,
> Am not tormented with ten thousand hells
> In being depriv'd of everlasting bliss?[7]

Similarly, Catherine and Heathcliff define their worst suffering as the mental torment caused by the mere absence of the other. The degree of pain this causes is in fact the measure of their mutual passion: the greater the pain, then demonstrably the greater the passion that is evoked. The two show a belief in the absolute unity of their identity at some deeper level than the physical which others such as Edgar cannot understand. Expressions such as being 'torn apart' seem to them to be literally true. Catherine is the first to assert (in the unlikely context of her revelation that she is to marry Edgar Linton) that Heathcliff is 'more myself than I am' and 'he's always in my mind—not as a pleasure any more than I am to myself—but as my own being'. She sees him as her 'soul' (traditionally an image of God), separation from whom turns her existence into a hell that, like

Mephistopheles', would be always with her. For her a dream of the traditional 'heaven' becomes literally a nightmare: 'I dreamt, once, that I was there . . . heaven did not seem to be my home; and I broke my heart with weeping to come back to earth; and the angels were so angry that they flung me out, into the middle of the heath on the top of Wuthering Heights; where I woke sobbing for joy' (chapter 9). The very location that is so evidently for Hindley, Hareton, Edgar, and others a place of hatred and violence is heaven for her if Heathcliff is there.

Similarly Heathcliff's focus is on the hell she has created for him by the physical absence involved in her marrying Edgar. Whereas Catherine does not believe that anything she does can separate her from him, he feels she has torn them apart in an unnatural way. The full force of his torment is felt when she is dying in Edgar's house and accuses Heathcliff of 'killing' her by his hostility to her marriage. He replies viciously, 'Are you possessed with a devil . . . You know you lie to say I have killed you; and, Catherine, you know that I could as soon forget you as my existence! Is it not sufficient for your infernal selfishness that while you are at peace I shall writhe in the torments of hell?' Catherine's replies capture their estrangement or 'absence' from each other: 'That is not *my* Heathcliff. I shall love mine yet; and take him with me—he's in my soul'. At this point Heathcliff's pain so enrages him that he is transformed from man to beast. As Ellen Dean reports: 'he gnashed at me, and foamed like a mad dog . . . I did not feel as if I were in the company of a creature of my own species'. Finally he indulges in a burst of violent hatred that is indistinguishable from passionate love: 'I have not one word of comfort—you deserve this. You have killed yourself: you loved me— then what *right* had you to leave me—answer me . . . Because nothing, misery, and degradation, and death, and nothing that God or Satan could inflict would have parted us, *you*, of your own will, did it . . . So much the worse for me, that I am strong. Do I want to live . . .—oh God! Would *you* like to live with your soul in the grave?' Then he crystallizes their bond in the ultimate paradox: 'I forgive what you have done to me. I love *my* murderer but *yours*! How can I?' (chapter 15).

Catherine's death removes her not to a Christian afterlife but to an occult world where the spirits of the dead are free to roam and haunt those left behind. Earlier in her delirium she had challenged (the absent) Heathcliff to seek her spirit at Gimmerton Kirk where they often 'braved the ghosts' by daring them to come: 'But Heathcliff, if I dare you now will you venture? If you do I'll keep you. I'll not lie there by myself: they may bury me twelve feet deep, and throw the church down on me; but I won't rest till you are with me . . . I never will' (chapter 12). When Heathcliff learns of her death, he responds as though to this challenge (which he did not hear) with a call to her to come to him: 'Catherine Earnshaw, may you not rest, as long as I am living! You said I killed you—haunt me then! The murdered *do* haunt their *murderers*. I believe—I know that ghosts *have* wandered on earth. Be with me always—take any form—drive me mad! Only do not leave me in this abyss, where I cannot find you. Oh, God? it is unutterable! I *cannot* live without my life! I *cannot* live without my soul!' (chapter 16). Evident in all exchanges between the two, but ignored by critics, is the mismatch in their understanding of the bond between them: Catherine sees it as overriding their physical proximity whereas Heathcliff sees physical closeness as essential to existence.

There is of course no authoritative comment in the narrative either on this mismatch or on whether the relationship between the two is a positive or a negative tie. Ironically in the course of the twentieth century many chose to see *Wuthering Heights* as the world's greatest love story, an assertion that attributes an underwriting of that idea to the author. But the text is far more elusive than such a simple reading presents and overlooks the absence of rapture on the part of the lovers. Many readings suggest themselves but they do so in the form of questions if the whole of the work is taken into account. Is it straining too much to see the novel as the evocation of the ultimate suffering in humans and a metaphorical version of the idea of hell as the absence of a loving God which, by translating it into human terms, illuminates the Christian concept? Or is the metaphor reversed so that the idea of an absent God or heaven is used to represent the torment of human passion which is always ultimately frustrated? Or is the novel arguing that such suffering and hatred rules out the existence of a loving God, a revision of the problem of evil? These and other possibilities offer themselves. Like Emily's poems on loss and separation, *Wuthering Heights* is a prism which refracts light variously: it is not merely open-ended but, like many early twentieth-century novels, an open text. Emily Brontë's attitude to Christianity and morality remains, like so much else about her, uncertain; and there is a sense in which, unlike her sisters, she writes a novel about morality without taking a moral stance but leaves a moral silence.

CHAPTER 8

RECONTEXTUALIZING THE BRONTËS

THE novels of the Brontë sisters, particularly those of Charlotte and Emily, made a great impact on the mid-nineteenth-century literary scene by transgressing conventional limits on what was printable. In *Jane Eyre* this related to issues of sexual morality; in *Wuthering Heights* to the depiction of extremes of emotion and violence, hints of necrophilia, and contempt for the marriage bond; in *The Tenant of Wildfell Hall* to the direct treatment of an alcoholic husband. All of these combined to excite as well as shock contemporary readers. Their effect was increased by the mystery of their authorship under what were rightly assumed to be pseudonyms; and then by the discovery that these narratives were the work of the apparently sedate, spinster daughters of a clergyman. Critics may have recognized the unconventional nature of the works but could not have predicted that these seven novels, whose authors' narrow lives were all ended by 1855, would create a myth which continues to develop today.

At the centre of the mythology were the works themselves, which for over a century and a half have continued to be the source of controversial modifications in stage, musical, operatic, and film adaptations for the large and small screen, as well as for innumerable other 'derivatives'. The term is provided by Patsy Stoneman in her seminal work, *Brontë Transformations: The Cultural Dissemination of Jane Eyre and Wuthering Heights* (1996). These spin-offs have a geographical focus in Haworth Parsonage (now the Brontë Parsonage Museum) and the Yorkshire moors which have become a pilgrimage centre as 'Brontë Country', where commercial businesses have been set up, trading on the Brontë name and the names of the novels.

The Brontë Myth is the title of a critical work by Lucasta Miller published in 2001 but perhaps originates in Terry Eagleton's well-known book *Myths of Power: A Marxist Study of the Brontës* (1975). The myth itself has become complex: though its centre lies in versions of the novels themselves or in adaptations of them, these have often been read as autobiographical. No doubt Gaskell's thrilling biography and the many which followed have been partly responsible for this assumption. The first requirement for myth status is a story that is so compelling in its original form that it is endlessly reinterpreted according to the tastes and concerns of each contemporary society and the literary genre which captures them. This is the fate that has overtaken *Jane Eyre* and *Wuthering Heights* as (frequently second-hand) knowledge of their plots has become widespread and they have reached mythic status, as have the Brontës themselves.

1850–1900 Adaptations and Criticism

Already, within a year of publication, *Jane Eyre* had been transposed into a new medium by adaptation for a stage play; and there followed ten or more dramatic versions with frequent performances both in the United States and in Britain. G. H. Lewes had rightly perceived, when comparing Charlotte's novel with Jane Austen's work, that there were signs in it of what he pedantically called 'melodrame'. It was indeed the sensational plot which caused it to be dramatized since melodrama was the most popular theatrical entertainment of the day and Charlotte's readership was small in a period of limited literacy. *Jane Eyre* was popular in both senses: in terms of numbers who watched it and in that the audiences came largely from the lower classes. The sensational features which the Brontës had inherited from the Gothic novels offered the kind of visual spectacle that audiences craved: the mysterious attacks at night; the violent animal-like figure in the attic revealed as the maniac; the destruction of Thornfield by fire; and Bertha's death.

Charlotte herself is forthright in a letter to her friend Williams about the first dramatic staging of her novel and expressed some fear of what it might be like:

A representation of 'Jane Eyre' at a Minor Theatre would no doubt be a rather afflicting spectacle to the author of that work. I suppose all would be wofully exaggerated and painfully vulgarized by the actors and actresses on such a stage. What—I cannot help asking myself—would they make of Mr Rochester. And the picture my fancy conjures up by way of reply is a somewhat humiliating one. What would they make of Jane Eyre? I see something pert and very affected as an answer to that query. (*Letters*, ii. 25)

Nevertheless she tells her correspondent that she will be interested to hear his account both of the performance and the audience's reaction. His reply, 'though so vivid I seem to realize it all', does not please her and she urges Williams to forget what he has seen: 'I wanted information and I have got it: you have raised the veil from a corner of your great world—your London—and have shown me a glimpse of what I might call *loathsome*, but which I prefer calling *strange*. Such then is a sample of what amuses the Metropolitan populace' (*Letters*, ii. 27). As this last reference to the audience's taste shows, Charlotte has clearly understood that her novel has been adapted for an audience far less educated than that for which it was written, and one unlikely even to have read it.

Though the sensational plot presumably attracted the theatrical entrepreneurs, there were other elements which lent themselves to an existing prototype of interpretation. This model required a class divide with a virtuous but impoverished woman, in need of protection, suffering at the hands of vicious aristocrats. Some critics assume that such plays are a reaction to the unrest and Chartism of the 'hungry forties' and intend by roundabout route to recommend paternalism as a panacea, for the plots routinely show the lowly heroine acquiring a protector in the shape of a reformed member of the upper classes, who is an exception to the general rule of upper-class heartlessness. Such an interpretation reads the plays as parallel to Elizabeth Gaskell's mainstream novel *North and South* (1854) in which a harsh employer learns to treat his workmen benignly through the influence of a good woman. Such works were open to the withering critique made by J. S. Mill in his *Principles of Political Economy* (1848), in which he refers to paternalism as 'the theory of dependence and protection'. He writes ironically that the theory implies that the upper classes 'should prepare themselves to perform conscientiously' this duty and that 'their whole demeanour should impress the poor with reliance on it, in order that, while yielding passive and active obedience to the rules prescribed for them, they may resign themselves to a trustful insouciance, and repose under the shadow of their protectors'.[1]

A paternalistic account of the plays certainly fits the nineteenth-century adaptations of *Jane Eyre*. Jane's lowly status is already a crucial issue in the novel, evidenced by Rochester's condescending manner and the Ingrams' contempt for one who is, as pro-mama, a lady and yet not a lady. But in contrast to Charlotte's account, the Jane of the early plays is not a divided self with a strong streak of rebelliousness but a vulnerable and helpless creature. It is impossible for instance to imagine Charlotte's heroine uttering the soliloquy that her counterpart does in John Brougham's popular play of the 1850s. Left alone after the incident (new to the story) of Lord Ingram's attempted flirtation, Jane stands 'despondingly' in the moonlight and bewails her present existence at Thornfield:

Is this the pleasant change which I had pictured? This is the hard sterile rock my distant hope had tinted over with the softest moonlight. Better, a thousand times better, my solitary cell once more, than to be gibed and mocked at by the vulgar-wealthy; to have the badge of servitude engraved upon my very heart, and know that tyrant circumstance has placed me in a world all prison, where every human being is a watchful jailor, and where you must endure the unceasing lash of insolence, the certain punishment of that stateless but unforgiven crime, poverty. But why should I weep? It is my destiny.[2]

This play roughly follows the original plot: Blanche is discarded; Rochester attempts bigamy; Bertha sets fire to the oratory where the wedding is to take place; and Rochester reveals all by crying out 'My wife!' A year elapses and Jane is seen poverty-stricken and still without relatives other than the Reeds when she hears Rochester calling. She returns to him, still penniless, to become his wife amid assembled peasants who fix 'a device' to his chair proclaiming their blinded master 'The Farmer's Friend'. Jane addresses them for him: 'My friends, he whose ambition is to be the kind landlord, and the good adviser, cannot, alas! behold your kindly glances, but he thanks you for your generous sympathy, as I do from my heart'.[3] Other versions stress the Lowood episode in order to bring out Jane's orphaned and friendless state or make the Rochester figure a patron of widows and orphans or improve his character in other ways to turn him into a suitable (and wealthy) protector for poor but virtuous Jane.

Alongside the plays, in the later part of the nineteenth century serious critical comment on the Brontës' novels opened up a divide which was to continue for nearly a century. These writers and critics practised a form of paternalism, though it differed from that implicit in the dramas. From the late 1860s on, there was a debate about the purpose of literary criticism and the prevailing view was that of the poet Matthew Arnold, who was now Professor of Poetry at Oxford.

He spoke with an almost papal authority in 1865 in an essay on 'The Function of Criticism at the Present Time'. Its function, he asserts, is to carry out 'a disinterested endeavour to learn and propagate the best that is known and thought in the world'.[4] Though Arnold is referring to various intellectual disciplines under the term 'criticism', he focuses on literary criticism. For him the task of the educated literary critic is to classify and rank literary works in order of merit for the benefit of the less knowledgeable sections of the readership. The method he recommends is to decide by comparison between individual works where, if anywhere, each fitted into what came to be called 'the canon'—a term taken from the 'canonical' or authentic books of the Bible as opposed to the unauthentic or 'apocryphal'. They were to do this in order to act as guardians of a precious heritage just as the upper classes were to be guardians of public order and social calm.

Since the Brontë sisters broke upon the cultural scene as literary triplets, it was a natural course for critics to compare, contrast, and rank them in relation to each other. It was widely agreed that Anne came lowest on the list and there was a consensus (of which Arnold was not a part) that Charlotte was the 'best' writer of the three. There was much uncertainty about the status of that oddity or monstrosity, *Wuthering Heights*. Interestingly, in spite of the flurry of stage adaptations of *Jane Eyre*, there appear to have been no similar versions of Emily's novel. Although it had a suitably lurid plot for a melodrama, its grimness, complexity, and the absence of a single viewpoint offered no easy way to adapt it for the popular theatre.

Towards the end of the century, however, the social climate among the middle classes changed in ways that made it possible to view *Wuthering Heights* with new eyes. Amongst other things, high Victorian values in relation to gender and subsequently sexuality were questioned: by this time there were well-developed challenges to the limitations on women's lives which barred them from the vote, the professions, and to a large extent from education. Just enough had improved in some of these areas (though not that of the franchise) for women to scent change in the air and clamour for more. A rebellious Cathy was now an interesting figure whom not everyone would condemn. Civil divorce, rather than one gained only by Act of Parliament, had been introduced in 1857 and women could now sue for divorce: married women had more rights in relation to custody of

children and to financial matters. These and other events made public discussion of hitherto taboo subjects possible and this even
included homosexuality, at least in law courts, when in 1885 the
Labouchère Amendment to the Criminal Law Amendment Act made
private or public homosexual acts a criminal offence. As others have
pointed out, the passing of this Act ironically had the potential to
create a sense of identity among the homosexual community and
certainly gave it a public profile.

Newspapers, periodicals, and literary works all reflected this more
open attitude to sexuality, thereby reducing for some the shock created earlier by Emily's transgressive novel of a woman with husband
and lover who wishes to keep both. In 1898 the *Daily Telegraph*
carried a series of articles by Mona Caird called 'Is Marriage a Failure?'. The answer, at least in the politicized New Women novels of
the 1890s, was uniformly affirmative. Their heroines routinely left
their husbands from choice: on account of the man's syphilis, or his
inability to inspire love, or even because the woman, as in Caird's own
novel *The Daughters of Danaus*, finds marriage 'stupid and degrading'. Such views were not held by the majority of the population but
they changed standards as to what was sayable in print. In fiction,
Hardy's *Tess of the d'Urbervilles* (1892) defended a fallen woman as
'pure'; and George Gissing in *The Unclassed* (1884) represented a
prostitute as respectable and shame-free.

As early as the 1870s serious critics had begun to rethink previous
assessments of *Wuthering Heights* by claiming that it did not deserve
'the wholesale condemnation and unqualified abuse which have been
heaped upon it' (Allott, pp. 392–3). One defended it by arguing the
'very repulsiveness [of the characters] adds to their force' (Allott,
p. 401); and the case was made that, though the novel depicted
human monsters and evil acts, it showed them accurately, 'with all the
vigour, and freshness, the living reality and impressiveness, which
can only belong to the spontaneous creations of genius' (Allott,
p. 400). This is an aesthetic judgement superimposed on what was for
a time a moral issue but the term 'genius' stuck and from then on it has
been unusual for Emily's name to be mentioned without this epithet.

Taking an aesthetic view of Emily's novel allowed critics to be
more detached and comment on matters other than moral issues.
Mary Ward, the novelist, now recognized literary innovation in the
bizarre events of *Wuthering Heights*. She saw in it the influence of the

German Romanticist E. T. A. Hoffmann, with his tales of crime and horror such as *The Devil's Elixir*. She praises Emily for introducing this element into English literature, a 'grafting of a European tradition upon a mind already richly stored with English and local reality' (Allott, p. 457), marvellously fusing the two. She is evidently referring to Emily's significant domestication of horror by her localized settings and by effecting a transformation of Gothic plots. Algernon Swinburne's recontextualizing of the *Wuthering Heights* myth was more personal. His unconcealed taste for sadomasochism led him to read the novel as the expression of a kindred spirit who saw pain and pleasure as inextricably linked. Ironically, this sadomasochistic reading captures the fact that in the narrative the love between Heathcliff and Cathy can only be measured by the degree to which each can inflict pain upon the other.

By 1900 also the novels and the lives of their authors had become intermingled, creating a complex myth at a time when the literary works were commonly seen as the expression of the author's character. This two-sidedness of the Brontë myth is neatly illustrated by Lucasta Miller's anecdote concerning an 'unliterary' friend's question: 'The Brontë sisters—weren't they fictional characters?'[5] Certainly there were plays in the 1930s, such as *The Tragic Race* or *Empurpled Moors*, which dramatized the Brontës' lives in the semi-fictional form now familiar in drama documentaries. These were followed in the 1940s by films which gave free play to scriptwriters to devise suitable stories about the sisters. The best known is *Devotion*, which gives Emily and Charlotte a tangled love life with Mr Nicholls. Another film, *Three Sisters of the Moor*, was never released in full but was used in a twenty-minute version to publicize the Orson Welles–Joan Fontaine *Jane Eyre*. Even as late as 1979 there was a French art film, *Les Sœurs Brontë*, depicting the sisters as languidly drooping beauties and playing up Branwell's vices to suit contemporary taste. To the majority of viewers, who were presumably unfamiliar with the facts of the Brontës' lives, these stories merged with the developing myth.

Anne, Emily, and Charlotte, by Branwell, who erased himself from the central position

From the film *Devotion*, 1946: (l. to r.) Olivia De Havilland as Charlotte, Paul Henreid as the Revd Arthur Nicholls, Ida Lupino as Emily, Nancy Coleman as Anne

divided self goes any challenging of the nature and roles of women in society which appear in *Jane Eyre*. Bad luck, in the form of the reappearance of an insane wife thought dead, is finally disposed of to leave lovers united.

The first adaptation of *Wuthering Heights* for a new medium did not occur for some seventy years after the publication of the novel. It took the form of a silent film directed by A. V. Bramble in 1920 for Ideal Films Limited. This UK version is said in the publicity poster to star Milton Rosmer as Heathcliff, without mentioning the actress who is to play Cathy, an omission that signifies her lack of importance. In keeping with the fact that Emily was now characterized as a genius amongst the intelligentsia, great attention was paid to literal fidelity to the plot of the original. For the first time a Brontë film was shot on location in Yorkshire and attempts were made to find the 'original' settings and buildings, a cumbersome task when heavy equipment had to be drawn by horses through rough country. In addition, as the publicity tells, the director was careful to consult 'the great authority, Mr. Jonas Bradley' in order 'to secure absolute accuracy'. The film does not survive but the British Film Institute holds the synopsis, cast list, stills, and publicity material. From these it can be inferred that, though the events of the narrative are followed in some detail, the film contrives to read them as did educated critical opinion. The Foreword to this archive refers to such views (citing the two critics already discussed):

Emily Brontë wrote her great story at the early age of 29. A year later she died leaving posterity to wonder what her mighty genius would have produced had fate spared her.

The late Mrs. Humphry Ward traced the source of 'Wuthering Heights' to 'The Tales of Hoffmann' . . . It is perhaps more artistically true to suppose that it had its origin in Emily Brontë's own untamed spirit, for as a piece of literature it stands all alone in its vehemence, its intensity, and in what Swinburne called 'the dark unconscious instinct of nature worship' that streaked her passionate genius.

As this account makes clear, the emphasis in this early film does not lie on the love affair between Heathcliff and Cathy. To these film-makers this novel is 'Emily Brontë's Tremendous story of Hate and its Overthrow'. It is seen as Heathcliff's story and his final redemption after a life of bitter hatred.

Possibly in the aftermath of a war which had killed millions, the violence of a novel in which no one is killed or severely injured no longer deterred film-makers from risking the public response to such a story. The synopsis shows the pivotal event in the film to be that in which Heathcliff overhears Cathy confiding in Mrs Dean. She tells her not only that she has agreed to marry Edgar Linton but that she shrinks from the 'horror of marriage with one brought so low' as Heathcliff. The rest of the story tells of his 'remorseless craving for vengeance' because 'on that day deep hatred was born in him'. The central figure's 'culminating act of revenge' is the forced marriage of Linton Heathcliff and the second Catherine; and Heathcliff's 'hate-begotten schemes' collapse only when he recognizes Hareton and the widowed Catherine as happy lovers. The original Cathy remains a relatively minor figure who happens to be the object of Heathcliff's passion.

The denouement develops into the hero's 'redemption' which underpins his heroic status: after his revelation about the young lovers, his face loses its 'hardness' and becomes 'beautified with hope and faith'. Cathy now appears to him as a ghost, he kisses her 'phantom cheek' before she fades away and he dies. Thus, the synopsis concludes, 'the evil in him had perished utterly, and in an all-conquering love—the love of the woman he had now rejoined—he had found the real Power, and the only happiness'.[13]

1930–1970 Films and Criticism

The next major innovation in the medium was the introduction in the 1920s of films with characters who not only moved but talked. Films had by now become longer: there was room for dialogue and scope for spectacle beyond that seen on stage. But the innovation brought difficulties as well as opportunities: how was a film to deal with the narrator implicit even in a third-person novel? Such a narrating voice could comment piously, adversely, or ironically on events and characters or reveal the inner thoughts of those involved. An obvious but uneasy solution was to use a detached voice-over but such a device was at odds with a supposedly realistic medium. Another solution was to allow characters to soliloquize by addressing the camera/audience but this too could prove inept. In the 2004 television version of Anthony Trollope's *He Knew He Was Right* not only major characters but minor ones also reveal their thoughts by direct address to the camera, an odd effect described by at least one critic as distracting and one that for some interfered with the suspension of disbelief.

The problem of how to replace the narrator becomes more complicated when the story is told in the first person and the narrator is a participant in events, as is the case with six of the seven Brontë novels, while *Wuthering Heights* has two narrators with one of them telling the story to the other who is himself partly involved. A further difficulty with Emily's novel is that it is impossible to determine from the text whether important episodes are real or imaginary: is it really Cathy's ghost rapping on Lockwood's window or is he dreaming? does her spirit really haunt Heathcliff and drive him to starve himself to death, or is he hallucinating? With the film-maker able to choose one or other option or to try to recreate the ambiguity, it was usual to opt for real ghosts.

The first 'talkie' adaptation of a Brontë novel was the 1934 version of *Jane Eyre* which, like many other films of the 1930s, bore a distinctive Hollywood stamp. Though it had several features characteristic of an American genre, with a 'romantic' central story and a glamorous female figure, it continued in the spirit of *Woman and Wife* by reducing Jane's significance. In the hands of the director, Christy Cabanne, she becomes an all-American blonde, prettily dressed and of a domestic disposition whose 'sacrificial love-interest' is 'painted in tender colours'.[14] This evidently necessitates the omission of all that happens to the heroine after leaving Thornfield. As in the melodramas, she is single-mindedly virtuous in her dealings with Rochester, showing no signs of internal conflict. Her aversion even to the thought of temptation is captured in a still where, demure in blonde ringlets and gingham, she dismisses with averted look and hand uplifted in rejection the massive diamond necklace proffered by Rochester and his jeweller or solicitor. Reviewers referred to the film as 'tragic' but the tragedy is undoubtedly Rochester's, an emphasis which was to persist.

Cabanne's film was followed several years later by two adaptations of Brontë novels which were to have a lasting influence on subsequent adaptations for the screen and played a powerful role in the transmission of the myths. They are *Wuthering Heights* (1939), starring Laurence Olivier and Merle Oberon, directed by William Wyler;

and *Jane Eyre* (1944), directed by Robert Stevenson, starring Orson Welles and Joan Fontaine. Signs of their classic—even mythic— status are provided by rapturous reviews, reissues, and the videos still available today. By 1948 22,000,000 people are estimated to have seen *Wuthering Heights* and 18,000,000 to have seen *Jane Eyre* but the iconic power of the two films was not the result of fidelity to the texts.

Visits to the cinema were now frequent even amongst the poorer sections of the population, and in the 1930s, as a slump in the British and American economies and the increasing threat of war in Europe darkened the lives of many, films offered escapism of a 'romantic' kind (in the popular sense). This type included what the makers of *Woman and Wife* had called 'the immortal' love story, a phrase suggesting a parallel to the story of Romeo and Juliet. Like that famous story, this one involved the 'tragic' separation of lovers but now with an ending in which love triumphed at last. In these two films such a story was seen as the timeless core of both novels in which supposedly irrelevant material could be adapted or if necessary deleted for the more powerful isolation of the central theme. Charlotte had already provided a happy ending, though of course it needed to be adapted to weed out the implications in the novel of the power relationship between the lovers. Emily's failure to provide such an ending could be made good by representing Cathy's ghost as real, so that she and Heathcliff could be shown finally reunited in death.

The iconic version of *Wuthering Heights* released in 1939 follows the 1920 silent version in making this Heathcliff's film but it was directed now at a mass audience, not an elite. It is a Hollywood production, shot by Metro-Goldwyn-Mayer Studios in California, with specially imported heather from England which in the sunshine grew as high as corn. As a consequence of its Hollywood origins the adaptation becomes allegedly 'one of the most compelling tragic romances ever captured on film'. The fact also that it was written by the sister of the author of the similarly 'romantic' *Jane Eyre* helped the transformation as Emily's strange novel was tailored for mass audiences. The film was made in the run-up to the Second World War: between the Munich Crisis and the start of the war in September 1939, when a grimly violent film of hate would not have gone down well. Instead, in the hands of well-practised film-makers, Emily's novel was revealed as what would have been called 'a weepie'. Sam

Goldwyn, the producer and head of United Artists, had strong views about what the film should be like to satisfy his audience: he turned it into what was immediately described as 'a story of undying love . . . that transcends the gloomy nature of its backgrounds'. Thus the medium determined, in accordance with Goldwyn's wishes, that the lovers should be made more likeable and sympathetic, for Goldwyn could not see 'why an audience would pull for a capricious, irresponsible girl or a hate-filled man bent on revenging his miserable childhood'.[15] Instead Heathcliff is turned into a more acceptably Byronic hero. It is Hindley who steals his horse, not the other way round; there is no threat to the infant Hareton who no longer figures in the story; there is no hanging of Isabella's spaniel, no killing of lapwing chicks; and no hint of necrophilia. In keeping with these improvements, Laurence Olivier's darkly handsome looks are not obscured, his unaccented voice remains attractively throaty, and he appears as something of a matinée idol with a pleasing touch of the bohemian.

Cathy is also toned down as to temperament but her appearance becomes crucial since Goldwyn did not use costumes of the Regency period, the time in which the novel was originally set, but used the Georgian style instead. He believed his preferred period 'was marked by fancier dresses for the women and [he] was eager to show off Merle Oberon in beautiful costumes'.[16] Spectacle was clearly a primary concern and all that remains of the class struggle outlined by Eagleton between the wealthy landowner and the nameless gypsy-turned-entrepreneur is the contrast between the Heights and the Grange. The Heights is a gloomy workaday place, the Grange an escapist fantasy of desirable luxury which Heathcliff and Cathy first glimpse from the outside. They look in on an elegant room where guests in stylish evening dress engage in graceful dancing to the sound of a small orchestral group. Later, after marrying Linton, Cathy is seen with her suave husband (David Niven) presiding over a similar entertainment. At this point the exotic half-oriental beauty Merle Oberon (née O'Brien) is dazzling in an elaborate ball-gown with sumptuous jewels sparkling on her head and neck. In addition to its spacious and elegant ballroom, the Grange boasts an adjacent balcony where Heathcliff can conveniently be tête-à-tête, first with Cathy, then with Isabella. Such treatment widened the gap between the expectations of those who knew the novels and those who knew only films and staged versions of the Brontës' work. The more

Joan Fontaine and
Orson Welles as Jane
Eyre and Rochester in
Jane Eyre, 1944

Merle Oberon and
Laurence Olivier as
Catherine and Heathcliff
in *Wuthering Heights*, 1939

serious-minded readers were presumably of the same mind as the member of the Brontë Society who wrote after the release of the film, 'The Lintons' house perplexes one. Neo-Italian architecture and eight flunkeys were not found on the moors'.[17]

Since, according to the reviews, the core of the now mythical story is 'the absoluteness of [Catherine's and Heathcliff's] love for which anything is worth sacrificing', the capacity of the lovers for happiness together needs to be demonstrated. The film chooses to evoke this by pictures of a childhood spent on the moors, which had been carefully contrived in a corner of Los Angeles. There, as children, the two romp together and chase each other among exceptionally tall hea-ther. Pictures of these childish games on the moors were to become a permanent feature of later films of *Wuthering Heights* and in particu-lar a rock called Penistone Crag where the children centre their games. There Cathy acts the role of 'chosen queen' to Heathcliff, curtseying and significantly calling him 'Milord'; there Heathcliff fills her arms with the giant heather; and there they later have their trysts. When the dying Cathy is carried to her window by Heathcliff, she asks for heather from the Crag which she claims to be able to see, and the Crag itself consequently became an iconic element in sub-sequent adaptations after a still of Olivier and Oberon there became famous.

Finally, though the story has been popularized in this film, it shares the happy ending of the silent version with the difference that it is not triggered by Hareton and Catherine. Instead Nelly Dean is given the role of marginal voice-over, telling the story to Lockwood to convince him that ghosts do exist when he is unsure about the hand and voice at his window. She reports how the local doctor saw the ghost of Catherine with the living Heathcliff on the moors but when he followed them he found only the man's body. As Nelly thus demonstrates, ghosts do exist and the finale shows the two ghosts fading mistily into a snowy landscape—together at last. Ironically this version of the myth became iconic in the very year, 1932, that the Brontë sisters were memorialized for their novels in Westminster Abbey, a fact which sanctified them with what the Brontë Society called 'the seal of national approval'. The memorial led *The Times* to comment that 'two of the sisters [are] among the highest ornaments of the literature that is common to the English speaking world'.[18]

The other classic Brontë film of this period, Robert Stevenson's

Jane Eyre, released in 1944, harks back to the earlier silent films in identifying the story as a deathless romance: it omits the Rivers episode, and the role of Rochester is taken by the overpowering Orson Welles, presumably chosen to indicate dominance. The film was made as the Second World War drew to a close, when women were working in factories making munitions, replacing male farm-labourers, or serving as chauffeurs to the military elite. But with the prospect of men returning from the battlefields to their previous employment, it was perhaps necessary that women should return to their natural nurturing and domestic sphere, since they were still what Simone de Beauvoir, in her 1949 work, referred to as *The Second Sex*. Certainly traditional views of women were re-emphasized.

This attitude is strikingly evident both in the 1944 film, which Aldous Huxley co-wrote with two others, and in the response of critics to the form it took. The original Jane, poor and plain as she is, insists on equality but here Orson Welles dominates the film physic-ally and thematically. He remains, as the reviews see it, the 'tragic' hero whose male superiority is visibly admired by the glamorous Jane Eyre (Joan Fontaine), as she gazes at him in passive reverence. Though she provides an initial voice-over to set the scene, she does so only to indicate her own lowly state in words provided by Huxley and his co-scriptwriters:

My name is Jane Eyre . . . I was born in 1820, a harsh time of change in England. Money and position seemed all that mattered. Charity was a cold and disagreeable word. Religion too often a mask of bigotry and cruelty. There was no proper place for the poor or the unfortunate. I had no father or mother, brother or sister.

This is the victim Jane of the old melodramas and the scenes which follow omit the rebellious outbreak against John Reed so that the story begins as she emerges from her cruel imprisonment in the Red Room and is hustled off to Lowood School. There the victim-ization continues as she is humiliated by Brocklehurst and laments the fact that she has nobody to love her. Critics found these early scenes not full of spirited rebellion as those in the novel were, but full of pathos which made them 'particularly effective'.[19] Con-sequently there is no need of the role model who in the novel moder-ates Jane's spirit, her mentor at Lowood, Miss Temple, of whom Charlotte wrote,

Miss Temple had always something of serenity in her air, of state in her mien, of refined propriety in her language, which precluded deviation into the ardent, the excited, the eager; something which chastened the pleasure of those who looked on her, and listened to her, by a controlling sense of awe. (book 1, chapter 8)

There is little trace of 'the ardent, the excited, the eager' in Stevenson's Jane, and Miss Temple does not appear.

Various aspects of the film serve to diminish Joan Fontaine's Jane, not least the appearance of Rochester's house which still resembles a castle with its castellated medieval front, stone floors, and large scale which suits the massive and booming figure of Welles as he strides masterfully through it. His manner to Jane is commanding as he first appears to her to the clattering of horses' hooves and militaristic music. After falling from his horse, which is startled by her presence, he shouts a brusque 'Get out of the way!' uttered in the dictatorial tone which persists throughout. On her return to the Hall after their first encounter, he snaps his fingers to summon her across to him as he sits bathing his injured foot. Wordlessly, she crosses to his side, stoops before him, and pours a kettle of hot water into his footbath in anticipation of his wish. This treatment ignites no resentment in Jane and Fontaine seems merely to take pride in carrying out his orders to the letter. There is little in the way of verbal sparring with him, no holding him at arm's length after the proposal, no preventing him from buying her flamboyant dresses; no internal agonizing before she leaves Thornfield after the attempted bigamy. She returns only to Gateshead where the kindly Doctor Rivers watches over her and her aunt, and she does not inherit a legacy but simply hears Rochester calling and returns to him.

Rochester's mistresses become merely a brief list of his unsatisfactory experiences in his search for a perfect woman: 'a French dancing girl, Viennese milliner, . . . a Neapolitan countess with a taste for jewellery'. They serve to show him as a dominant male, perfectly masculine—in the traditional sense—and this is then seen to be complemented by the aspect of femininity that Jane represents here. The apparently perfect match is reflected in the approval of the contemporary reviewer who admires 'the long suffering heroine' as an exemplar of 'the inner resource of weak femininity',[20] referring presumably to the belief that to be truly feminine is 'to suffer and be still'.

This version became so hugely popular that it coloured and over-shadowed the two 1960s adaptations: a serialized BBC television version and a film made by the Greek director Giorgos Lios.

1970–2000 Criticism, Films, Television, and Opera

Up to the 1970s, as has been shown, the mythical status of *Jane Eyre* and *Wuthering Heights* had been determined by the powerful impact of mid-twentieth-century films: tragic romance had given way to sentimental love stories with less impact. From the sixties onwards, changes in society became more apparent as the privations of war faded and ultimately prosperity became more widespread. At the same time, more open attitudes to sexuality spread widely enough to affect what was thought to be sayable, printable, or showable on screen. Popular tastes, as film-makers recognized, were changing and the push for equal opportunities could no longer be ignored. In 1975 the Sex Discrimination Act was passed, prohibiting such discrimination in employment, education, and provision of goods. What came to be sarcastically called 'political correctness' meant that film-makers were likely to consider afresh how they represented what had hitherto been the second sex.

Meanwhile standards of criticism amongst those familiar with the Brontë novels were also changing, particularly as to ideas on the function of criticism: ranking continued for a time, but the assess-ment was seen to depend on other factors than realism or aesthetic value. Interest was now focused on 'social meaning', implicit in the text by reason of the values and assumptions of the originating soci-ety, which were embedded there through its language. Context was understood to be part of the meaning in relation to issues of class, gender, and race. In Brontë criticism the Marxist Terry Eagleton led the way by illuminating the class issues at stake in *Wuthering Heights* in his *Myths of Power: A Marxist Study of the Brontës* (1975). In this work he concentrates on class as the single issue, ignoring the gender of the characters under discussion and he still wished to rank Emily ahead of Charlotte, though later, however, he confirmed that he had been 'gender-blind' and was no longer.

By the time he did so, the social construction of gender or the conventional understanding and description of femininity had become a controversial issue with Kate Millett's ground-breaking book, *Sexual Politics* (1975). The topic became a significant feature of literary criticism in the next ten years and was addressed in relation to the Brontës in Gilbert and Gubar's famous critical study, *The Madwoman in the Attic: The Woman Writer and the Nineteenth-Century Literary Imagination* (1979). This work shed new light on Bertha who had been brought to notice by Jean Rhys in her prequel to *Jane Eyre*, *Wide Sargasso Sea* (1966). This work anticipates Brontë's novel by constructing a life for Antoinette/Bertha before her incarceration and the story is told partly by Antoinette herself, who appears as a victim not accepted by either black or white races and betrayed by Rochester's promiscuity. Rhys fills in Antoinette's earlier misery as Brontë's novel filled in the ill-usage of the child Jane Eyre.

In fact the seminal recognition of the importance of gender in the Brontë novels is found long before this in the writings of Virginia Woolf who in 1929, just a year after women over 21 were given the vote, flouted the popular processing of *Jane Eyre* into romantic camera fodder when in *A Room of One's Own*, with a nod to Emily's 'genius', she rehabilitated Charlotte in strikingly modern terms. Though she still follows the traditional practice of ranking works according to their degree of greatness, her main concern is to give an account of how vividly Charlotte evokes the divided consciousness of women like Jane Eyre in the early nineteenth century. Woolf recognizes patriarchal society for what it is and what it imposes on women: 'since a novel has this correspondence to real life, its values are to some extent those of real life. But it is obvious that the values of women differ very often from the values which have been made by the other sex ... Yet it is the masculine values that prevail'.[21]

Woolf sees this situation changing in some nineteenth-century novels, such as Charlotte's, where the depiction of women becomes more varied and complicated than the convention of dividing them into 'womanly' or 'unwomanly'. She is able to interpret the significance of the early reviewers' bewilderment with Charlotte's creations: 'The whole structure, therefore of the early nineteenth-century novel was raised, if one was a woman, by a mind which was slightly pulled from the straight, and made to alter its clear vision in deference to external authority'. In accordance with practice at the time, Woolf reads such inconsistencies as flaws. Nevertheless, she captures the effect of the painfully divided self that film versions had so far ignored by reverting to a picture of Jane as a womanly woman, conforming to the earlier untroubled view of femininity:

the writer was meeting criticism; she was saying this by way of aggression, or that by way of conciliation. She was admitting that she was 'only a woman' or protesting that she was 'as good as a man'. She met that criticism as her temperament dictated, with docility and diffidence or with anger and emphasis.[22]

Fifty years after the publication of *A Room of One's Own*, the appearance of *The Madwoman in the Attic* brought this feminist critique of women in novels to a wider audience. Only then did it begin to infiltrate the popular medium of film which by this time included the small as well as the large screen. Even so, the central element in the myth of *Jane Eyre* continued to be the 'timeless' love story. Only four years after the publication of Gilbert and Gubar's book, the most independent Jane of the twentieth century appeared on screen.

Feminist influence was beginning to be felt in Delbert Mann's 1970 version of *Jane Eyre* but only in a mild form as the expectations of filmgoers changed. Previously, different attitudes had existed between those who knew the novel and those who did not; but by this time, more people presumably had read the novel and feminist issues were discussed in broadsheet and tabloid newspapers alike. This can also be inferred from the increased efforts of film-makers to remain 'faithful' to the original details of the story. Mann's film reintroduces the Rivers episode and makes Jane's return to Rochester a considered choice between the two men but she does not return as a financially independent woman as the result of a legacy. The token feminist input resides in the verbal sparring between Jane and Rochester which suggests some less submissive figure than her predecessors: she teases her lover after his proposal, for instance, over what he will be like once she is securely his wife: 'For a while you'll be as you are now . . . and then you'll turn cool and capricious and stern'. As one reviewer points out, however, the camera work undermines this independence by seeing Jane repeatedly through Rochester's eyes or physically dominated by him. This is token feminism at best and, more surprisingly, there is little sexual explicitness: Jane appears, as one critic says, 'bloodless', a state which he attributes to her 'protracted inhibitions'.[23]

The tokenism was remedied in 1983 when discussion of women's rights was in full flood and the BBC produced a television serial version of Charlotte's novel with Zelah Clarke as Jane and Timothy Dalton as Rochester. Dalton had already played Heathcliff in a 1970 film of *Wuthering Heights* and was later to play James Bond in two films. As this latter role suggests, he represents what in the 1980s and 1990s was thought to be a handsome man. As the length of the 1983 serial, which ran for four hours, indicates, the BBC, as a public-service broadcaster not a commercial organization, wished to give a comprehensive version of the novel. This is also borne out by the inclusion of incidents omitted from some previous versions since the film, like the novel, begins with Jane at a window-seat at her aunt's house and includes Rochester's gypsy impersonation and the tearing of the wedding veil (though this had appeared in at least one silent film). Most significantly, there is time given to covering the Rivers section in detail, which records Jane's physical privation after leaving Thornfield to the extent of a scene in which she eats food intended as pig-swill. Her time as village teacher is shown as well as St John's overdue proposal after she has inherited her fortune, thus reinstating the contrasting temptations represented for her by Rochester and St John, whom she tells sternly, as in the novel, 'I scorn your idea of love!'

This treatment of Rivers shows that Jane is no longer the passive creature of earlier films and that is the main significance now read into the narrative. The new awareness of how restricted women had been (and in some ways still were) resonated with Charlotte's recognition of the similar struggle Jane undergoes. Fairly unobtrusively but effectively, the film presents a new kind of Jane Eyre, replacing the Joan Fontaine image which had dominated for so long. The contrast between Zelah Clarke's diminutive figure and the lanky Dalton referred to by one critic as 'willowy' does not suggest vulnerability on her part because she conveys perfect self-sufficiency by the demeanour of her small bustling figure and by her firm voice: she has the air of a woman who always knows what she is about, while the willowy Rochester uses his physical pliability to suggest that he bends to accommodate her physically and emotionally.

As Jane delivers the limited voice-over, she includes brief indications of her own thoughts/perspective: at the house party she comments to herself, not the audience, that Blanche Ingram is 'shallow and haughty' and that she knows Rochester does not love this woman. In this way it is shown that she is aware of Rochester's manipulativeness and she receives his proposal at first by distancing herself with the same combativeness that she has shown in their repartee. The portrayal of Rochester also works to alter the power-relationship of male dominance that was standard in earlier films. His manner, like his physique, is politely pliable even in their banter-ing exchanges and, after her wordless departure on the morning after the failed wedding, he manages to appear strong-willed but he is not shown making his lengthy self-justification or listing his for-eign mistresses. Rather than a wearily knowledgeable man of the world, he appears simply as a disappointed lover with even a faint tinge of the New Man (who was theoretically arriving on the public scene some 100 years after the New Woman).

This 1983 film focused on the love story in a domestic form, not the upper-class setting of the usual Gothic, and unlike the Orson Welles film it does not attempt high tragedy, while Jane's moral struggle, though real, is not underpinned by a substantial evocation of religious belief. This domestic and secular model is followed in 1996 by Franco Zeffirelli's *Jane Eyre*. His *Romeo and Juliet* of 1968 had already provided a fairy-tale extravaganza with stunning Italian locations and gorgeous period clothes. Along with this went refer-ences to contemporary culture, since he read the story as one of teenagers rebelling against society as students in 1968 were rebelling against the establishment on the streets of Europe. The date of the production also explains the shots of the teenage actors naked in bed together.

His production of Charlotte's novel seems to be an attempt at a Cinderella fairy tale in which a heroine suffers in her youth but finds her wealthy Prince Charming in the end. Like *Romeo and Juliet*, the 1996 film reflects something of society's concern with issues such as women's rights to independence, but an escapist fantasy was likely to go down best in the UK, where the film was made, at a time of economic decline when a collapse in house prices caused negative equity for many, and loss of their homes for some. Consequently the British scriptwriter, Hugh Whitemore, tones down or omits painful episodes. The cruelty of Lowood is necessary to create the picture of Jane as ill-used but is quickly concluded and accounts for her melan-cholic attitude. It is not thought necessary to include the period of privation she undergoes after leaving Thornfield and she goes straight to Gateshead where she is nursed for six months by St John Rivers (transformed into the local rector) and his sister Mary. His proposal to her is made without coercion and she does not agonize over it but offers him as much of her legacy as he will need for his missionary work, as well as giving part to Lowood School. Thornfield itself is shown as a haven of comfort and warmth with an efficient and cosily friendly North Country housekeeper (Joan Plowright) and the significance of its battlemented luxury for Jane is made clear by her reaction to her spacious four-postered bedroom: 'Is this for me?'.

This Jane is distinguished from earlier versions on screen because she is not played by a contemporary beauty but by a pale gawky actress, Charlotte Gainsbourg, who is distinctly plain. Her lack of conventional beauty is underlined by casting as her rival Blanche Ingram (a dark-haired beauty in the novel) the six-foot-tall blonde 'supermodel', Elle 'The Body' Macpherson. Zeffirelli's Jane also resembles Charlotte's by showing signs that, despite her childhood ill-usage, she has retained some independence of spirit. She is not afraid to stand up to Rochester or even to criticize him for making Adèle feel 'unloved' but her cool demeanour remains impassive and calm, creating what critics called 'passionless effect'. Though her voice-over fills in gaps in the narrative, it reveals nothing of her inner thoughts.

The effect of this impassiveness is increased by the scriptwriter's addition of pious remarks such as her rebuke to Rochester, the declaration to St John of her intended donation to charity, and her reply —'We shall work hard . . . say your prayers Adèle'—to her pupil's question 'Shall we be happy?'—Rochester is similarly muted: he is quietly polite from the meeting in the lane onwards and after the failed marriage only pleads 'Tell me you love me!' and 'Don't leave me Jane!'. This is all he says as Jane, having calmly told him she loves him, leaves wordlessly. There is no painful scene between the two and he does not ask her to become his mistress. Some attempt is made to make him appear heroic by showing his risking his life in the fire to try to save Bertha. Perhaps the most interesting aspect of the film is the treatment of Bertha who is seen full-face several times: she is no longer the savage animal of the novel but a beautiful dark-haired and visibly Caucasian woman who is mentally disturbed.

Perhaps this reflects Zeffirelli's recognition of the current sensitivity over the issues of race and of mental disability, and harks back to *Wide Sargasso Sea*.

Only two years later, in 1997, LWT produced the first film adaptation of Charlotte's novel to be scripted by a woman, Kay Mellor. She was approached by another woman, Sally Head, presumably because of her previously successful scripts for a TV series, *Band of Gold*, which consisted of episodes, realistically and sympathetically represented, relating the life stories of a group of prostitutes. They included a teenager, Tracey, played by a young and relatively inexperienced actress, Samantha Morton, who was now cast as Jane Eyre in Mellor's version. Significantly, Morton also provides a voice-over more conspicuous than in other adaptations which is able to reveal something of Jane's own thoughts and feelings as well as linking events. The choice of Mellor as scriptwriter is evidently the result of a determination to make this a woman's story and reclaim it for Jane by choosing a writer known for her contemporary approach to feminist issues. For by now Britain had experienced its first female prime minister; the Sex Discrimination Act was over twenty years old; and some women had gone far enough in their professions to argue for something more than basic rights, and to complain of the 'glass ceiling'.

Mellor's script fulfils much of what was expected of her. From the first, when Rochester rebukes Jane after falling from his horse, she is visibly resentful and defends herself from the charge of causing the accident. This resistance continues when he orders her later to sit in a particular place, for she is then prepared to tell him that, though he pays her to do his bidding, he must do so 'with respect'. When he derides what he assumes is her Brocklehurst-style of evangelical religion, she answers that she dislikes the clergyman and adds 'I have found my own faith'. Such a faith had long been suppressed in Jane Eyre films but is now shown as the motive for her insistence, after the attempted bigamy, that it would be wrong to become Rochester's mistress. The restoration of Jane's religion-based morality reintroduces the internal struggle that she undergoes in the novel and in this film there is no doubt of the powerful sexual attraction between her and Rochester, which is vividly evoked by their body language, especially in the night-time episodes after Bertha's burning of Rochester's bed and the attack on Mason. These visual indications are reinforced by Jane's willingness to reveal her passionate feelings in the voice-over.

Rochester (Ciaran Hinds), who is for once visibly much older than Jane, is a large, moustached figure whose domineering manner turns to bluster under the impact of Jane's cool self-assertiveness. She tells him, for instance, that she will not stay in his drawing room 'to be insulted' by the Ingrams' derision of governesses. Later her insistence on visiting her dying aunt, despite his wish to prevent her, leaves him knowing 'the game is over' as he tells Blanche at this point, cutting short their game of billiards. He is clearly referring to the power struggle with Jane and recognizing that he has lost it. The gradual loss of control over her culminates in his frantic pleading as she leaves Thornfield when in desperation he becomes violent and tries to restrain her physically. The novel implied potential, not real, violence, but a more open climate on the subject of domestic abuse allowed the director to show it happening (a feature which was also to become dominant in adaptations of Emily's and Anne's novels). The power is now in Jane's hands as an out-of-control Rochester alternately shouts blustering abuse and pleas as she follows her conscience and leaves him.

When she finally returns after rejecting St John, she takes the initiative with the blinded Rochester. *She* seizes him in her arms, *she* refuses to leave him when told to, and *she* kisses *him* in a scene that says more plainly than the words (omitted in this version) 'Reader *I* married him' not '*He* married me'. Kay Mellor, in an interview, spoke of how she intended to prevent the film from being 'railroaded into [becoming] Rochester's before the end'. The camera tells the very story she intended and in the final shot, instead of Jane's face shown gazing rapturously at Rochester, he looks gratefully at hers, which the camera does not show: her female gaze is in control. This is not the equality that the novel asserts: the scale has tipped in the heroine's favour.

It was the composer Michael Berkeley and his librettist David Malouf who finally resolved the problem of the first-person narration which had foxed all the film-makers. The two-act opera *Jane Eyre*, first performed in 2000, does not attempt to tell the story in full but scales it down to 'the bare bones of a timeless love story', using only the events at Thornfield. The creation of the opera was a tribute to what had turned *Jane Eyre* into a myth in the first place: it represented what Berkeley thought necessary for the operatic genre: 'a bloody good story'. It has a cast of only five characters: Jane, Rochester, Bertha, Mrs Fairfax, and Adèle. It includes Jane's lonely arrival, the mystery of the maniacal laughter, the strange anguish of Rochester (and of Bertha), Rochester's proposal, and the discovery of his wife's existence.

Jane, the narrator, opens the opera alone on stage some months after her flight from Thornfield, busy with her needlework. Throughout the performance Jane, as in the novel, is recollecting what happened between her and Rochester from whom she is now estranged. As in a dream or interior monologue, she recalls the past, which is enacted by the other four characters who join her on stage as the story dictates, playing her own part as it arises and always present. Hence the work fuses past and present times in a genre in which 'realism' of a novelistic kind is not expected, since thoughts and emotions are necessarily expressed by singers not speakers. Memories are in effect treated as a visible dream.

The structure of the story hinges on recurrent motifs attached to the three central characters which recur with variations throughout. In the opening scene Jane's precarious self-control is captured as she sings:

> Silence. Quietness.
> Some of us choose quietness
> when storms rock the air,
> and the wind out on the moor shakes
> the wainscot, rattles the pane, a place
> of the still heart, out of
> the world's eye and the sky's
> perpetual knocking.[24]

This aria is used particularly effectively at a moment of crisis when Jane discovers that Rochester has a wife. She struggles to control her rising distress by using it as a calming mantra when, as the stage directions indicate, she is 'urgent now, hysterical'. She gets no further than 'Quietness, Quietness. | Some of us choose | When storms rock the air | . . . Quietness we stop our ears | To the voices that call us back'.[25] Similarly Rochester's passionate desire is expressed by his recurrent cries of 'Jane! Jane!' which cut through the scenes until the final cry breaks into Jane's present time and she finds him in reality on stage as they are reunited. Bertha's motif is at first her strange laugh offstage which creates a sense of her haunting presence at Thornfield. Later this changes to her desperate cries for Rochester: 'Edward! Edward!'

As the programme notes for the opera point out, 'the most significant rethinking of Brontë's work is the representation of Bertha'. She becomes a tragic figure like the Antoinette/Bertha of *Wide Sargasso Sea* (1966), 'somebody you sympathise with'. Though Gilbert and Gubar had 'rethought' Bertha in 1979, no visual version before this opera seems to take this new reading fully on board. The other aspect of Bertha integrated into this work is that of her as a frightening doppelgänger representing the suppressed side of Jane's nature. Certainly she is omnipresent here, vocally at least, as Jane's shadow and for the first time in an adaptation, Jane Eyre herself makes the identification:

> Oh sir, is this true?
> Can this be true?
> Is that unhappy woman
> What I was to be tomorrow—
> Your wife, Mrs Rochester?[26]

In the various film adaptations of Charlotte's novel, music is heavy-handedly used to emphasize that something frightening is about to erupt or that a romantic scene will soon occur. A prime example is the militaristic music that accompanies Orson Welles's macho performance as Rochester. In the opera, however, the music is integral to the whole and is accurately said to express 'the inner turmoil of frustrated desires'. Further, the postmodernist device of intertextual reference (of a musical kind) adds depth. There is an allusion to the music of Debussy's *Pelléas et Mélisande* in which two half-brothers engage in a jealous struggle over the wife of one of them, echoing the Bertha–Jane–Rochester triangle. There is also an echo of *Lucia di Lammermoor* when Adèle innocently foretells Bertha's murderous attempt on Rochester by musical phrases from the mad scene after Lucia has murdered her husband.

Berkeley and Malouf's opera recontextualizes the novel in terms of this different medium by boldly exploiting its potential, something film-makers had never been radical enough to do. The work demonstrates the power of the myth to evoke, long after it was written, vibrant and contemporary interpretations. It does so despite the fact that the name of the family has become a commercial logo for commodities ranging from Brontë biscuits to Brontë tweed. There was also an operatic version of *Wuthering Heights* by Bernard Herrmann in 1966, and a French opera in three acts by Thomas Stubbs entitled *Les Hauts de Hurlevant* in 1967.

Like the 1997 *Jane Eyre*, the film versions of *Wuthering Heights* released in 1992 and 1998, while drawing on earlier adaptations, reflected the contemporary interest in violence. On screen this had been evident in horror films and increasingly horrific documentary footage of wars, massacres, disasters, and accidents. In society at large there were increasing concerns over violent crimes and domestic violence. Both the 1990s adaptations make visible and add to the cruelties already referred to in Emily's novel with all the force of the photographic image.

The early idyll of the Olivier film has now become part of the myth and is evidenced by frequent kisses and embraces between Cathy and Heathcliff, and the Kosminsky film (1992) adds a routine embrace on a bed to what might otherwise seem to the audience a brother-and-sister relationship. Childish romps on the moors in the David Skynner version (1998) are made slightly odd by the accent of the vivacious French actress Juliet Binoche, who is plainly not English, let alone North Country. More significant, however, is the depiction of her as a giddy girl fascinated by what Heathcliff (Ralph Fiennes) calls 'silly frocks', fur-lined hoods, and the glamorous life at the Grange which, as in the Olivier version, is the scene of formal entertaining and dances. Her youth is presumably meant to be suggested by her frequent and often inappropriate girlish giggle, which is awkwardly at odds with Heathcliff's grim intensity and rough appearance. The effect of this representation of Jane creates an asymmetry between herself and Heathcliff which, as one critic puts it, 'weakens anything that *Wuthering Heights* for the 90s might have to say about the sexual politics of Emily's novel'.[27]

Like its 1939 predecessor, this is Heathcliff's film and Ralph Fiennes's version of the character is unkempt, loutish, violent, and able to invoke violence in others. He not only fights with Hindley but even manages to provoke Edgar into striking him. For his own part, he kills the lapwing chicks, bullies Isabella after she has become his wife, digs up Cathy's coffin, and savagely attacks her daughter,

Catherine, when she attempts to escape from her imprisonment at the Heights. He is Heathcliff as a domestic bully driven mad by Cathy's caprices and her taste for luxury.

Fiennes's Heathcliff, however, pales by comparison with Robert Cavanah's version in the 1998 film directed by David Skynner. Cavanah's appearance lacks physical presence and could not be further removed from Olivier's handsomely Byronic Heathcliff. He is unattractively slovenly and with a vicious temper that makes him appear bitterly spiteful rather than calculatingly vengeful like his predecessor in the 1920 silent story of hate. The violence which he perpetrates and which surrounds him was presumably intensified for an audience now hard to shock. To the killing of the birds in a gratuitous act of cruelty is added the bitter fight with Hindley and the physical brutality he metes out to the second Catherine when she resists him. When the Grange becomes his property, he vandalizes it like some enraged pop star in a hotel room. The suggestion of necrophilia involved in Emily's account of the removal of the side of Cathy's coffin is intensified by a scene in which he embraces her shrouded corpse after digging it up. Most horrific of all is his casual rape of his newly married wife, Isabella, which he carries out with brutal coldness and which turns him into a monster of domestic violence for an audience which by the 1990s knew that such monsters existed. Nevertheless, Heathcliff is finally shown reunited with Cathy in death after he encounters her ghost on the moor, while the subsequent scene of Hareton and Catherine as they kiss only serves to increase the sense of imbalance in the film.

A more coherent account of domestic violence, now recognized as a fact, had already appeared from what, for those who did not know the novel, was an unexpected source. From the 1850s until the late twentieth century Anne Brontë's novels had not been the subject of adaptations. She was regarded as a limited novelist with little of interest to say. The first film version of *The Tenant of Wildfell Hall* in 1968–9 was dismissed by contemporary critics, even though it was adapted by the well-known playwright Christopher Fry. One spoke of 'the essentially cliché-ridden nature of Anne (sister of Emily and Charlotte) Brontë's inspiration';[28] another described it as 'a mere tear-duct-teaser, Victorian pornography of the emotions at its sickliest';[29] a third found the only thing to praise was 'the endless tittle-tattle and backbiting' of 'the shut-in rural life of the 19th century'.[30]

The three-part BBC television adaptation nearly thirty years later in 1996 received quite a different reception of a kind that indicated changes in how society now regarded certain issues. These involved a recognition of social evils that were still obscured in the 1960s despite the new sexual permissiveness. This permissiveness had now become naturalized to the extent that the producer of the BBC version of *The Tenant of Wildfell Hall* could say approvingly that 'Anne Brontë . . . is far more erotic and explicit' than Jane Austen whose novels were being adapted at the same time. He is credited with saying 'In Austen, sex is just a kiss on the back of the hand, whereas here everything happens'.[31] This is certainly true of the film where Huntingdon's priapic nature is evident from the moment he lays eyes on Helen. It persists throughout the film as his passionate encounter in the garden with Annabella is overheard by his wife who rightly assumes he is adulterous. Even when he has become estranged from the heavily pregnant Helen, he attempts to rape her.

But by this time his sexual predatoriness is simply part of a larger picture of the kind of abuse which by 1996 was publicly discussed. Domestic violence caused by alcoholism receives more emphasis than Huntingdon's claim to droit de seigneur. His drinking companions also prey on women and Hargrave's attempt to seduce Helen is made more explicit without distorting the narrative. Brontë does not describe physical abuse but this was now recognized as a part of marriages where alcohol fuelled a husband's behaviour. In the novel Huntingdon's drunken friend Hattersley, 'Swearing and cursing like a maniac' (chapter 31), is irritated by his wife Millicent's tears. He attempts to discover why by 'shaking her and remorselessly crushing her slight arms in the gripe of his powerful fingers'. The film shows a more vicious attack in keeping with the heightened physicality of abuse known to be meted out to some wives. Similarly, when Helen tells Huntingdon she intends to leave him, the novel recounts his verbal bullying but on screen he strikes her, seizes her by the throat, and hurls her to the floor. Presumably this gives 1990s viewers the same degree of shock that would have been felt by contemporary readers at Anne's more moderate depiction of Huntingdon's behaviour.

Other domestic issues are dealt with in the same way so that they speak to a contemporary audience who recognized the behaviour of 'a violent man whose abuse of his son may have stopped short of the sexual but was still very nasty'.[32] The film shows the young Arthur enticed into heavy drinking, as in the novel, and hints at sexual abuse as he is applauded for repeating obscene rhymes that his father's friends have taught him. Stress is also laid on Helen's struggle after leaving her husband to support herself and her son by her painting, an unladylike trade.

This updating was perceptively balanced against an indication of the period by what one review praised as the absence of a predominating 'sense of costume'.[33] By this is meant that it shows 'no wigs, . . . very little make-up' and clothes that 'actually get dirty'. But reviewers also fully realized the way the film resonated with contemporary concerns. They claimed that, unlike alterations in a screen version of *Pride and Prejudice*, this adaptation does not 'pander to the audience without adding to the author's intentions . . . [but] intensifies Brontë's work'. Repeatedly the 'modern' quality of Anne's novel is understood. A member of the cast claims that 'the problems of alcoholism and the home-breaking, and the violence it causes, are as relevant today as they were then'.[34] A popular newspaper writes, 'single mothers, women's rights and domestic abuse, such matters were as relevant in nineteenth-century England as today'.[35] And a female reviewer exults, 'You want real life? Did you witness the dysfunctional home life Arthur Huntingdon . . . made . . ., as he, the alcoholic, drained all life and love from his wife, the co-dependent? And what about the struggles of the single mother, Helen Graham . . . as she painted to keep her non nuclear family going?'[36] The general consensus seems to have been that, had there not been a taboo against explicit treatment of these issues, 'Brontë would have broached [them] herself'.[37] These reactions show a popular convergence finally with specialist writers who by the 1990s had long been unearthing the 'modern' treatment of class, gender, and sexuality in the Brontë novels, or rather had recognized how their works were already challenging conventional views on these issues in their own time. The academic critic Elaine Showalter wrote in her *Observer* review that Anne's depiction of her 'abused and mutinous heroine was so far in advance of her time that she is only now getting her due'.[38] On this interpretation it would seem that 'gentle' Anne was the boldest of the three sisters for whom full recognition did not come until the end of the twentieth century.

In addition to the films discussed above, there were several minor television adaptations of both *Jane Eyre* and *Wuthering Heights*, as well as a film version of *Shirley* (1922) and two of *Villette* (1957 and 1970). *Wuthering Heights* was also translated into films in other languages and the cultures attached to them: the Mexican *Abismos de Pasión* (1953); the Indian *Dil Diya Dard Liya* (1966); the French *Hurlevant* (1985); and the Japanese *Arashi-Ga-Oka* (1988). These adaptations continue to be made, including one in 2002 which took the form of a three-part television serial in which Heathcliff is transformed into a lower-class girl, Carol Bolton, and Cathy is similarly transgendered into a middle-class boy, Andrew Collins. *Sparkhouse*, as this version is called, suggests that the class struggle is a timeless matter which is more important than gender.

Jane Eyre and *Wuthering Heights* have also been seen as having an impact on twentieth-century novels. Charlotte's novel is said to have influenced the plots of many others: Stella Gibbons's spoof *Cold Comfort Farm* (1932), Winifred Holtby's *South Riding* (1936), and famously Daphne du Maurier's best-seller *Rebecca* (1938). *Rebecca*, which itself became a popular film, recounts the experiences of a prim young girl who becomes the second wife of a rich older man, Maxim de Winter. The novel hinges on the dark secret relating to the death of his first wife which, like the secret existence of Bertha, finally emerges.

By the late twentieth century *Wuthering Heights* had become more a focus of interest and source of public reference than *Jane Eyre*. In the mid-1970s a popular song called 'Wuthering Heights', written and sung by Kate Bush in a weird register that appears to be exceptionally high-pitched and other-worldly, evoked the uncanny atmosphere of the novel and became highly popular. The music critic Nicky Losseff, however, who produces a detailed musical analysis of the song, demonstrated that the uncanny effect is due to 'the interaction between meanings inherent in the music and in the lyrics'. He argues that these meanings relate 'to the real and the other world' and are 'explored musically in two particularly powerful ways: harmonic structure and vocal timbre'.[39] Kate Bush compresses Emily's novel into the words of Cathy's ghost tapping on the window of Heathcliff's house:

> Out on the wiley, windy moors
> We'd roll and fall in green
> You had a temper like my jealousy
> Too hot, too greedy
> How could you leave me?
> When I needed to possess you
> I hated you, I loved you too
>
> Bad dreams in the night
> They told me I was going to lose the fight,
> Leave behind my wuthering, wuthering
> Wuthering Heights.
>
> *Chorus* Heathcliff, it's me, Cathy come home
> I'm so cold!, let me in-a-your window[40]

Wuthering Heights also evoked poems of that name by Sylvia Plath and Ted Hughes, based on their pilgrimage in 1961 to the supposed site of the house. Plath's poem invokes her relationship with the landscape there as she identifies herself with what she derives of Emily's view from the novel:

> There is no life higher than the grasstops
> Or the hearts of sheep, and the wind
> Pours by like destiny, bending
> Everything in one direction.
> I can feel it trying to funnel my heat away.
> If I pay the roots of the heather
> Too close attention, they will invite me
> To whiten my bones among them.[41]

Hughes's own poem makes the identification of Plath and Emily more explicit by comparing them:

> That climb
> A mile beyond expectation, into
> Emily's private Eden. The moor
> Lifted and opened its dark flower
> For you too. That was satisfactory.
> Wilder, maybe, than Emily ever knew it.[42]

Interestingly both these poems, which are entitled 'Wuthering Heights', continue the synthesis of Emily's life and her novel which Henry James had so abhorred. The same process is in evidence in the films based on the Brontë lives, set in 'the Brontë landscape' like the novels. Perhaps the best known of these is *Devotion* (1946) in which the sisters became virtuous Jane-Eyre-like figures, sacrificing themselves for Branwell and each other.

At a more popular level, *Wuthering Heights* has spawned flippant comic versions such as sketches by the comedians Morecambe and Wise, and the one in 'Monty Python'. A longer satire is *Spike Milligan's Wuthering Heights* published in book form in 1994 which turns its melodramatic elements into farce, partly by taking meta-phorical language literally and introducing twentieth-century obscenities. One inference to be drawn from these and other deriva-tives is that *Jane Eyre*, *Wuthering Heights*, and the lives of the Brontës themselves are not only inextricably entwined but now so established in popular culture that reference on any level—even a soap opera—can be seen to work.

NOTES

CHAPTER 1. The Lives of Charlotte, Emily, and Anne Brontë

1. Felicia Gordon, *A Preface to the Brontës* (London and New York: Longman, 1989), 39.
2. Joan Stevens (ed.), *Mary Taylor: Friend of Charlotte Brontë: Letters from New Zealand and Elsewhere* (Oxford: Oxford University Press, 1972), 158.

CHAPTER 2. The Fabric of Society

1. J. M. Golby, *Culture and Society in Britain, 1850–1890* (Oxford: Oxford University Press, 1988), 5.
2. F. Engels, *The Condition of the Working Class in England*, ed. V. Kiernan (Harmondsworth: Penguin, 1987), 108.
3. David Vincent, *Bread, Knowledge and Freedom: A History of Nineteenth-Century Working-Class Autobiography* (London: Europa Publications, 1981), 52–3.
4. John Burnett, *Plenty and Want: A Social History of Food in England from 1915 to the Present Day* (London: Routledge, 1994), 53.
5. Golby, *Culture and Society in Britain*, 41.
6. Vincent, *Bread, Knowledge and Freedom*, 113.
7. Arthur Helps, *The Claims of Labour: An Essay on the Duties of the Employers to the Employed* (London: William Pickering, 1844), 16.
8. Ibid. 156.
9. J. S. Mill, *Principles of Political Economy, Books IV and V*, ed. D. Winch (Harmondsworth: Penguin, 1985), 119.
10. S. S. Ellis, *The Daughters of England: Their Position in Society, Character, and Responsibilities* (London: Fisher, 1845), 11–12.
11. A. H. Manchester, *A Modern Legal History of England and Wales 1750–1950* (London: Butterworth, 1980), 368.
12. E. K. Helsinger, R. L. Sheets, and W. Veeder (eds.), *The Woman Question: Society and Literature in Britain and America, 1837–1883* (Manchester: Manchester University Press, 1983), i. 15.
13. Dale Spender (ed.), *The Education Papers: Women's Quest for Equality in Britain, 1850–1912* (New York and London: Routledge & Kegan Paul, 1897), 62.
14. Helsinger, Sheets, and Veeder (eds.), *Woman Question*, ii. 62.
15. Ibid. 61.
16. Ibid. 66.
17. Sally Shuttleworth, *Charlotte Bronte and Victorian Psychology* (Cambridge: Cambridge University Press, 1996), 32.
18. Roy Porter, *A Social History of Madness: Stories of the Insane* (London: Phoenix, 1999), 47.

19. Andrew Scull, *Museums of Madness: The Social Organization of Insanity in the Nineteenth Century* (London: Allen Lane, 1979), 30.
20. Shuttleworth, *Charlotte Brontë*, 76.
21. Janet Oppenheim, *Shattered Nerves: Doctors, Patients and Depression in Victorian England* (Oxford: Oxford University Press, 1991), 49.
22. Linda Colley, *Britons: Forging the Nation 1807–1837* (Yale: Yale University Press, 1992), 358.
23. Ibid. 360.
24. Alexander Walker, *Physiognomy Founded on Physiology and Applied to Various Countries* (London: Smith, Elder), 220.
25. Thomas Carlyle, 'Occasional Discourse on the Negro Question', *Fraser's Magazine*, 40 (Dec. 1849), 671.
26. Ibid. 672.
27. Ibid. 673.
28. D. Parker, 'Dickens and America: The Unflattering Glass', *Dickens Studies Annual*, 15 (1986), 62.
29. Florence Nightingale, *Letters from Egypt: A Journey on the Nile 1849–1850*, ed. A. Sattin (London: Parkway Publishing, 1998), 208.

CHAPTER 3. The Literary Context

1. Felicia Gordon, *A Preface to the Brontës* (London and New York: Longman, 1989), 107.
2. Maria Grey and Emily Shirreff, *Thoughts on Self-Culture Addressed to Women* (London: Hope & Co., 1854), 336.
3. Richard D. Altick, *The English Common Reader: A Social History of the Mass Reading Public 1800–1900* (Chicago: University of Chicago Press, 1967), 134.
4. Guinevere L. Griest, *Mudie's Circulating Library and the Victorian Novel* (Indiana: Indiana University Press, 1970), 86.
5. Ibid. 71.
6. C. E. Mudie, 'Mr Mudie's Library', *Athenaeum*, 1719 (1860), 451.
7. *The Tenant of Wildfell Hall*, Oxford World's Classics (Oxford 1998), ed. Herbert Rosengarten and Margaret Smith, 3–4.

CHAPTER 4. The Brontës' Novels and Social Class

1. Elizabeth Rigby, '*Vanity Fair, Jane Eyre* and the Governesses Benevolent Institution', *Quarterly Review*, 84 (1848), 176.
2. Deirdre David, *Fictions of Resolution in Three Victorian Novels: North and South, Our Mutual Friend, Daniel Deronda* (London: Macmillan, 1981).
3. Terry Eagleton, *Myths of Power: A Marxist Study of the Brontës* (Basingstoke: Macmillan, 1975), 47.
4. Lawrence Stone, *The Family, Sex and Marriage in England 1500–1800* (London: Weidenfeld and Nicolson, 1977), 667.
5. Ibid. 669.

6. Samuel Smiles, *Self-Help* (Oxford: Oxford University Press, 2002), ch. 1.
7. Eagleton, *Myths of Power*, 114.

CHAPTER 5. Gender, Nationality, and Race in the Brontës' Novels

1. S. S. Ellis, *The Women of England: Their Social Duties and Domestic Habits* (London: Fisher, 1839), 72–3.
2. W. R. Greg, 'Why are Women Redundant?', *National Review*, 14 (1862), 434–60.
3. Isabella Beeton, *Beeton's Book of Household Management* (London: Chancellor Press, 1861), 1.
4. Ibid. 16.
5. Philip Collins, *The Critical Heritage: Dickens* (New York: Barnes and Noble, 1971), 549.
6. N. Humble, *Mrs Beeton's Book of Household Management* (Oxford: Oxford University Press, 2000), 363.
7. S. S. Ellis, *The Mothers of England: Their Influence and Responsibility* (London: Fisher, 1843), 321–2.
8. Mary Taylor, *Miss Miles or A Tale of Yorkshire Life 60 Years Ago*, ed. J. H. Murray (New York and Oxford: Oxford University Press, 1990), iii. 124–5.
9. Geraldine Jewsbury, *Marian Withers* (London: Colburn & Co., 1851), iii. 124–5.
10. Florence Nightingale, *Cassandra and Other Selections from Suggestions for Thought*, ed. Mary Poovey (New York: New York University Press, 1993), 214.
11. Ibid. 228.
12. Ibid. 208.
13. Ibid. 207.
14. Ingham (ed.), *The Brontës: A Critical Reader* (London: Longman, 2003), 70–90: 72.
15. E. K. Helsinger et al. (eds.), *The Woman Question: Society and Literature in Britain and America 1837–1883* (Manchester: Manchester University Press, 1983), ii. 61.
16. Ingham (ed.), *Brontës: A Critical Reader*, 24–44: 30.
17. Ibid. 234–52.
18. Ibid. 216–33: 217.

CHAPTER 6. The Brontës and the Psyche: Mind and Body

1. Sally Shuttleworth, *Charlotte Brontë and Victorian Psychology* (Cambridge: Cambridge University Press, 1996), 222.
2. Roy Porter, *Mind Forg'd Manacles: A History of Madness in England from the Restoration to the Regency* (Harmondsworth: Penguin Books, 1987), 41.
3. Shuttleworth, *Charlotte Brontë*, 61.
4. George Combe, *Elements of Phrenology* (London: Simpkin & Marshall, 1824), 9–10.

5. Combe, *Elements of Phrenology*, 16.
6. Ibid. 17.
7. Ibid. 223–4.
8. Shuttleworth, *Charlotte Brontë*, 64.
9. Roy Porter, *A Social History of Madness: Stories of the Insane* (London: Phoenix, 1999), 26.
10. Porter, *Mind Forg'd Manacles*, 190.
11. Ibid. 224.
12. Combe, *Elements of Phrenology*, 223.
13. Porter, *Mind Forg'd Manacles*, 35.
14. Ibid. 282.
15. Jeremy Bentham, *Panopticon; or, the Inspection-House* (*Works*, Edinburgh: William Tait, and London: Simpkin Marshall, 1843), iv. 44.
16. Porter, *Mind Forg'd Manacles*, 209–10.
17. Samuel Smiles, *Self-Help* (Oxford: Oxford University Press, 2002), 3.
18. Ibid. 21.
19. Ibid. 16.
20. Quoted by Sally Shuttleworth in *Jane Eyre* (Oxford: Oxford University Press, 2000), ed. Margaret Smith, with notes and introd. by Shuttleworth, 476.
21. Shuttleworth, *Charlotte Brontë*, 51.
22. Ibid. 230.

CHAPTER 7. Religion in the Brontës' Works

1. Heather Glen, *Charlotte Brontë: The Imagination in History* (Oxford: Oxford University Press, 2002), 75.
2. Anne Brontë, *Agnes Grey and Poems*, ed. Anne Smith (London: Everyman, 1985), 175.
3. *The Poems of Charlotte Brontë*, ed. Tom Winnifrith (Oxford: Basil Blackwell for the Shakespeare Head Press, 1984), 328.
4. Marianne Thomählen, *The Brontës and Religion* (Cambridge: Cambridge University Press, 1999), 177.
5. Lisa Wang, 'The Holy Spirit in Emily Brontë's *Wuthering Heights* and Poetry', *Literature and Theology*, 14/2 (2000), 161.
6. Ibid. 169.
7. Christopher Marlowe, *Doctor Faustus*, ed. D. Bevington and E. Rasmussen (Manchester: Manchester University Press, 1933), I. iii. 78 ff.

CHAPTER 8. Recontextualizing the Brontës

1. John Stuart Mill, *Principles of Political Economy*, ed. D. Winch (Harmondsworth: Penguin, 1985), 119.
2. John Brougham, *Jane Eyre* (London: John Dicks, 1850), Act II, scene 2, p. 13. Copy in the Brontë Parsonage Museum.
3. Ibid., Act V, scene 2, p. 32.

4. *Complete Works of Matthew Arnold* (Ann Arbor: University of Michigan Press, 1966–77), iii. 283.

5. L. Miller, *The Brontë Myth* (London: Jonathan Cape, 2001), 140.

6. *Bioscope*, 14 Oct. 1915.

7. BFI archive.

8. *Bioscope*, 14 Oct. 1918.

9. *Bioscope*, 14 Oct. 1915.

10. Ibid.

11. BFI archive.

12. *The Moving Picture World*, 26 Jan. 1918.

13. BFI archive.

14. *Kine Weekly*, 6 Sept. 1934.

15. *Cinema*, 26 Apr. 1939.

16. *Literary Film Quarterly*, 24/4 (1996). P. Mills, 'Wyler's version of Brontë's storms in *Wuthering Heights*', ibid. 417.

17. *BST* 49/4 (1939), 240.

18. *BST* 20/5 (1992), 284.

19. *The Cinema*, 1 Dec. 1943.

20. Ibid.

21. Virginia Woolf, *A Room of One's Own* (London: Hogarth Press, 1929), 110.

22. Ibid. 111.

23. *Monthly Film Bulletin* (Apr. 1971), 75.

24. Chandos CD: Act I, scene 1.

25. Ibid., Act II.

26. Ibid.

27. *Sight and Sound* (Oct. 1992).

28. *Sun*, 6 Feb. 1969.

29. *New Statesman*, 31 Jan. 1969.

30. *Daily Mail*, 30 Dec. 1968.

31. *Observer Review*, 25 Aug. 1996.

32. *Financial Times*, 17 Nov. 1996.

33. *Independent*, 18 Nov. 1996.

34. *Independent*, 20 Nov. 1996.

35. *Evening Standard*, 14 Nov. 1996.

36. *Daily Telegraph*, 18 Nov. 1996.

37. BBC advertisement.

38. *Observer*, 25 Aug. 1996.

39. N. Losseff, 'Cathy's Homecoming and the Other World', *Popular Music*, 182 (1999), 227–40.

40. EMI CD: Kate Bush, *The Kick Inside*.

41. *Collected Poems of Sylvia Plath*, ed. Ted Hughes (London: Faber and Faber, 1981), 167.

42. Ted Hughes, *Birthday Letters* (London: Faber and Faber, 1998), 59.

FURTHER READING

MATERIAL RELATING TO THE BRONTËS' LIVES

Alexander, C., *The Early Writings of Charlotte Brontë* (Oxford: Blackwell, 1983).

—— and Smith, M., *The Oxford Companion to the Brontës* (Oxford: Oxford University Press, 2003).

Altick, R., *The English Common Reader: A Social History of the Mass Reading Public 1800–1900* (Chicago: University of Chicago Press, 1957).

Barker, J., *The Brontës* (London: Orion, 1994) (the fullest and most detailed biography of the whole family and their background).

Bock, C., *Charlotte Brontë and the Storyteller's Audience* (Iowa City: University of Iowa Press, 1992).

Brontë, Charlotte, *The Letters of Charlotte Brontë*, ed. M. Smith, 3 vols. (Oxford: Clarendon Press), 1995, 2000, 2004).

Gaskell, Elizabeth, *Life of Charlotte Brontë*, ed. E. Jay (Harmondsworth: Penguin, 1998).

Glen, H. (ed.), *The Cambridge Companion to the Brontës* (Cambridge: Cambridge University Press, 2000).

Lewis, J. (ed.), *Labour and Love: Women's Experience of Home and Family 1850–1940* (Oxford: Blackwell, 1986).

Orel, H., *The Brontës: Interviews and Recollections* (Iowa: University of Iowa Press, 1996) (including Ellen Nussey's memories of Charlotte).

Ricks, C., 'E. C. Gaskell's Charlotte Brontë', in *Essays in Appreciation* (Oxford: Clarendon Press, 1996), 118–45.

Wheat, P., *The Adytum of The Heart: The Literary Criticism of Charlotte Brontë* (Madison: Fairleigh Dickinson University Press, 1992).

Wise, T. J., and Symington, A. (eds.), *The Brontës: Their Lives, Friendship and Correspondence*, 4 vols. (1933; Oxford: Basil Blackwell, 1980).

SOCIAL CLASS

Burnett, J., *Plenty and Want: A Social History of Food in England from 1815 to the Present Day* (London: Routledge, 1966; repr. 1994) (an analysis of the history which reveals much about social history).

Corfield, P. J. (ed.), *Language, History and Class* (Oxford: Basil Blackwell, 1991).

Dolin, T., 'Fictional Territory and a Woman's Place: Regional and Sexual Difference in *Shirley*', *English Literary History*, 62/1 (1995), 197–215.

Eagleton, T., *Myths of Power: A Marxist Study of the Brontës* (London: Macmillan, 1975).

Greene, S., 'Apocalypse When?: *Shirley's* Vision and the Politics of Reading', *Studies in the Novel*, 26/4 (1994), 350–71.

Hughes, K., *The Victorian Governess* (London: Hambledon Press, 1993).

Joyce, P., *Visions of the People: Industrial England and the Question of Class 1848–1914* (Cambridge: Cambridge University Press, 1989).

Politi, J., '*Jane Eyre* Class-ified', in H. Glen (ed.), *Jane Eyre: New Casebook* (London: Macmillan, 1997), 78–91.

Rose, J., *The Intellectual Life of the British Working Classes* (New Haven and London: Yale University Press, 2001).

Smiles, Samuel, *Self-Help*, ed. P. W. Sinnewa (Oxford: Oxford University Press, 2002).

Thompson, E. P., *The Making of the English Working Class* (London: Pelican Books, 1980).

Vincent, D., *Bread, Knowledge and Freedom: a Study of Nineteenth-Century Working-Class Autobiography* (London: Europa Publications, 1981).

—— *Literacy and Popular Culture: England 1750–1914* (Cambridge: Cambridge University Press, 1989).

GENDER

Boumelha, P., *Charlotte Brontë* (Hemel Hempstead: Harvester Wheatsheaf, 1990).

Caine, B., *English Feminism 1780–1980* (Oxford: Oxford University Press, 1997).

Carnell, R. K., 'Feminism and the Public Sphere in Anne Brontë's *The Tenant of Wildfell Hall*', *Nineteenth Century Literature*, 53/1 (1998), 1–24.

Clapp, A. M., 'The Tenant of Patriarchal Culture: Anne Brontë's Portrait of the Problematic Female Artist', *Michigan Academician*, 28/2 (1996), 352–68.

Colby, C., *The Ends of History: Victorians and the Woman Question* (New York and London: Routledge, 1991).

Cosslet, T., *Woman to Woman: Female Friendship in Victorian Fiction* (Brighton: Harvester Press, 1988).

Frederico, A. R., 'The Other Case: Gender and Narration in Charlotte Brontë's *The Professor*', *Papers on Language and Literature*, 30/4 (1994), 323–45; repr. in Ingham (ed.), *Brontës: A Critical Reader*.

Gilbert, S., and Gubar, S., *The Madwoman in the Attic: The Woman Writer and the Nineteenth Century Literary Imagination* (New Haven: Yale University Press, 1979).

Hammerton, A. J., *Cruelty and Companionship: Conflict in Nineteenth Century Married Life* (London: Routledge, 1992).

Helsinger, E. K., et al., *The Woman Question: Society and Literature in Britain and America 1837–1883* (Manchester: Manchester University Press, 1983) (a most useful anthology with a wide-ranging collection of nineteenth-century material).

Homans, M., *Bearing the Word: Language and Female Experience in Ninteenth-Century Women's Writing* (Chicago: University of Chicago Press, 1986).

Ingham, P., *The Language of Gender and Class: Transformation in the Victorian Novel* (London: Routledge, 1996).

Jacobs, N. M., 'Gendered and Layered Narrative in *Wuthering Heights* and *The Tenant of Wildfell Hall*', *Journal of Narrative Technique*, 16/3 (1986), 204–19; repr. in Ingham (ed.), *Brontës: A Critical Reader*.

Jacobus, M., 'The Buried Letter: Feminism and Romanticism in *Villette*', in Jacobus (ed.), *Women Writing and Writing about Women* (London: Croom Helm, 1979), 121–40.

Kucich, J., *Repression in Victorian Fiction: Charlotte Brontë, George Eliot and Charles Dickens* (Berkeley and Los Angeles: University of California Press, 1987).

Langland, E., *Nobody's Angels: Middle-Class Women and Domestic Ideology in Victorian Culture* (Ithaca, NY, and London: Cornell University Press, 1995).

Marcus, S., 'The Profession of the Author: Abstraction, Advertising and *Jane Eyre*', *PMLA* 110/2 (1995), 206–19; repr. in Ingham (ed.), *Brontës: A Critical Reader*.

Maynard, J., *Charlotte Brontë and Sexuality* (Cambridge: Cambridge University Press, 1984).

Meyer, S., ' "Words on Great Vulgar Sheets": Writing and Social Resistance in Anne Brontë's Agnes Grey', in B. L. Harman and S. Meyer (eds.), *The New Nineteenth Century: Feminist Readings of Underread Victorian Fiction* (New York and London: Garland, 1996), 3–16; repr. in Ingham (ed.), *Brontës: A Critical Reader*.

Mitchell, J., *The Stone and the Scorpion: Female Subjects of Desire in the Novels of Charlotte Brontë, George Eliot and Thomas Hardy* (Westport, Conn.: Greenwood Press, 1994).

O'Toole, T., 'Siblings and Suitors in the Narrative Architecture of *The Tenant of Wildfell Hall*', *Studies in English Literature*, 39/4 (1999), 715–31; repr. in Ingham (ed.), *Brontës: A Critical Reader*.

Poovey, M., *Uneven Developments: The Ideological Work of Gender in Mid-Victorian England* (London: Virago, 1989).

Sadoff, D., *Monsters of Affections: Dickens, Eliot and Brontë on Fatherhood* (Baltimore: Johns Hopkins University Press, 1982).

Steinitz, R., 'Diaries and Displacement in *Wuthering Heights*', *Studies in the Novel*, 32/4 (2000), 407–19; repr. in Ingham (ed.), *Brontës: A Critical Reader*.

Stone, L., *The Family, Sex and Marriage in England 1500–1800* (Harmondsworth: Penguin, 1979).

Wein, T., 'Gothic Desire in Charlotte Brontë's *Villette*', *Studies in English Literature*, 39/4 (1999), 733–46, repr. in Ingham (ed.), *Brontës: A Critical Reader*.

Woolf, V., '*Jane Eyre* and *Wuthering Heights*', *The Common Reader*, 1 ser. (London: Hogarth Press, 1925), 196–204.

RACE

David, D., *Rule Britannia: Women, Empire and Victorian Writing* (Ithaca, NY: Cornell University Press, 1995).

Gibson, M. E., 'Seraglio or Suttee: Brontë's *Jane Eyre*', *Postscript*, 4 (1987), 1–8.

Meyer, S. L., 'Colonialism and the Figurative Strategy of *Jane Eyre*', *Victorian Studies*, 33/2 (1990), 247–68.

Zonana, J., 'The Sultan and the Slave: Feminist Orientalism and the Structure of Jane Eyre', *Signs: Journal of Women in Culture and Society*, 18/3 (1993), 592–617, repr. in Ingham (ed.), *Brontës: A Critical Reader*.

SCIENCE AND THE MIND

Dames, N., 'The Clinical Novel: Phrenology and *Villette*', *Novel*, 29/3 (1996), 367–91.

Foucault, M., *Discipline and Punish: The Birth of the Prison*, trans. A. Sheridan (Harmondsworth: Penguin, 1991).

Jack, I., 'Physiognomy, Phrenology and Characterization in the Novels of Charlotte Brontë', *BST* 15/80 (1970), 377–91.

Oppenheim, J., *Shattered Nerves: Doctors, Patients and Depression in Victorian England* (Oxford: Oxford University Press, 1991).

Otis, L. (ed.), *Literature and Science in the Nineteenth Century* (Oxford: Oxford University Press, 2002).

Porter, R., *A Social History of Madness: Stories of the Insane* (London: Weidenfeld and Nicolson, 1987).

—— *Mind Forg'd Manacles: A History of Madness in England from the Restoration to the Regency* (London: Athlone Press, 1987).

Rothstein, L., *Vital Signs: Medical Realism in Nineteenth-Century Fiction* (Princeton: Princeton University Press, 1992).

Scull, A. T., *Museums of Madness: The Social Organization of Insanity in Nineteenth-Century England* (London: Penguin Books, 1979).

—— *The Most Solitary of Afflictions: Madness and Society in Britain 1700–1900* (New Haven and London: Yale University Press, 1993).

Showalter, E., *The Female Malady: Women, Madness and English Culture* (London: Virago, 1987).

Shuttleworth, S., *Charlotte Brontë and Victorian Psychology* (Cambridge: Cambridge University Press, 1996).

Small, H., *Love's Madness: Medicine, the Novel and Female Insanity 1800–1865* (Oxford: Clarendon Press, 1998).

Tytler, G., *Physiognomy in the European Novel: Faces and Fortunes* (Princeton: Princeton University Press, 1982).

RELIGION AND MORALITY

Bamber, M., 'William Grimshaw, Patrick Brontë and the Evangelical Revival', *History Today*, 42 (1992), 25–31.

Bradley, I., *The Call to Seriousness: The Evangelical Impact on the Victorians* (London: Jonathan Cape, 1976).

Chard, M. J., ' "Apple of Discord": Centrality of the Eden Myth in Charlotte Brontë's Novels', *BST* 19/5 (1988), 197–205.

Cunningham, V., *Everywhere Spoken Against: Dissent in the Victorian Novel* (Oxford: Clarendon Press, 1975).

Dale, P. A., 'Heretical Narration: Charlotte Brontë's Search for Endlessness', *Religion and Literature*, 16/3 (1984), 1–24.

Fike, F., 'Bitter Herbs and Wholesome Medicines: Love as Theological Affirmation in *Wuthering Heights*', *Nineteenth-Century Fiction*, 23/2 (1968), 127–48.

Glen, H., *Charlotte Brontë: The Imagination in History* (Oxford: Oxford University Press, 2002), 50–96.

Henderson, H., *The Victorian Self: Autobiography and Biblical Narrative* (Ithaca, NY: Cornell University Press, 1989).

Hilton, B., *The Age of Atonement: The Influence of Evangelism on Social and Economic Thought 1795–1865* (Oxford: Clarendon Press, 1988).

Jay, E., *The Religion of the Heart: Anglican Evangelism and the Nineteenth-Century Novel* (Oxford: Clarendon Press, 1979).

—— *Faith and Doubt in Victorian England* (London: Macmillan, 1986).

Nemesvari, R., 'Strange Attractions on the Yorkshire Moors: Chaos Theory and *Wuthering Heights*', *Victorian Newsletter*, 92 (1997), 15–21.

Phillips, M. J., 'Charlotte Brontë's Favourite Preacher: Frederick Denison John Maurice (1805–1872)', *BST* 20/2 (1990), 77–88.

Qualls, B. V., *The Secular Pilgrims of Victorian Fiction: The Novel as a Book of Life* (Cambridge: Cambridge University Press, 1982).

Rowell, G., *Hell and the Victorians: A Study of the Nineteenth-Century Theological Controversies Concerning Eternal Punishment and the Future Life* (Oxford: Oxford University Press, 1974).

Taylor, I., *Holy Ghosts: The Male Muses of Emily and Charlotte Brontë* (New York: Columbia University Press, 1990).

Thormählen, M., *The Brontës and Religion* (Cambridge: Cambridge University Press, 1999).

Wang, L., 'The Holy Spirit in Emily Brontë's *Wuthering Heights* and Poetry', *Literature and Theology*, 14/2 (2000), 160–73.

Wheeler, M., *Death and the Future Life in Victorian Literature and Theology* (Cambridge: Cambridge University Press, 1990).

ADAPTATIONS, DERIVATIVES, AND CRITICAL HISTORY

Ingham, P. (ed.), *The Brontës: A Critical Reader* (London: Longman, 2003) (a selection of significant critical chapters and articles, some of which are cited separately in this Further Reading list).

Kendrick, R., 'Edward Rochester and the Margins of Masculinity in *Jane Eyre* and *Wide Sargasso Sea*', *Papers on Language and Literature*, 30/3 (1994), 235–56; repr. in Ingham (ed.), *Brontës: A Critical Reader*.

Miller, L., *The Brontë Myth* (London: Jonathan Cape, 2001) (a gripping account of some of the material relating to a range of traditions concerning the Brontës and their novels).

Nudd, D. M., 'Bibliography of Film, Television and Stage Adaptations of *Jane Eyre*', *BST* 20/3 (1991), 169–72.

—— and Lace, B. (eds.), *Brontë's Jane Eyre: Approaches to Teaching* (New York: Modern Language Association, 1993).

Rhys, Jean, *Wide Sargasso Sea*, ed. A. Smith (Harmondsworth: Penguin, 2000).

Stoneman, P., *Brontë Transformations: The Cultural Dissemination of Jane Eyre and Wuthering Heights* (Hemel Hempstead: Prentice Hall, 1996) (an invaluable and comprehensive account of the amazing range of adaptations, sequels, and other derivatives including plays, films, operas, musicals, and poems).

WEBSITES

http://www.bronte.org.uk   Brontë Parsonage Museum

http://www.lang.nagoya-u.ac.jp/~matsuoka/bronte.html   Brontë sisters

http://www.stg.brown.edu/projects/hypertext/landow/victorian/cbronte/bronteov.html   Charlotte Brontë

http://www.cs.cmu.edu/people/mmbt/bronte/bronte-anne.html   Anne Brontë

http://www.shef.ac.uk/misc/personal/cslma/anne/bronte.html   Anne Brontë

http://www.victorianweb.org/authors/bronte/ebronteov/html   Emily Brontë

FILM AND TELEVISION ADAPTATIONS OF THE BRONTËS' NOVELS

CHARLOTTE BRONTË

Jane Eyre (Italy; director Theodore Marston, 1910)
Jane Eyre (US; director Martin J. Faust, 1914)
Jane Eyre (US; director Frank H. Crane, 1914)
Jane Eyre (with Richard Tucker as Rochester, 1915)
Jane Eyre (with Conway Teale as Rochester, 1915)
Jane Eyre (US; director Travers Vale, 1915)
The Castle of Thornfield based on *Jane Eyre* (Italy, 1915)
The Master of Thornfield (US; 1915)
Woman and Wife, based on *Jane Eyre* (US; director Edward José, 1918)
Jane Eyre (Italy; director Riccardo Tolentino, 1918)
Jane Eyre (US; director Hugo Ballin, 1921)
Die Waise von Lowood (Germany; director Kurt Bernhardt, 1926)
Jane Eyre (US; director Christy Cabanne, 1934)
Jane Eyre (NBC TV; director Edward Sobol, 1939)
Jane Eyre (US; director Robert Stevenson, 1944)
Jane Eyre (Studio One TV, 1949)
Jane Eyre (BBC six-part version, 1956)
Jane Eyre (NBC TV; adaptor Robert Esson, 1957)
Jane Eyre (NBC TV, one hour; director David Susskind, 1961)
Jane Eyre (BBC TV six-part version; director Rex Tucker, 1963)
Jane Eyre (Greece; director Giorgos Lios, 1968)
Jane Eyre (GB; director Delbert Mann, 1970)
Jane Eyre (BBC TV five-part version; director Joan Craft, 1973)
Jane Eyre (BBC TV eleven-part version; director Julian Amyes, 1983)
Jane Eyre (GB, Italy, France, US; director Franco Zeffirelli, 1996)
Jane Eyre (LWT TV film; director Robert Young, 1997)

Shirley (GB; director A. V. Bramble, 1922)

Villette (BBC TV starring Jill Bennett and Michael Warre, 1957)
Villette (TV serial; director Moira Armstrong, 1970)

ANNE BRONTË

The Tenant of Wildfell Hall (BBC TV four-part serial; director Peter Sasdy, 1968–9)

The Tenant of Wildfell Hall (BBC TV three-part serial; director Mike
Barker, 1996)

EMILY BRONTË

Wuthering Heights (GB; director A. V. Bramble, 1920)

Wuthering Heights (US; director William Wyler, with Laurence Olivier
and Merle Oberon, 1939)

Wuthering Heights (BBC TV; producer George More O'Ferrall, 1948)

Wuthering Heights (US TV; director Paul Nickell, 1950)

Abismos De Pasión (Mexico; director Luis Buñuel, 1953)

Wuthering Heights (BBC TV; adaptor Nigel Kneale, 1953)

Wuthering Heights (US; director Daniel Petrie, 1958)

Wuthering Heights (BBC TV serial with Claire Bloom and Keith Michell,
1962)

Dil Diya Dard Liya ('Give your heart and receive anguish') (Bombay;
director A. R. Kardar, 1966).

Wuthering Heights (GB; director Robert Fuest, 1970)

Wuthering Heights (BBC TV serial; director Peter Hammond, 1978)

Hurlevent (based on *Wuthering Heights*; France; director Jacques Rivette,
1985)

Arashi-Ga-Oka (based on *Wuthering Heights*; Japan; director Yoshishige
Yoshida, 1988)

Emily Brontë's Wuthering Heights (US/GB; director Peter Kosminsky,
1992)

Wuthering Heights (LWT TV film; director David Skynner, 1998)

Wuthering Heights CA (US TV; director Suri Krishnamma, 2003)

INDEX

ANTHONY TROLLOPE

ÉMILE ZOLA

L'Assommoir
The Attack on the Mill
La Bête humaine
La Débâde
Germinal
The Ladies' Paradise
The Masterpiece
Nana
Pot Luck
Thérèse Raquin

The Oxford World's Classics Website

www.worldsclassics.co.uk

- Information about new titles
- Explore the full range of Oxford World's Classics
- Links to other literary sites and the main OUP webpage
- Imaginative competitions, with bookish prizes
- Peruse the Oxford World's Classics Magazine
- Articles by editors
- Extracts from Introductions
- A forum for discussion and feedback on the series
- Special information for teachers and lecturers

www.worldsclassics.co.uk

American Literature

British and Irish Literature

Children's Literature

Classics and Ancient Literature

Colonial Literature

Eastern Literature

European Literature

History

Medieval Literature

Oxford English Drama

Poetry

Philosophy

Politics

Religion

The Oxford Shakespeare

A complete list of Oxford Paperbacks, including Oxford World's Classics, Oxford Shakespeare, Oxford Drama, and Oxford Paperback Reference, is available in the UK from the Academic Division Publicity Department, Oxford University Press, Great Clarendon Street, Oxford OX2 6DP.

In the USA, complete lists are available from the Paperbacks Marketing Manager, Oxford University Press, 198 Madison Avenue, New York, NY 10016.

Oxford Paperbacks are available from all good bookshops. In case of difficulty, customers in the UK can order direct from Oxford University Press Bookshop, Freepost, 116 High Street, Oxford OX1 4BR, enclosing full payment. Please add 10 per cent of published price for postage and packing.